Y0-BGG-123

Global
Mormonism

Global Mormonism

in the

21st Century

Edited by Reid L. Neilson
Foreword by Paul Hyer

RELIGIOUS STUDIES CENTER
BRIGHAM YOUNG UNIVERSITY

RELIGIOUS STUDIES CENTER
BRIGHAM YOUNG UNIVERSITY

Published by the Religious Studies Center, Brigham Young University, Provo, Utah (http://religion.byu.edu/rsc_rec_pub.php)

© 2008 by Brigham Young University. All rights reserved.

Any uses of this material beyond those allowed by the exemptions in U.S. copyright law, such as section 107, "Fair Use," and section 108, "Library Copying," require the written permission of the publisher, Religious Studies Center, 167 HGB, Brigham Young University, Provo, Utah 84602. The views expressed herein are the responsibility of the authors and do not necessarily represent the position of Brigham Young University or the Religious Studies Center.

ISBN 978-0-8425-2696-8

Cover painting by Roger Loveless, *Brotherhood*

In memory of Paul H. Peterson (1941–2007),
a scholar who believed in this young historian

Past International
Society Conferences

The proceedings of these conferences can be ordered from the International Society at http://www.ldsinternationalsociety.org/.

Contents

Foreword

Paul Hyer

OVER THE LAST half century, as the restored Church of Jesus Christ has "come out of obscurity," thousands of Latter-day Saints have secured important professional positions and accomplished great things around the world. But for decades little was known as to who they were or what they have achieved. Consequently, in the late 1980s William Atkin, while managing a law office in the Republic of China (Taiwan) at the time, discussed with a group of friends the possibility of organizing an interested group of international Latter-day Saints.

The International Society was thus organized in 1989 as an association of professionals with international interests who are members and friends of The Church of Jesus Christ of Latter-day Saints. The threefold mission of the society is (1) to encourage collegiality among professionals involved in international business, law, education, humanitarian service, or other activities; (2) to promote shared professional and social interest and concerns of society members; and (3) to provide support for international programs of the Church and Brigham Young University, where possible. The society is now the fastest growing and most comprehensive network of Latter-day Saint international professionals.

The society networks with members throughout the world and has an executive board and an office with staff support located on BYU's campus at the Kennedy Center for International Studies. Field representatives are located in cities or areas with significant numbers of professionals. The society also holds an annual conference in April to share the interests of members. To date, eighteen annual conferences have been held. Proceedings are published annually and are available online at ldsinternationalsociety.org.

In addition, the society publishes a print and online newsletter with information about various member activities, regional reports, Latter-day Saints, BYU, Church news and announcements, and updates on the society's various activities. It also presents a Distinguished Service Award to a deserving individual each April at its conference to recognize his or her service and devotion. Past award recipients whose service has international dimensions include John K. Carmack, who directs the Perpetual Education Fund; Garry R. Flake, who directs crisis humanitarian work for the Church; Donald L. Staheli, who has done significant work in China; and William F. Atkin, who has long been involved in legal matters across the world that concern the Church.

Many of the essays included in this volume provide information or insights that are not generally found in the media, general conference addresses, or other such places. They will be of interest to a broad audience, prompt some important thought and discussion, and represent only a sampling of what is available in the publications of the International Society.

Paul Hyer is executive director of the International Society and a professor emeritus of Chinese history at Brigham Young University.

Introduction:
A Recommissioning of Latter-day Saint Historians

Reid L. Neilson

SCHOLARLY OBSERVERS OF the Christian tradition—of which The Church of Jesus Christ of Latter-day Saints is a part—are beginning to expand their visions of a Christian past, present, and future to embrace a truly global Christianity.[1] In a groundbreaking article, "Eusebius Tries Again," missiologist Andrew F. Walls argues that "The situation of the global church at the end of the second millennium calls us to a reconception of the task of the Christian historian and offers a new vision to direct the study, teaching, and writing of Christian history." However, he is not merely calling for a retooling of existing chroniclers of the religious past. He believes this paradigm shift will "require a new breed of church historians with all the skills and virtues nourished in the older school but with a range of others as well, skills and virtues demanded by the new environment of Christianity in the southern continents." Walls concludes with a professional call to arms: "It is time for the recommissioning of church historians."[2]

---

1. See especially Philip Jenkins, *The Next Christendom: The Coming of Global Christianity* (New York: Oxford University Press, 2002); and Philip Jenkins, *The New Faces of Christianity: Believing the Bible in the Global South* (New York: Oxford University Press, 2006).
2. Andrew F. Walls, "Eusebius Tries Again: Reconceiving the Study of Christian History," *International Bulletin of Missionary Research* 24, no. 3 (2000): 111.

This same revolution needs to happen in Mormon studies. While a doctoral candidate in religious studies, I was invited to help coauthor a historiographic survey on international Mormonism, given my research interest in the expansion of American religions into the Pacific basin.[3] The lead author of the essay asked me to collect, reference, and summarize everything that has been written about The Church of Jesus Christ of Latter-day Saints in post–World War II Asia and Oceania. I wish I could say it was an overwhelming task, but it was not. I was disappointed to learn how little has been written about the international Church in these regions.[4] Most of the sources I discovered were short periodical pieces brimming with testimony and faith but lacking scholarly depth and analysis. Many were written by returned-missionaries-turned-amateur-historians and by second- and third-generation members who had immigrated to America. Coming to terms with the lack of histories written by local members was perhaps the most disheartening part of the project.

As I have contemplated the international lacuna in our documented past, I have come up with a number of reasons to suggest why we have struggled. To begin with, some Mormon historians mistakenly feel that international Church history is too recent to chronicle. Many of the countries currently friendly to Church proselyting have only been open since World War II or, in the case of Eastern Europe, since the fall of communism. Most of the historical actors are still alive, they point out. Second, the hub of Mormon studies is in northern Utah, particularly at Brigham Young University (BYU), Utah Valley University, and Utah State University. Although

---

3. See Kahlile B. Mehr, Mark L. Grover, Reid L. Neilson, Donald Q. Cannon, and Grant Underwood, "Growth and Internationalization: The LDS Church Since 1945," in *Excavating Mormon Pasts: The New Historiography of the Last Half Century,* ed. Lavina Fielding Anderson and Newell G. Bringhurst (Salt Lake City: Greg Kofford Books, 2004), 199–228.

4. The scholarship of R. Lanier Britsch on Mormonism in the Pacific Basin and Asia is a noteworthy exception to this rule.

these intermountain universities offer a number of courses on Mormonism, I am aware of only one class on global Mormonism, The International Church, at BYU. Most Utah students are more familiar and seemingly interested in the foundational periods of Mormonism, essentially the presidential administrations of Joseph Smith and Brigham Young. A lack of foreign-language proficiency is a third reason why English-speaking scholars have shied from the international Church. The level of fluency required and attained by most young missionaries abroad is conversational at best and often does not include mastery of foreign writing systems. Lastly, many historians within the Church wrongly assume that international Church history lacks the pizzazz of early American Mormonism, with its angels, visions, golden plates, and seer stones. Yet the study of global Mormonism offers a wonderful window into larger scholarly themes such as ethnicity, enculturation, transnationalism, globalization, and regionalism.

I am, therefore, not surprised when many of my colleagues say, "I don't do international Church history." But just as scholar Ann Braude argued for the primacy of women's history in the larger field of American religious studies, I likewise maintain that international Church history *is* Church history. Church members need to realize that much of our most interesting history occurred abroad. We must remember that the Restoration of the gospel continues every time a new country is dedicated by apostolic authority for proselyting. In other words, the original 1830 New York Restoration, was replicated in Great Britain in 1837, Japan in 1901, Brazil in 1935, Ghana in 1970, Russia in 1989, and Mongolia in 1992. Therefore, Latter-day Saint historians need to refocus their scholarly gaze from Palmyra, Kirtland, Nauvoo, and Salt Lake City to Tokyo, Santiago, Warsaw, Johannesburg, and Nairobi. In the coming years, these international cities and their histories will become increasingly important to our sacred history. We need to tell these non–North American stories with greater frequency and with better skill. I hope this volume of essays will be a small wave in a sea change.

Fortunately, there are some bright spots in the study of global Mormonism. Over the past seventeen years, the International Society, backed by Brigham Young University's David M. Kennedy Center for International Studies, Marriott School of Management, J. Reuben Clark Law School, Department of Educational Leadership, and Alumni Association, has hosted an annual conference in Provo, Utah, on the globalization of Mormonism. Past themes include "Education, the Church, and Globalization," "The Challenge of Sharing Religious Beliefs in a Global Setting," "Out of Obscurity: Public Affairs and the Worldwide Church," "Muslims and Latter-day Saints: Building Bridges," "BYU's Role in Assisting the International Mission of the Church," and "Church Development in the Developing World" (see appendix for complete list of past conference themes). Following each symposium, the proceedings have been collected, edited, published in magazine form, and made available to International Society members, as well as the larger Church and academic community.

As both an undergraduate and graduate student—and now as an assistant professor—at Brigham Young University, I have attended a number of these yearly gatherings. I have left these meetings both educated and edified about the many opportunities and challenges facing The Church of Jesus Christ of Latter-day Saints in the twenty-first century. Desiring my students, colleagues, and fellow Latter-day Saints to likewise be up-to-date on the recent trajectories and contours of international Mormonism, I concluded that these conference papers warranted a wider distribution channel to reach a larger audience. Taken together, these annual addresses constitute perhaps the most important public dialogue on the globalization of Mormonism. After surveying the past decade of conference proceedings, I selected twenty essays for publication, which I have organized into five themed parts: "Joseph Smith, Mormonism, and the World," "Missionary Work in a Global Village," "Humanitarian Outreach and the Latter-day Saints," "Church Education Initiatives in an Era of Globalization," and "International Challenges Facing the Church." Although some of the statistics in a few of the essays are outdated, the larger questions they raise and issues they tackle still resonate today.

In the first part, "Joseph Smith, Mormonism, and the World," four Church leaders and scholars survey the impact of the Prophet Joseph Smith and his American religion from a global perspective. In the opening essay, "Joseph Smith and the Rise of a World Religion," religious educator Robert L. Millet surveys the scriptures and words of latter-day prophets concerning the prophesied rise of the Church of Jesus Christ in the final dispensation. He offers ten markers of a world religion and suggests how Mormonism will eventually fulfill them all. Historian Grant Underwood, in "Joseph Smith's Legacy in Latin America and the Pacific," describes the Prophet's inspired view of the identity and destiny of the native inhabitants of Oceania and the New World. He argues that Church leaders have consistently taught that the descendants of Lehi have a special place in God's latter-day work. In "The Prophet's Impact on Europe, Then and Now," Elder Keith K. Hilbig looks back on Joseph Smith's contributions to the gospel in Great Britain through the Quorum of the Twelve Apostles. Moreover, he describes the Church's more recent expansion throughout Eastern Europe. Lastly, Elder Robert S. Wood discusses the issues of developmentalism and multiculturalism from a Church perspective in "'A Babe upon Its Mother's Lap': Church Development in a Developing World." He reflects on how far the Church has come since 1834, when Joseph Smith prophesied that it would someday fill not only the Americas but also the world.

Part 2, "Missionary Work in a Global Village," focuses on how Mormonism has spread throughout the world through its impressive proselyting program, while also discussing contemporary evangelism challenges. In "Sharing the Gospel in a Global Setting," Elder Lance B. Wickman describes his and Apostle Dallin H. Oaks's contribution to the Emory University School of Law's project on law and religion. He offers an excellent overview of the historical background, aims, and message of the Church's missionary program. Attorney Hugh M. Matheson, in "Challenges from Religious Communities in Spreading the Gospel," relates his experiences working as the Church's international legal counsel in Africa and as the director of public affairs for the Africa Area. He shares some of the Church's ongoing challenges as it seeks to proclaim its message to the African people. Latter-day Saints not only need to protect their own religious freedom but also others' religious freedom, according to the eleventh article of faith, argues legal scholar W. Cole Durham Jr. in "The Impact of Secularization on Proselytism in Europe: A Minority Religion Perspective." Using Europe as a case study, he warns of modern-day Sherems and Korihors dressed in the guise of secularization, who threaten religious minorities and proselyting success. Finally, Middle East scholar James A. Toronto provides a survey of Church involvement in the Muslim world in "Challenges to Establishing the Church in the Middle East." He concludes his comments by suggesting a number of opportunities and challenges facing Mormonism in that region of the world.

"Humanitarian Outreach and the Latter-day Saints," part 3, describes the Church's involvement with humanitarian projects around the globe. Elder James O. Mason discusses the scriptural mandate for the Church and its membership to help the poor in "Humanitarian Aid: The Challenge of Self-Reliance." He also explains how the Lord and His prophets have outlined this temporal uplifting according to spiritual principles. In the "Panel on Church Welfare Initiatives," three Church welfare and humanitarian-aid administrators reflect on their own temporal stewardships in the international Church. Harold C. Brown tells of his experiences helping to administer the Church's welfare program worldwide. A. Terry Oakes discusses what the Church is doing to help the downtrodden find employment. The third panelist, E. Kent Hinckley, discusses the activities of the Production and Distribution division of Welfare Services. The final essay in this section, "Building Bridges of Understanding through Church Humanitarian Assistance," by Garry R. Flake, provides an overview of how the Church blesses lives and strengthens relationships with individuals, peoples, and governments through its generous aid programs.

This volume's fourth part, "Church Education Initiatives in an Era of Globalization," looks at how Church leaders and laity have sought—and are still seeking—to expand learning and training opportunities to help worldwide church members improve their spiritual and temporal lives. Elder Joe J. Christensen, in "The Globalization of the Church Educational System," chronicles the growth and development of the Church's schooling organization. He describes the rise and internationalization of seminaries and institutes. In "Education, the Church, and Globalization," Elder John K. Carmack makes it clear that President Gordon B. Hinckley and other Church leaders are committed to lifting up the global poor through education. The Perpetual Education Fund will provide increased opportunities for Church members to create a Zion society by both giving and receiving learning opportunities. The Church is constantly trying to improve its educational offerings in order to help its members find spiritual and temporal success, religious educator A. Bryan Weston relates in "Education and Provident Living in an Expanding Church." He describes how the international institute programs help young adults stay anchored to the gospel. Two scholars of education, E. Vance Randall and Chris Wilson, in "Private Education Initiatives by Latter-day Saints," offer a historical survey of Church involvement in primary, secondary, and postsecondary schooling. They also highlight what individual Latter-day Saints are accomplishing through private educational programs based on gospel principles.

"International Challenges Facing the Church," the final section, contains five essays that complicate the picture of future Church expansion in the twenty-first century. Elder Alexander B. Morrison begins by appraising major global trends and issues that humankind will be facing in the coming years in "The Tumultuous Twenty-first Century: Turbulence and Uncertainty." He suggests some worrisome implications of globalization, including a failing environment, political upheaval, pandemics, and a growing gap between rich and poor worldwide. In "Family and the Global Church: Cultural and Political Challenges," Elder Bruce D. Porter links the growth of the Church internationally with doctrines professed in the Church's "Proclamation on the Family," which seem at odds with many secular philosophies. He suggests five ways in which the Church will continue to progress, despite global challenges. There are a variety of moral issues inherent in the globalization of any organization, including the Church, David A. Shuler contends in "An Ethical Dilemma: The Imposition of Values on Other Cultures." He reexamines the notions of change, idealism, values, and development as they relate to the gospel of Jesus Christ. Elder Charles Didier, in "The Paradox of Religious Pluralism and Religious Uniqueness," describes how Latter-day Saints must advocate the truthfulness of the Restoration while maintaining ecumenical relationships in a religiously plural world. He maintains that Church members are obligated to proclaim what they believe to be true. Lastly, President Dieter F. Uchtdorf makes the case that although there are great challenges in the world today, there are also great opportunities for the Church and its members, in "The Church in a Cross-Cultural World." Latter-day Saints need to be lights unto the world through their beliefs and actions in order for the message of the Restoration to take hold in every land.

WHEN I FIRST conceived of this book project, I casually bounced the idea off Richard Neitzel Holzapfel, publications director for the Religious Studies Center at Brigham Young University. In characteristic fashion, Richard immediately grasped the idea, calculated its scholarly contribution, and committed both of us to its prompt publication. My mind was spinning as I walked back to my office that spring day—not only does Richard publish prodigiously himself, he empowers others to do likewise, I had quickly learned. Within days, he had secured the administrative approval and financial backing of Religious Education's Administrative Council. I am grateful for their support and trust, especially from Terry B. Ball, Dennis A. Wright, and Arnold K. Garr.

Having secured the sponsorship of the Religious Studies Center and Religious Education, I next contacted Paul Hyer, the current executive director of the International Society, to see if his organization would be interested in my plan. Not only did Paul likewise see merit in the proposal, but he also became a tireless advocate of the project, acted as a facilitator between our campus organizations, and kindly agreed to write the book's foreword. This volume would have never seen the light of day without his smile and work. The International Society's current board of directors—Paul D. Rytting (President), Paul Hyer (Executive Director), William F. Atkin, Roger E. Baker, J. Michael Busenbark, Lew W. Cramer, W. Cole Durham Jr., William "Mac" Epps, Cynthia Saldanha Halliday, Michael Judson, Cory Leonard, E. Vance Randall, Jeffrey Ringer, and Blaine Tueller—are to be thanked for their encouragement, as are the many conference planning committee members and editors who originally prepared the annual conference proceedings for publication.

Nearly two dozen Church leaders, administrators, and scholars generously consented to having their previously published essays reprinted in this volume. I thank Harold C. Brown, Elder John K. Carmack, Elder Joe J. Christensen, Elder Charles Didier, W. Cole Durham Jr., Garry R. Flake, Elder Keith Hilbig, E. Kent Hinckley, Elder James O. Mason, Hugh M. Matheson, Robert L. Millet, A. Terry Oakes, Elder Bruce D. Porter, E. Vance Randall, Dave Shuler, James A. Toronto, President Dieter F. Uchtdorf, Grant Underwood, A. Bryan Weston, Elder Lance B. Wickman, Chris Wilson, and Elder Robert S. Wood for their assistance. Moreover, the Religious Studies Center staff, including Devan Jensen, Elizabeth N. Hixson, Nathan Richardson, and Elisabeth R. Sutton are to be commended for making the book look as good as it does. Lastly, I thank my wife, Shelly, and our children, John and Kate, for supporting my academic adventures.

Reid L. Neilson is an assistant professor of Church history and doctrine at Brigham Young University.

Part I

Joseph Smith,
Mormonism,
and the World

Chapter 1

Joseph Smith and the Rise of a World Religion

Robert L. Millet

A MIGHTY VISION must have filled the mind of Joseph Smith the Prophet as he spoke the following words only weeks before his death: "I calculate to be one of the instruments of setting up the [kingdom of God foreseen by] Daniel by the word of the Lord, and I intend to lay a foundation that will revolutionize the whole world. . . . It will not be by sword or gun that this kingdom will roll on: the power of truth is such that all nations will be under the necessity of obeying the Gospel."[1]

The revolution that we know as the Restoration began slowly, has progressed steadily, and will yet spread dramatically. The Restoration was not destined to take place in a corner; it would not be confined to a tiny element of this world's population, nor would it be possible for people to ignore it. In the words of the risen Lord: "And when that day shall come, it shall come to pass that kings shall shut their mouths; for that which had not been told them shall they see; and that which they had not heard shall they consider. For in that day, for my sake shall the Father work a work, which shall be a great and a marvelous work among them; and there shall be among them

---

1. Joseph Smith, *Teachings of the Prophet Joseph Smith*, comp. Joseph Fielding Smith (Salt Lake City: Deseret Book, 1976), 366.

those who will not believe it, although a man shall declare it unto them" (3 Nephi 21:8–9).

In short, the marvelous work and a wonder—literally from Isaiah, the "miraculous miracle"—would become a world religion, one whose truth and influence for good would spread to every corner of the globe.

I am not a sociologist of religion, an anthropologist, or a statistician. I am not trained in demographics. But I do know something about what the scriptures and the prophets have declared relative to this "wonderful flood of light"[2] that has come into the world through the call and instrumentality of Joseph Smith Jr. We live in the early stages of the formation of a world religion. In this chapter, I would like to suggest briefly ten characteristics of a world religion and how it is that The Church of Jesus Christ of Latter-day Saints will eventually become a mighty power, an ensign to the nations (see Isaiah 5:26).

1. A world religion spreads to all nations.

Rodney Stark, a noted sociologist of religion, after a serious investigation of patterns of Latter-day Saint growth, observed: "The Church of Jesus Christ of Latter-day Saints, the Mormons, will soon achieve a worldwide following comparable to that of Islam, Buddhism, Christianity, Hinduism, and the other dominant world faiths. . . . Indeed, today they stand on the threshold of becoming the first major faith to appear on earth since the Prophet Mohammed rode out of the desert." Stark then suggested that a 30 percent per decade growth rate will result in over 60 million Mormons by the year 2080. A 50 percent per decade growth rate, which is actually lower than the real growth rate since World War II, will result in 265 million

---

2. *Messages of the First Presidency*, 6 vols., ed. James R. Clark (Salt Lake City: Bookcraft, 1965–75), 4:205.

Mormons by 2080.[3] Some fifteen years later, Stark acknowledged that his projections had missed the mark slightly: He had underestimated the growth of the Church by more than a million persons.[4]

Some Christians are deeply troubled that the Church's missionary efforts are not confined to non-Christians, that we bring our message to all people, regardless of their religious background. Because Latter-day Saints believe that what we have to share with others represents a *fulness* of the gospel of Jesus Christ and that the fulness is not found elsewhere, we feel a responsibility to make the message available to all who will hear. The great commission given to the Apostles when Jesus ascended into heaven, a commission to make disciples of all nations (see Matthew 28:19–20; Mark 16:15–18), has been repeated and renewed to the Latter-day Saints: "Go ye into all the world, preach the gospel to every creature, acting in the authority which I have given you, baptizing in the name of the Father, and of the Son, and of the Holy Ghost" (D&C 68:8).

Elder Dallin H. Oaks pointed out that "our message [is] for everyone, believers as well as non-believers." He noted that there are "two reasons for this answer—one a matter of principle and the other a matter of practicality. . . . We [preach] to believers as well as unbelievers because our message, the restored gospel, makes an important addition to the knowledge, happiness, and peace of all mankind. As a matter of practicality, we preach to believers as well as unbelievers because we cannot tell the difference." Elder Oaks asked a distinguished religious leader: "'When you stand before a congregation and look into the faces of the people, can you tell the difference between those who are real believers and those who are not?' He smiled wryly, and I sensed an admission that he had

---

3. Rodney Stark, "The Rise of a New World Faith," *Review of Religious Research* 26, no. 1 (1984): 18–23.

4. See James T. Duke, ed., *Latter-day Saint Social Life: Social Research on the LDS Church and Its Members* (Provo, UT: Religious Studies Center, Brigham Young University, 1998), chapters 1–2.

understood the point."[5] Every person must have the opportunity to hear the gospel, either here or hereafter. Eventually "the truth of God will go forth boldly, nobly, and independent, till it has penetrated every continent, visited every clime, swept every country, and sounded in every ear, till the purposes of God shall be accomplished, and the Great Jehovah shall say the work is done."[6]

But there is more. Elder Bruce R. McConkie explained that before the Lord Jesus can return in glory, two things must take place:

> The first . . . is that the restored gospel is to be preached in every nation and among every people and to those speaking every tongue. Now there is one immediate reaction to this: Can't we go on the radio and preach the gospel to . . . the nations of the earth? We certainly can, but that would have very little bearing on the real meaning of the revelation that says we must preach it to every nation, kindred, and people. The reason is the second thing that must occur before the second coming: The revelations expressly, specifically, and pointedly say that when the Lord comes the second time to usher in the millennial era, he is going to find, in every nation, kindred, and tongue, and among every people, those who are kings and queens, who will live and reign a thousand years on earth (Revelation 5:9–10).
>
> That is a significant statement that puts in perspective the preaching of the gospel to the world. Yes, we can go on the radio; we can proclaim the gospel to all nations by television or other modern invention. And to the extent that we can do it, so be it, it's all to the good. But that's not what is involved. What is involved is that the elders of Israel, holding the priesthood, in person have to trod the soil, eat in the homes of the people, figuratively put their arms around the honest in heart, feed them the gospel, and baptize them and confer the Holy Ghost upon them. Then these people have to progress and advance,

---

5. Dallin H. Oaks, in Conference Report, April 1998, 79.
6. Joseph Smith, *History of the Church of Jesus Christ of Latter-day Saints*, 7 vols., ed. B. H. Roberts, 2nd ed. rev. (Salt Lake City: Deseret Book, 1957), 4:540.

and grow in the things of the Spirit, until they can go to the house of the Lord, until they can enter a temple of God and receive the blessings of the priesthood, out of which come the rewards of being kings and priests.

The way we become kings and priests is through the ordinances of the house of the Lord. It is through celestial marriage; it is through the guarantees of eternal life and eternal increase that are reserved for the Saints in the temples. The promise is that when the Lord comes he is going to find in every nation and kindred, among every people speaking every tongue, those who will, at that hour of his coming, have already become kings and priests. . . . All this is to precede the second coming of the Son of Man.[7]

2. Doctrine and practice must remain orthodox and consistent as the Church spreads to foreign cultures.

Doctrinal finality rests with apostles and prophets, not theologians or scholars. One professor of religion at a Christian institution remarked to me, "You know, Bob, one of the things I love about my way of life as a religious academician is that no one is looking over my shoulder to check my doctrine and analyze the truthfulness of my teachings. Because there is no organizational hierarchy to which I am required to answer, I am free to write and declare whatever I choose." I nodded kindly and chose not to respond at the time. I have thought since then, however, that what my friend perceives to be a marvelous academic freedom can become license to interpret, intuit, and exegete scripture in a myriad of ways, resulting in interpretations as diverse as the interpreters' backgrounds, training, and proclivities. There are simply too many ambiguous sections of scripture to let the Bible speak for itself. This was, in fact, young Joseph Smith's dilemma: "The teachers of religion of the different sects understood the same passages of scripture so differently as to destroy all

---

7. Bruce R. McConkie, "To the Koreans, and All the People of Asia," in Spencer J. Palmer, *The Expanding Church* (Salt Lake City: Deseret Book, 1978), 141–42.

confidence in settling the question by an appeal to the Bible" (Joseph Smith—History 1:12).

In many cases, neither linguistic training nor historical background will automatically produce the (divinely) intended meaning or clarification of difficult scriptural matters. Some of these matters are not insignificant. Who decides which interpretation Matthew or Paul or Jesus intended? Further, who decides who decides? What is the standard by which we judge and interpret? Who has the right to offer inspired commentary on words delivered by holy men and women of God who spoke and wrote anciently as they were moved upon by the Holy Spirit? (see 2 Peter 1:21). While each reader of holy writ should be in tune with the Spirit while reading scripture, Latter-day Saints believe that the final word on prophetic interpretation rests with prophets. As C. S. Lewis wisely remarked, "Unless the measuring rod is independent of the things measured, we can do no measuring."[8]

In writing of *sola scriptura* as a tenet of the Reformation—the principle of "scripture alone" to establish doctrinal understanding— Randall Balmer of Barnard College at Columbia University observed that "Luther's sentiments created a demand for Scriptures in the vernacular, and Protestants ever since have stubbornly insisted on interpreting the Bible for themselves, forgetting most of the time that they come to the text with their own set of cultural biases and personal agendas." Balmer continued:

> Underlying this insistence on individual interpretation is the assumption . . . that the plainest, most evident reading of the text is the proper one. Everyone becomes his or her own theologian. There is no longer any need to consult Augustine or Thomas Aquinas or Martin Luther about their understanding of various passages when you yourself are the final arbiter of what is the correct reading. This tendency, together with the absence of any authority structure within Protestantism, has

8. C. S. Lewis, "The Poison of Subjectivism," in *Christian Reflections* (Grand Rapids, MI: Eerdmans, 1967), 73.

created a kind of theological free-for-all, as various individuals or groups insist that *their* reading of the Bible is the only possible interpretation.[9]

Again, there is a great advantage to a priesthood hierarchy, in terms of maintaining doctrinal orthodoxy. While members of The Church of Jesus Christ of Latter-day Saints are perfectly free to think and reflect on whatever they choose and to draw doctrinal conclusions on their own, they are at the same time instructed to say in sermons and lessons, and to publish, "none other things than that which the prophets and apostles have written" (D&C 52:9). The declaration, clarification, and interpretation of doctrine for the Church as a whole rest with the presiding councils of the Church: the First Presidency and the Quorum of the Twelve Apostles (see Mosiah 18:18–19; 25:21–22; Ephesians 4:11–14).

3. The teachings of the faith must answer some of life's most vexing questions and help to meet some of the deepest needs of humanity.

Sometimes I do not think we as Latter-day Saints appreciate fully what we have. I wonder whether we sense the import of the restored knowledge of the plan of salvation. A while ago I spoke with a member of the Church who had converted from Judaism about a decade before. We chatted for a couple of hours about what things within the faith were attractive to the average Jew and what things tended to turn them off. In regard to the latter category, my friend—a dedicated and devoted Saint—answered kindly but directly: "Some of my Jewish friends feel as if Mormonism provides quick and easy answers to questions that have been raised for millennia, and that a snappy answer to such mysteries as the nature of God, the problem of evil and suffering, life before and after death, and so forth bespeak

---

9. Randall Balmer, *Mine Eyes Have Seen the Glory: A Journey into the Evangelical Subculture in America*, 2nd ed. (New York: Oxford University Press, 1993), 24; emphasis in original.

a lack of awe and humility in the face of gargantuan issues." I think the assessment is accurate. "The things of God are of deep import," Joseph Smith wrote from Liberty Jail, "and time, and experience, and careful and ponderous and solemn thoughts can only find them out."[10]

For example, in considering but one doctrinal mystery, namely, life after death, Colleen McDannell and Bernhard Lang have written:

> Expressions of the eternal nature of love and the hope for heavenly reunion persist in contemporary Christianity. Such sentiments, however, are not situated within a theological structure. Hoping to meet one's family after death is a wish and not a theological argument. While most Christian clergy would not deny that wish, contemporary theologians are not interested in articulating the motif of meeting again in theological terms. The motifs of the modern heaven—eternal progress, love, and fluidity between earth and the other world—while acknowledged by pastors in their funeral sermons, are not fundamental to contemporary Christianity. Priests and pastors might tell families that they will meet their loved ones in heaven as a means of consolation, but contemporary thought does not support that belief as it did in the nineteenth century. There is no longer a strong theological commitment. . . .
>
> The major exception to this caveat is the teaching of The Church of Jesus Christ of Latter-day Saints, whose members are frequently referred to as the Mormons. The modern perspective on heaven—emphasizing the nearness and similarity of the other world to our own and arguing for the eternal nature of love, family, progress, and work—finds its greatest proponent in Latter-day Saint understanding of the afterlife. While most contemporary Christian groups neglect afterlife beliefs, what happens to people after they die is crucial to Latter-day Saint teachings and rituals. Heavenly theology is the result not of mere speculation, but of revelation given to past and present church leaders. . . .

---

10. Smith, *Teachings*, 137.

> There has been . . . no alteration of the Latter-day Saint understanding of the afterlife since its articulation by Joseph Smith. If anything, the Latter-day Saints in the twentieth century have become even bolder in their assertion of the importance of their heavenly theology. . . . In the light of what they perceive as a Christian world which has given up belief in heaven, many Latter-day Saints feel even more of a responsibility to define the meaning of death and eternal life.[11]

4. A world religion must somehow strike the difficult balance between building upon the past, upon settled, bedrock doctrine, and reaching out for new insight and revelation.

To some extent, the growth and spread of The Church of Jesus Christ of Latter-day Saints may be attributed largely to what some would feel to be contradictory and irreconcilable processes: (1) constancy and adherence to "the ancient order of things" and (2) development and change, according to needs and circumstances. Mormonism may thus be characterized as a religious culture with both static and dynamic—priestly and prophetic—elements, a church acclimated to both conservative and progressive postures.

The Saints have held tenaciously to and grounded themselves in what we perceive to be the particular beliefs and rites of both ancient Judaism and first-century Christianity. At the same time, through a belief in modern and continuing revelation, Latter-day Saints have made shifts and developments in policies and procedures according to pressing needs and anticipated challenges. For example, much of the Judeo-Christian world would consider the Bible (particularly the parts they accept as scripture) as embodying the *canon*—the rule of faith and practice. As one of my professors in graduate school emphasized and reemphasized, if the word *canon*, the accepted books of scripture, means anything at all, it is then set, fixed, closed, and established. The Latter-day Saint canon, on the other hand, is open,

---

11. Colleen McDannell and Bernhard Lang, *Heaven: A History* (New Haven, CT: Yale University Press, 1988), 312–13, 322.

flexible, and, when Church leaders feel divinely directed, expanding.

This Church could not operate properly for twenty-four hours without divine guidance, nor could each of us fulfill our assignments in the home and the Church without the spirit of revelation. As Elder McConkie has written:

> In the true Church, where there are apostles and prophets to give the mind and will and voice of the Lord to the Church and the world . . . nothing is better known or more greatly appreciated than the fact that the canon of scripture is not now and never will be full. . . . The last word has not been spoken on any subject. Streams of living water shall yet flow from the Eternal Spring who is the source of all truth. There are more things we do not know about the doctrines of salvation than there are things we do know. . . . What a wondrous thing it is to worship a God who still speaks, whose voice is still heard, whose words are without end![12]

President Spencer W. Kimball reminded us that "there are those who would assume that with the printing and binding of these sacred records, that would be the 'end of the prophets.' But again we testify to the world that revelation continues and that the vaults and files of the Church contain these revelations which come month to month and day to day."[13]

5. The fruits of the faith must reach beyond doctrinal insight; the visible Christian community must be impacted.

Joseph Smith's vision of the kingdom of God was cosmic. It consisted of more than sermons and study and Sabbath services; it entailed the entire renovation of the order of things on earth, the transformation of humankind, and the elevation of society. And at the heart of that sublime kingdom was the doctrine of Zion, a doc-

---

12. Bruce R. McConkie, "A New Commandment: Save Thyself and Thy Kindred!" *Ensign*, August 1976, 7, 11.
13. Spencer W. Kimball, in Conference Report, April 1977, 115.

trine and a worldview that would shape the early Church and point the Saints of the twentieth century toward the eschatological ideal.

Joseph Smith seems to have first encountered the concept of Zion (in a sense other than the holy mount or holy city in Jerusalem) in his translation of the Book of Mormon. The Book of Mormon prophets spoke of Zion as a holy commonwealth, a *society* of the Saints, a *way of life* that was to be established or brought forth under God's direction; those who fought against it were to incur God's displeasure. The municipals "labor for the welfare of Zion" rather than for money. In addition, in the words of the resurrected Savior, Zion was identified as a specific *place* in the land of America, a land of promise and inheritance for the descendants of Joseph of old (see 1 Nephi 13:37; 2 Nephi 10:11–13; 26:29–31; 28:20–24; 3 Nephi 16:16–18).

Zion is spoken of in scripture as a banner, or *ensign*, around which a weary and beleaguered people may rally. It is also a *standard* against which the substance and quality of all things are to be evaluated. The Saints are expected to judge all things by a set of guidelines obtained from a source beyond that of unenlightened man. Note the language of the revelation: "Behold, I, the Lord, have made my church in these last days like unto a judge sitting on a hill, or in a high place, to judge the nations. For it shall come to pass that the inhabitants of Zion shall judge all things pertaining to Zion" (D&C 64:37–38). As an illustration of this principle, Elder Joseph Young explained that Joseph Smith the Prophet "recommended the Saints to cultivate as high a state of perfection in their musical harmonies as the standard of the faith which he had brought was superior to sectarian religion. To obtain this, he gave them to understand that the refinement of singing would depend upon the attainment of the Holy Spirit. . . . When these graces and refinements and all the kindred attractions are obtained that characterized the ancient Zion of Enoch, then the Zion of the last days will become beautiful, she will be hailed by the

Saints from the four winds, who will gather to Zion with songs of everlasting joy."[14]

Zion was and is to be the focus, the convergence, and the concentration of all that is good, all that is ennobling, all that is instructive and inspirational. In Zion all things are to be gathered together as one in Christ (see Ephesians 1:10). In short, according to President Brigham Young, "every accomplishment, every polished grace, every useful attainment in mathematics, music, and in all science and art belong to the Saints."[15] The Saints "rapidly collect the intelligence that is bestowed upon the nations," President Young said on another occasion, "for all this intelligence belongs to Zion."[16]

Further, Zion is people, the people of God, people who have come out of the world of Babylon into the marvelous light of Christ. In this vein the Lord encouraged his little flock: "Verily, thus saith the Lord, let Zion rejoice, for this is Zion—THE PURE IN HEART; therefore, let Zion rejoice, while all the wicked shall mourn" (D&C 97:21). Thus, Zion is a state of being, a state of purity of heart that entitles one to be known as a member of the household of faith. President Brigham Young therefore spoke of the Saints having Zion in their hearts: "Unless the people live before the Lord in the obedience of His commandments," he said, "they cannot have Zion within them." Further, "As to the spirit of Zion, it is in the hearts of the Saints, of those who love and serve the Lord with all their might, mind, and strength."[17] On another occasion he affirmed: "Zion will be redeemed and built up, and the Saints will rejoice. This is the land of Zion; and *who are Zion?* The pure in heart are Zion; they have Zion within them. Purify yourselves, sanctify the Lord God in your

---

14. Cited in "Vocal Music," *History of the Organization of the Seventies* (Salt Lake City: Deseret Steam Printing Establishment, 1878), 14–15.
15. Brigham Young, in *Journal of Discourses* (London: Latter-day Saints' Book Depot, 1854–86), 10:224.
16. Young, in *Journal of Discourses*, 8:279.
17. Young, in *Journal of Discourses*, 2:253.

hearts, and have the Zion of God within you."[18] Finally, President Young asked: "*Where is Zion?* Where the organization of the Church of God is. And may it dwell spiritually in every heart; and may we so live as to always enjoy the Spirit of Zion!"[19]

Zion is a place. Zion is a people. Zion is a holy state of being. In the words of President Spencer W. Kimball, Zion is "the highest order of priesthood society."[20] It is the heritage of the Saints. "The building up of Zion," Joseph Smith taught, "is a cause that has interested the people of God in every age; it is a theme upon which prophets, priests and kings have dwelt with peculiar delight; they have looked forward with joyful anticipation to the day in which we live; and fired with heavenly and joyful anticipations they have sung and written and prophesied of this our day; but they died without the sight; we are the favored people that God has made choice of to bring about the latter glory."[21] This is the destiny of those who endure faithfully to the end. In that sense, as Joseph Smith stated, "We ought to have the building up of Zion as our greatest object."[22]

The answer to this world's greatest concerns—be it poverty, fatherless homes, the disintegration of the nuclear family, the redefinition of marriage, or even the bickering between nations—is not to be found in social programs per se, as important as such matters can be in dealing with temporary needs. Rather, a religion that cannot assist in the transformation of the human soul can have little effect in transforming a decaying society. President Ezra Taft Benson taught: "The Lord works from the inside out. The world works from the outside in. The world would take people out of the slums. Christ takes the slums out of people, and then they take themselves out of the slums. The world would mold men by changing their environment.

---

18. Young, in *Journal of Discourses*, 8:198; emphasis added

19. Young, in *Journal of Discourses*, 8:205; emphasis added.

20. Spencer W. Kimball, in Conference Report, October 1977, 125.

21. Smith, *Teachings*, 231.

22. Smith, *Teachings*, 160.

Christ changes men, who then change their environment. The world would shape human behavior, but Christ can change human nature. ... Yes, Christ changes men, and changed men can change the world."[23]

6. A successful world religion is one that, while holding tenaciously to its own singular and exclusive truth, maintains a healthy, affirming perspective toward other faiths.

President Howard W. Hunter explained: "The gospel of Jesus Christ, which gospel we teach and the ordinances of which we perform, is a global faith with an all-embracing message. It is neither confined nor partial nor subject to history or fashion. Its essence is universally and eternally true. Its message is for all the world, restored in these latter days to meet the fundamental needs of every nation, kindred, tongue, and people on the earth. It has been established again as it was in the beginning—to build brotherhood, to preserve truth, and to save souls."[24]

We have a responsibility to love and care for our neighbors and make a difference for good in their lives. There is a very real sense in which the Latter-day Saints are a part of the larger "body of Christ," the Christian community, whether certain groups feel comfortable with acknowledging our Christianity or not. Given the challenges we face in our society, it seems so foolish for men and women who profess a belief in the Lord and Savior, whose hearts and lives have been surrendered to that Savior, to allow doctrinal differences to prevent them from working together. President Gordon B. Hinckley pleaded with us: "We can respect other religions and must do so. We must recognize the great good they accomplish. We must teach our children to be tolerant and friendly toward those not of our faith.

23. Ezra Taft Benson, in Conference Report, October 1985, 5.
24. Howard W. Hunter, "The Gospel, a Global Faith," *Ensign*, November 1991, 18.

We can and do work with those of other religions in the defense of those values which have made our civilization great and our society distinctive."[25]

It is my conviction that God loves us, one and all, for I believe He is our Father in Heaven and that He has tender regard for us. I also feel strongly that, in spite of growing wickedness, men and women throughout the earth are being led to greater light and knowledge, to the gradual realization of their own fallen nature and thus of their need for spiritual transformation. C. S. Lewis once stated that "There are . . . people who are slowly becoming Christians though they do not yet call themselves so. There are people who do not accept the full Christian doctrine about Christ but who are so strongly attracted by Him that they are His in a much deeper sense than they themselves understand. There are people in other regions who are being led by God's secret influence to concentrate on those parts of their religion which are in agreement with Christianity, and who thus belong to Christ without knowing it."[26]

I am immeasurably grateful for the fulness of the gospel—for the priesthood, for living apostles and prophets, for the ordinances of salvation, for temples and sealing powers, and for mind-expanding and liberating doctrines. But I have found myself, more and more often, looking into the eyes of those of other faiths, sensing their goodness, perceiving their commitment to God, and feeling those quiet but profound impressions bearing witness to my soul, an expanding awareness that God knows them, loves them, and desires for me to love, respect, and better understand them. The archbishop of Canterbury, Rowan Williams, has observed: "Conversation may or may not lead to conversion in the sense of one party adopting the viewpoint of the other, and if we only conversed when that was our aim, we should experience nothing but very tense and polarized

---

25. Gordon B. Hinckley, in Conference Report, April 1998, 3.
26. C. S. Lewis, *Mere Christianity* (San Francisco: HarperSanFrancisco, 2001), 208–9.

communication in this world; . . . conversation assumes that I shall in some degree change because of the other—not by becoming the same, but simply by entering a larger world."[27]

"If it has been demonstrated that I have been willing to die for a 'Mormon,'" Joseph Smith taught, "I am bold to declare before Heaven that I am just as ready to die in defending the rights of a Presbyterian, a Baptist, or a good man of any other denomination; for the same principle which would trample upon the rights of the Latter-day Saints would trample upon the rights of the Roman Catholics, or of any other denomination who may be unpopular and too weak to defend themselves."[28] "If I esteem mankind to be in error," Joseph explained, "shall I bear them down? No. I will lift them up, and in their own way too, if I cannot persuade them my way is better; and I will not seek to compel any man to believe as I do, only by the force of reasoning, for truth will cut its own way. Do you believe in Jesus Christ and the Gospel of salvation which he revealed? So do I. Christians should cease wrangling and contending with each other, and cultivate the principles of union and friendship in their midst."[29]

7. A vibrant world religion is able to balance its increasing membership with a focus upon spiritual spontaneity.

One of the inevitable consequences of religious groups that undergo unusual growth is a kind of institutionalization, a fossilized sterilization, what Max Weber called "the bureaucratization of charisma." In short, they tend to become rule-driven, legalistic, and overly prone to "do things by the book." Sadly, they lose what made them so dynamic and attractive to begin with—a reliance upon principles and a kind of spiritual flexibility, the capacity to be open to new ideas, new approaches, new understandings, all as given from on

---

27. Rowan Williams, *Christ on Trial* (Grand Rapids, MI: Eerdmans, 2000), 65.
28. Smith, *Teachings*, 313.
29. Smith, *Teachings*, 313–14.

high. Handbooks and guidelines are invaluable, but we must never quench the Spirit or become so tied to written instructions that we cannot be prompted and led in difficult decisions (see Moroni 6:9; D&C 46:2).

Elder Boyd K. Packer offered the following counsel in 1984:

Organization, programs, procedures, policies, and principles— all are important. But they are not of equal importance. Leaders may very well spend time and budget on things that are not crucial and actually neglect the weightier matters. . . .

If a leader does not know the *principles*—by principles I mean the principles of the gospel, the doctrines, what's in the revelations—if he does not know what the revelations say about justice or mercy, or what they reveal on reproof or forgiveness, how can he make inspired decisions in those difficult cases that require his judgment? . . .

There are principles of the gospel underlying every phase of Church administration. These are not explained in the handbooks. They are found in the scriptures. They are the substance of and the purpose for the revelations.

Procedures, programs, the administrative policies, even some patterns of organization are subject to change. The First Presidency are quite free, indeed quite obliged, to alter them from time to time. But the *principles*, the *doctrines, never* change. If we overemphasize programs and procedures that *can* change, and will change, and must change, and do not understand the fundamental principles of the gospel, which *never* change, we can be misled. . . .

Now, I do not imply that we should ignore the handbooks or manuals; not for one minute would I say that. What I do say is this: There is a spiritual ingredient not found in handbooks that we must include in our ministry if we are to please the Lord.[30]

---

30. Boyd K. Packer, "Principles" (address given at regional representatives seminar, April 1984), in *The Things of the Soul* (Salt Lake City: Bookcraft, 1996), 64–66; emphasis in original.

As to how the Church can maintain a personal touch, a one-by-one ministry with continued Church growth and expansion, President Packer remarked several years later:

> Actually the Church is no bigger than a ward. Each bishop has counselors. He wears a special mantle and is designated as the presiding high priest in the ward. There are other high priests, and there is a presidency of elders. There are auxiliary leaders and teachers sufficient for the need. When we serve obediently, ever willingly, our pay, like the bishop's, comes in blessings.
>
> No matter if the Church grows to be a hundred million (as it surely will!), it will still be no bigger than a ward. Everything needed for our redemption, save for the temple, is centered there—and temples now come ever closer to all of us.[31]

8. A world religion must somehow engender a deep sense of commitment and loyalty among its members.

What are some of the reasons for Church growth? What generally attracts people to the Church? Many people in the world, weary of moral decline and what they perceive to be an erosion of time-honored values, are drawn to a church and a people who seem to be, as one journalist put it, "a repository of old-fashioned values, an American success story."[32] Latter-day Saints hold to absolute truths concerning God, man, and right and wrong. And, as we have pointed out, the Latter-day Saint doctrines concerning God's plan for His children, as well as the answers to such dilemmas as where we came from, why we are here, and where we are going—these things appeal to large numbers of men and women who are searching for meaning in life and for answers to the perplexities of our existence. The focus on the family is refreshing and badly overdue in a world that seems to be drifting rapidly from its moorings.

---

31. Boyd K. Packer, in Conference Report, April 1999, 79; emphasis added.
32. Peter Steinfels, "Despite Growth, Mormons Find New Hurdles," *New York Times*, September 15, 1991, sec. 1, p. 1.

Though it may seem odd at first glance, there is another reason why the Church is growing so rapidly—because of the requirements and the demands it makes upon its members. "Let us here observe," the early Saints were taught, "that a religion that does not require the sacrifice of all things never has power sufficient to produce the faith necessary unto life and salvation."[33] In other words, a religion that does not ask anything of its congregants can promise very little to them. Easy religion and convenient theology are not satisfying to the soul. People yearn for something to which they can commit themselves completely, something worthy of their devotion and their investment of time, talents, and means. It is worth noting, therefore, that recent studies in the sociology of religion indicate that the religious organizations that are growing the fastest are, ironically, those whose costs of membership—material, social, and spiritual—are greater. The greater the investment in terms of participation and involvement, the greater the sticking power and the attractiveness to the seeker of truth.[34]

9. The spirit and legacy of the founder of the faith must remain central to the Church. At the same time, the members must demonstrate an intelligent loyalty to the founder's successors.

While we thank God for living apostles and prophets today— for seers and revelators who see things not visible to the natural eye (see Moses 6:36)—we build upon a foundation laid by the Prophet Joseph Smith and by the revelations and heavenly powers communicated to him. Joseph Smith stands in a singular position to the Latter-day Saints: our worship is reserved for the members of the Godhead, but a special form of respect and loyalty is extended to Brother Joseph. He is what might be called a prophet's prophet. The

---

33. Joseph Smith, comp., *Lectures on Faith* (Salt Lake City: Deseret Book, 1985), 69.

34. Roger Finke and Roger Stark, *The Churching of America, 1776–1990* (New Brunswick, NJ: Rutgers University Press, 1992), 255.

Prophet Joseph Smith taught us that the head of the kingdom of God is Jesus Christ, the Great High Priest of our profession. We learn that Michael (Adam) and Gabriel (Noah) come next in line of authority. Although we are not told who comes next, we would suppose that the dispensation heads would follow.

A dispensation is a period of time in which God reveals Himself, His beloved Son, and the plan of life and salvation to men and women on earth. Such direction comes through the dispensation head, the man called to serve as the preeminent prophetic revealer of Christ. My guess is that there have always been testimony meetings, even from the beginning of time. I suppose it would not have been unusual to listen to a testimony meeting in 3000 BC and hear the following: "I know that God lives, that Jehovah is His Son, and that Enoch is His chosen prophet." If we had attended a testimony meeting in 1800 BC, we might have heard the following: "I have a testimony that God our Heavenly Father lives, that Jesus Christ is the Messiah and Savior, and that Abraham is His prophet." Interesting, isn't it? We hear testimony borne of God and His Son and then of the dispensation head almost in the same breath, and this is as it should be. God sends subsequent prophets during that dispensation, and each of these is a powerful and special witness of Christ and a mighty man of God; at the same time, their testimonies and witnesses are echoes and mirrors of the testimony first borne by the dispensation head.

In a magnificent address delivered to the Church at the April 1916 general conference, President Joseph F. Smith spoke of the link, the vital link, between Joseph Smith, the founder of the faith, and the current Church and its leaders:

> I feel sure that the Prophet Joseph Smith and his associates, who, under the guidance and inspiration of the Almighty, and by his power, began this latter-day work, would rejoice and do rejoice, if they are permitted to look down upon the scene that I behold in this tabernacle. And I believe they do have the privilege of looking down upon us, just as the all-seeing eye of God beholds every part of his handiwork. . . .

So, I feel quite confident that the eyes of Joseph the Prophet, and of the martyrs of this dispensation, and of Brigham and John and Wilford, and those faithful men who were associated with them in their ministry upon the earth, are carefully guarding the interests of the Kingdom of God in which they labored and for which they strove during their mortal lives. I believe they are as deeply interested in our welfare today, if not with greater capacity, with far more interest, behind the veil, than they were in the flesh. . . . And I have a feeling in my heart that I stand in the presence not only of the Father and of the Son, but in the presence of those whom God commissioned, raised up, and inspired, to lay the foundations of the work in which we are engaged.[35]

In writing of this pivotal moment in Church history, Jan Shipps observed:

President Smith knew that the fifteen years of his presidency had been hard years for the Latter-day Saints. . . . He knew that they were worried about what had happened in the Church as well as to the Church and that they were concerned about the changes that were rushing in upon the Mormon world. Therefore, instead of delivering a sentimental homily about the founders of the Church and the trials they had endured, he delivered 'a remarkable sermon' that had continuity as one of its main themes. This was a sermon that the Saints very much needed to hear. . . .

Couched in a manner that makes it applicable in all times and in diverse places, Joseph F. Smith's sermon called up the sacred past and brought it forward to vindicate the present. Just as surely as the early Christian canon, in order to establish a correspondence between two apparently different eras, brought the Hebraic past into the Christian present . . . , so the Prophet-President's sermon established a basis for a metaphysical bonding between the nineteenth-century Mormon experience and its distinctly dissimilar twentieth-century counterpart.

---

35. *Messages of the First Presidency*, 5:5–6.

In short, "Joseph F. Smith conveyed to the Saints his confidence that the changes which had occurred during his tenure were not changes which had in any way diminished the strength of the relationship between God and His chosen people. Notwithstanding shifting times and seasons, Mormonism remained the same."[36]

Now, having acknowledged the role of the dispensation head— and in this case the significant labor of Brother Joseph—we readily acknowledge that ours is a forward-looking Church and that we do not dwell constantly upon what was or even forevermore on *how* it was done. Elder Bruce R. McConkie explained:

> The Lord, in his infinite wisdom and goodness, knows what ought to be done with his servants. The other thing to note is that when the Lord calls a new prophet he does it because he has a work and a labor and a mission for the new man to perform.
>
> I can suppose that when the Prophet Joseph Smith was taken from this life the Saints felt themselves in the depths of despair. To think that a leader of such spiritual magnitude had been taken from them! . . . And yet when he was taken the Lord had Brigham Young. Brigham Young stepped forth and wore the mantle of leadership. With all respect and admiration and every accolade of praise resting upon the Prophet Joseph, still Brigham Young came forward and did things that then had to be done in a better way than the Prophet Joseph himself could have done them.[37]

10. The great strength of a world religion lies in the individual witness of its members.

"Herein lies the great strength of this kingdom," President Hinckley said. "It is the conviction, solid and real and personal, that is found in the hearts of millions of Latter-day Saints who live in

---

36. Jan Shipps, *Mormonism: The Story of a New Religious Tradition* (Urbana and Chicago: University of Illinois Press, 1985), 138–45.

37. Bruce R. McConkie, "Succession in the Presidency," *1974 BYU Speeches of the Year* (Provo, UT: BYU Publications, 1975), 24.

many lands and who speak a variety of tongues. Each is a part of a great society of believers."[38] President Brigham Young is reported to have said that his greatest fear was that the members of this Church would settle into a kind of spiritual complacency and accept everything the Brethren said and did without obtaining a witness of its truthfulness for themselves.[39] It is intelligent obedience, not "blind obedience" that the Lord and His prophets need from the Saints; such obedience lends strength and power and dynamism to the work of the Lord. In other words, while it is essential that we are led by fifteen men who have been called, ordained, and set apart as special witnesses of the name of Christ in all the world, the true strength of this Church lies in the hearts of its members.

There is an episode in the Old Testament that underlines the importance of enlightened and thus empowered members. On one occasion Moses gathered together the seventy elders of Israel "round about the tabernacle." Jehovah descended in a cloud, spoke to Moses, and poured out His Spirit upon the seventy. Eldad and Medad were overcome with that Spirit and prophesied. Joshua became concerned and anxiously said to the Lawgiver: "My Lord Moses, forbid them. And Moses said unto him, Enviest thou for my sake?" That is, "What's the matter, Joshua? Are you afraid they will take my job as prophet-leader?" And then followed immortal words, language that has everlasting relevance to those who seek to know the mind and will of the Almighty: "*Would God that all the Lord's people were prophets, and that the Lord would put his Spirit upon them*" (Numbers 11:24–29; emphasis added; compare D&C 1:19–20).

One of the remarkable attributes of God and of His chosen prophets is that they are not possessive of spiritual gifts or graces; it is as though Joseph Smith and his prophetic successors have bidden

---

38. Gordon B. Hinckley, *Teachings of Gordon B. Hinckley* (Salt Lake City: Deseret Book, 1997), 133.

39. Harold B. Lee, *Stand Ye in Holy Places* (Salt Lake City: Deseret Book, 1975), 163; see also *Journal of Discourses*, 6:100; 9:149–50.

us to brush away the cobwebs of complacency, open the shutters of heaven, and gaze with them upon the scenes of eternity. Thus, the Choice Seer could affirm that "God hath not revealed anything to Joseph, but what He will make known to the Twelve, and even the least Saint may know all things as fast as he is able to bear them."[40]

The testimony of Jesus, that which undergirds this latter-day work, is in fact the spirit of prophecy (see Revelation 19:10). My colleague Joseph Fielding McConkie wrote: "Our faith and our doctrine is that every member of the Church has both the ability and responsibility to be a prophet. To join the Church is but to enroll in the school of the prophets. . . . Our doctrine is not simply that if we live righteously we can receive revelation; rather it is that if we live right there is no power that can prevent our receiving it." In addition, just as our dispensation stands independent of all previous dispensations, "all who would lay claim to the promise of salvation must do so as prophets or prophetesses. Each must claim a personal dispensation of the gospel. All who profess a testimony of the gospel must have a knowledge of saving truths that stands independent of the revelations given to others."[41]

Conclusion

Try to imagine how a small group of Latter-day Saints must have felt as they gathered together at the home of Peter Whitmer Sr. for the formal organization of the Church on April 6, 1830. Try to imagine what went through the minds of the early missionaries as they were told by revelation that "the voice of the Lord is unto all men, and there is none to escape; and there is no eye that shall not see, neither ear that shall not hear, neither heart that shall not be penetrated. . . . And the voice of warning shall be unto all people, by the mouths of my disciples, whom I have chosen in these last days"

---

40. Smith, *Teachings*, 149.
41. Joseph Fielding McConkie, *Prophets and Prophecy* (Salt Lake City: Bookcraft, 1988), 90–91.

(D&C 1:2, 4). Try to imagine the wonder and amazement that must have overcome the little flock as they were instructed that "the sound must go forth from this place unto all the world, and unto the uttermost parts of the earth—the gospel must be preached unto every creature, with signs following them that believe" (D&C 58:64). Truly, the arm of the Lord would be revealed "in convincing the nations . . . of the gospel of their salvation. For it shall come to pass in that day, that every man shall hear the fulness of the gospel in his own tongue, and in his own language, through those who are ordained unto this power" (D&C 90:10–11).

President Wilford Woodruff described an early meeting of the Saints in Kirtland:

> On Sunday night the Prophet called on all who held the Priesthood to gather into the little log school house they had there. It was a small house, perhaps 14 feet square. But it held the whole of the Priesthood of the Church of Jesus Christ of Latter-day Saints who were then in the town of Kirtland, and who had gathered together to go off in Zion's camp. . . . When we got together the Prophet called upon the Elders of Israel with him to bear testimony of this work. Those that I have named spoke, and a good many that I have not named, bore their testimonies. When they got through the Prophet said, "Brethren I have been very much edified and instructed in your testimonies here tonight, but I want to say to you before the Lord, that you know no more concerning the destinies of this Church and kingdom than a babe upon its mother's lap. You don't comprehend it." I was rather surprised. He said "it is only a little handful of Priesthood you see here tonight, but this Church will fill North and South America; it will fill the world."[42]

The little stone foreseen by Nebuchadnezzar and interpreted by Daniel was being cut out of the mountain "without hands," meaning, without human hands; it was an act of God. The foundation was laid for the establishment of the kingdom of God, a kingdom that would never be lost from the earth through apostasy, a kingdom that would

---

42. Wilford Woodruff, in Conference Report, April 1898, 57.

expand and be sanctified until the pure in heart were prepared to welcome to the earth the King of Zion (see Moses 7:53), the King of Kings and Lord of Lords. While we speak often of living in the last days, of being a part of the winding up scenes in the eleventh hour, there is yet much to do: many, many millions must yet join the Church and gather to holy temples throughout the globe (see Revelation 5:9–10); the Saints must put their lives (including their financial resources) in order so that "the church may stand independent above all other creatures beneath the celestial world" (D&C 78:14); and, finally, we must so center our lives in Jesus Christ and His gospel that the tinsel, trappings, and tauntings of our telestial world will have little or no effect on us; like Nephi, we will give them no heed whatsoever (see 1 Nephi 8:33).

It is reported that Count Leo Tolstoi once observed, "If the [Latter-day Saints] follow the teachings of this Church, nothing can stop their progress—it will be limitless. There have been great movements started in the past but they have died or been modified before they reached maturity. If Mormonism is able to endure, unmodified, until it reaches the third and fourth generation, it is destined to become the greatest power the world has ever known."[43]

President Hinckley asked:

> Now, what of the future? What of the years that lie ahead? It looks promising indeed. People are beginning to see us for what we are and for the values we espouse. The media generally treat us well. We enjoy a good reputation, for which we are grateful.
>
> If we will go forward, never losing sight of our goal, speaking ill of no one, living the great principles we know to be true, this cause will roll on in majesty and power to fill the earth. Doors now closed to the preaching of the gospel will be opened. The Almighty, if necessary, may have to shake the nations to

---

43. Cited in Thomas J. Yates, "Count Tolstoi and the 'American Religion,'" *Improvement Era*, February 1939, 94.

humble them and cause them to listen to the servants of the living God. Whatever is needed will come to pass.[44]

In another address President Hinckley said:

The time has come for us to stand a little taller, to lift our eyes and stretch our minds to a greater comprehension and understanding of the grand millennial mission of this, The Church of Jesus Christ of Latter-day Saints. This is a season to be strong. It is a time to move forward without hesitation, knowing well the meaning, the breadth, and the importance of our mission. . . . We have nothing to fear. God is at the helm. He will overrule for the good of this work. . . . No force under the heavens can stop it if we will walk in righteousness and be faithful and true. The Almighty Himself is at our head.[45]

Robert L. Millet is a professor of ancient scripture at Brigham Young University. This essay was presented at "Joseph Smith and the World," the International Society's sixteenth annual conference, April 2005, Brigham Young University, Provo, Utah.

44. Gordon B. Hinckley, in Conference Report, October 1997, 92.
45. Gordon B. Hinckley, in Conference Report, April 1995, 95.

Chapter 2

Joseph Smith's Legacy in Latin America and the Pacific

Grant Underwood

MUCH IS BEING said about the Prophet Joseph Smith, the man who "has done more, save Jesus only, for the salvation of men in this world, than any other man that ever lived in it" (D&C 135:3). I wish to add a single furrow to that well-ploughed field. I will do so not by reviewing the impressive though well-known numerical growth or extensive construction program of the Church in Latin America and the Pacific, but by focusing on the undergirding vision that for many years motivated the outreach to these areas. I speak of Joseph Smith's remarkable conception of the identity and destiny of the indigenous peoples of Polynesia and the western hemisphere.

Before doing so, I desire to express my profound gratitude for having had the extraordinary opportunity these past four years of working closely with all the known private and public papers of the Prophet Joseph Smith. How my love for him has deepened is best illustrated by an experience I had before my mission. As a youth, I had never met my Uncle Harold Nelson, because he was shot down over the North Sea just six weeks before V-E Day. However, my grandparents lovingly kept his four slender mission diaries prominently displayed on one of their bookshelves. As I was preparing to serve a mission, I asked if could read Uncle Harold's diaries. They gladly consented, and over the next few months I became well acquainted with him.

I read of his triumphs and his challenges, as well as the humor and heartache in his mission life. I felt I glimpsed something of his personality as well as his spirituality, and I grew attached to him. The same outcome has resulted from my recent work with the Joseph Smith Papers. Though I have been involved in religious education for more than two decades, the Prophet has come alive to me in a way he never had before. Scrutinized at the closest range, I can say that not only was he a remarkable prophet and gifted Church leader, but he was also a very appealing human being, a man whom I have come to love and admire deeply.

To segue into my presentation, I would say that, for me, one of Joseph's most attractive attributes was his sensitivity to the poor and oppressed. Nowhere was this more powerfully expressed than in the exalted vision he communicated of the true nature of the indigenous peoples of the Americas. In an era that was dominated by negative stereotypes of the Indians, bloody conflict and territorial acquisition, and too many "trails of tears," Joseph Smith set forth a dramatically different vision of who the Native Americans were and what their future should be. He infused new life and meaning into the biblical image of Gentile "nursing fathers and mothers" and left a legacy of compassion and nurture that continues to inspire us today. Of course, as President Boyd K. Packer reminded us in the April 2005 general conference, ultimately the credit goes not to Joseph Smith but to God, who is love. Still, Joseph as prophet was no human fax machine. He was a unique human being who had to have the cluster of personal qualities and the kind of heart that could receive and promote such a vision.

That vision was first set forth in the Book of Mormon. Indeed the book itself was destined to play a pivotal role in helping reverse the fortunes of indigenous peoples throughout the Americas and the Pacific. When the book's first 116 translated pages were lost, the Lord severely chastised the Prophet but affirmed, "Nevertheless, my work shall go forth, ... and for this very purpose are these plates preserved, ... that the Lamanites might come to the knowledge of their fathers, and that they might know the promises of the Lord" (D&C 3:16, 19–20).

Later, Joseph translated the book's title page. It boldly announces that while Jew and Gentile would also benefit from its message, it was particularly "written to the Lamanites, who are a remnant of the house of Israel ... to show unto the remnant of the House of Israel what great things the Lord hath done for their fathers; and that they may know the covenants of the Lord, that they are not cast off forever" (Book of Mormon, title page).

Anyone who has read the Book of Mormon knows that it consistently places ethnic Israel at the center of human history. One of the book's prophecies goes so far as to justify the formation of the United States in terms of its potential service to the indigenous remnants of Israel. Christ tells Lehi's descendants that in the future the Gentiles would be "established in [America], and be set up as a free people by the power of the Father, that [the Book of Mormon] might come forth from them unto a remnant of your seed, that the covenant of the Father may be fulfilled which hath covenanted with his people, O House of Israel" (3 Nephi 21:4). Envisioning the foundation of a free country in the Americas to facilitate the carrying of the restored gospel and its accompanying text to native peoples was a rather remarkable inversion of the social hierarchies of the day. The Gentile colonizers—white Americans—could repent, "come in unto the covenant and be numbered among this the remnant of Jacob" (3 Nephi 21:22), but their blessings were to come through adoption into the house of Israel by being numbered with Indians and islanders, not vice versa (see 1 Nephi 14:1–2; 2 Nephi 10:18–22; 2 Nephi 30:1–2; 3 Nephi 16:13; 21:6, 22–24; 29:1–9; 30:1–2, for examples of Book of Mormon passages where this perspective is evident). In the Book of Mormon, Gentiles are portrayed as servants, not masters, as nursemaids to royal heirs, and as adopted rather than natural children.

Though the Book of Mormon presents Israel's current condition as a faint shadow of its former self, the book is also replete with promises of its restoration, both spiritually and temporally.[1]

In the heyday of "manifest destiny," such rhetoric was not calculated to win friends for the Prophet. And it certainly was out of tune with the tenor of the times to assert, as did Joseph Smith, that America actually belonged to the Lamanites and that one day it would be their millennial inheritance. Some of the Prophet's associates, fired with his grand, if unconventional, vision, interpreted portions of 3 Nephi in ways that now seem overenthusiastic. Parley P. Pratt, for instance, assured the Native Americans that with respect to the dominant white population, "The very places of their dwellings will become desolate except such of them as are gathered and numbered with you; and you will exist in peace, upon the face of this land, from generation to generation. And your children will only know that the Gentiles once conquered this country, and became a great nation here, as they read it in history; as a thing long since passed away, and the remembrance of it almost gone from the earth."[2] Another of the Prophet's followers warned his fellow Americans that "the cries of the red men, whom you and your fathers have dispossessed and driven from their lands which God gave unto them and their fathers for an everlasting inheritance, have ascended into the ears of the Lord of Sabaoth."[3] To say the least, such rhetoric seemed unduly solicitous of the lowly Indian.

---

1. The Book of Mormon view of the eschatological restoration of Israel and the role Gentiles will play in this is discussed at greater length in Grant Underwood, *The Millenarian World of Early Mormonism* (Urbana and Chicago: University of Illinois Press, 1993), 29–31, 67–69, 77–83, 90–92.
2. Parley P. Pratt, *A Voice of Warning and Instruction to All People* (New York: W. Sandford, 1837), 191. This portion of the text was deleted by Pratt in his second edition (1839) and was not restored in subsequent editions.
3. Charles B. Thompson, *Evidences in Proof of the Book of Mormon* (Batavia, NY: 1841), 229–30.

Outreach to the Lamanites

Given such sentiments and given the Book of Mormon's persistent proclamation of the restoration of latter-day Israel, it is not surprising that in this dispensation the first formal mission to a specific group of people was to the Lamanites. Oliver Cowdery, Parley P. Pratt, and others trudged a thousand miles, mostly on foot, to arrive at the newly organized Indian Territory in present-day eastern Kansas to deliver the message. When just days into their mission the government Indian agent confronted them with the ultimatum to either move east out of Indian Territory and into Missouri or west into the Fort Leavenworth guardhouse, the mission was temporarily aborted. For many Saints, here ends the story of the Prophet's outreach to the Indians. Not so. Fortunately, in recent years, scholars have reconstructed that interesting but little-known history.[4] Suffice it to say, the Prophet never lost sight of what the Lord had in store for the children of Lehi.

A most telling example occurred in the summer of 1843. Because of previously sympathetic dealings with them, a delegation of Pottawatamie Indians sought out the Prophet to be their "father," as they called it to counsel them in temporal affairs. The Prophet replied that he would be pleased to do all that was legally in his power. "I feel interested in the welfare and prosperity of all my red children," he wrote, "and will most cheerfully do them all the good in my power as to do good is what I always delight in."[5] As inevitably has been the case with indigenous peoples the world over, what to do with their land has been a primary concern. The Prophet replied: "In regard to parting with your lands and selling them, I do not think it is best for

---

4. Ronald W. Walker, "Seeking the 'Remnant': The Native American during the Joseph Smith Period," *Journal of Mormon History* 19 (Spring 1993): 1–33.

5. Joseph Smith to Pottawatomie Indians, August 28, 1843, Joseph Smith Collection, Church Archives, The Church of Jesus Christ of Latter-day Saints, Salt Lake City.

you to let them go but to keep them to live upon for yourselves and your children." After sharing additional counsel, Joseph concluded with a statement that epitomizes the legacy he has passed on to generations of Latter-day Saints who have labored in the Americas and the Pacific. "The Mormons," he wrote, "are your friends and they are the friends of all men, and I have the very best of feelings to all men and especially towards you my children. I wish you well, and hope the great God will bless you and abundantly supply you with every good thing, and that peace and prosperity may forever attend you and your children."[6]

Such sympathy has tended to characterize faithful Latter-day Saints ever since, with Joseph's successor Brigham Young leading the way. On one occasion, President Young told the Utah Legislature, "I have uniformly pursued a friendly course of policy towards [the Indians], feeling convinced that independent of the question of exercising humanity towards [them], it was manifestly more economical and less expensive, to feed and clothe, than to fight them."[7] In the 1850s, Young wrote to Ute Indian Chief Walkara. His letter echoes Joseph Smith's earlier expression to the Pottawatamie. Young told Walkara to remind his people that the Mormons "are their very best friends they have on the earth. . . . While the sun shall shine and the moon shall give her light we are still their friends. And the reason, Friend Walker, that I have before told you. It [is] because the Red Men have descended from the same fathers and are of the same family as the Mormons, and we love them, and shall continue to love them, and teach them things that may do them good. And now, Brother Walker, you have never known me to be ought but your steadfast, undeviating friend."

---

6.   Joseph Smith to Pottawatomie Indians, August 28, 1843.

7.   Brigham Young, as cited in Leonard J. Arrington and Davis Bitton, *The Mormon Experience: A History of the Latter-day Saints* (Urbana, IL: University of Illinois Press, 1992), 148.

Then, in a gesture typifying the culturally respectful attitude toward native peoples that would be evidenced by generations of Church leaders and missionaries, he added: "I now send you six large plugs of tobacco, that you may smoke in peace with your friends, remembering that I am one [friend] whilst ever you sojourn upon the earth, earnestly seeking your true welfare, and praying for blessings to descend upon you whilst your actions are guided by the Spirit of Truth."[8]

Jacob Hamblin, not a member of the Quorum of the Twelve but popularly known as the "Apostle to the Lamanites," epitomized the best of Latter-day Saint behavior. On one occasion, a group of Navajo came to trade with him. As was their custom, they stopped on a hill just outside Kanab where Hamblin was then living. They built a smoke and with a blanket signaled their arrival. Hamblin sent his son, Jacob Jr., with a pony to exchange for blankets. "The boy, eager to make a good bargain, kept demanding more and more, and the Indian gave what he asked without much protest. When [Jacob Jr.] arrived home, pleased with himself as a good trader, his father looked at the blankets, and without comment counted out one pile. 'You take these back,' he told the boy. 'You charged too much for the pony; this is all he is worth.' At the camp the Indian was evidently expecting him. 'I know you come back,' the native said. 'Jacob your father? He my father, too.'"[9]

At times, it was envisioned that the family relationship might even become literal rather than just figurative. According to a later recollection by W. W. Phelps, when Joseph Smith arrived in Missouri for the first time in the summer of 1831, the Prophet conveyed the

---

8. Brigham Young to Chief Walkara, January 22, 1855, as cited in Leonard J. Arrington, *Brigham Young: American Moses* (New York: Knopf, 1985), 217.

9. Juanita Brooks, "Jacob Hamblin: Apostle to the Indians," *Improvement Era*, April 1944, 253–54, as cited in Arrington and Bitton, *Mormon Experience*, 155.

word of the Lord thus: "It is my will, that, in time, ye should take unto you wives of the Lamanites."[10] That directive has been fulfilled off and on over the years, beginning with Benjamin Grouard's 1846 marriage to the Tuamotuan princess, Tearo, during the first Mormon mission to the South Pacific.[11] Wilford Woodruff kept an extensive and detailed diary from the 1830s to the 1890s. In it, he recorded the essence of a speech President Brigham Young gave just days after entering the Salt Lake Valley in 1847. According to Woodruff, Young desired "that our people would be connected with every tribe of Indians throughout America & that our people would yet take their squaws wash & dress them up teach them our language & learn them to labour & learn them the gospel of there [sic] forefathers & raise up children by them & teach the children & not many generations Hence they will become A white & delightsome people & in no other way will it be done & that the time was nigh at hand when the gospel must go to that people."[12]

Once formal missions were launched among western Indians during the 1850s, Woodruff noted, "President Young said He w[an]ted the Elders to marry the squaws of the Tribes to fulfill the commandment of God &c."[13] And in response to a "fuss" being made over John D. Lee's marrying an Indian woman, President Young, with droll hyperbole, said: "We have sent Elders for several years to go among the Indians [to] marry their squaws & identify themselves with the Indians. Go and live with them but up to this day I could not get an Elder to do it I have said if any man could get appointed to take my place I would show them how it was done."[14]

---

10. W. W. Phelps to Brigham Young, August 12, 1861, Church Archives.

11. Addison Pratt, *The Journals of Addison Pratt*, ed. S. George Ellsworth (Salt Lake City: University of Utah Press, 1990), 275–77.

12. Wilford Woodruff Journal, July 28, 1847, Church Archives.

13. Woodruff Journal, September 16, 1857.

14. Woodruff Journal, November 18, 1858.

Missions to the Pacific

How did the Lamanite work come to be extended to the Pacific? In the 1840s, converted whaler Addison Pratt told Joseph Smith he thought the Hawaiians were related to the American Indians. This may have prompted the Prophet to authorize a mission to the Pacific Islands as a significant step toward implementing his stirring April 1843 challenge to the Quorum of the Twelve: "Don't let a single corner of the earth go without a mission."[15] Less than a month later, the Quorum met in the Prophet's Nauvoo office and called Addison Pratt, Noah Rogers, Benjamin F. Grouard, and Knowlton F. Hanks to the Pacific Islands.

On June 1, 1843, without fanfare, but not without deep feelings about leaving loved ones, Pratt and the others quietly commenced their journey to Massachusetts, whence in October they set sail on the whaler *Timoleon* bound for the Pacific Ocean. Nearly seven months would elapse before Pratt disembarked on the island of Tubuai and commenced his mission in what is now French Polynesia. Pratt knew some Hawaiians from his whaling days, and Grouard learned the local tongue quickly and began teaching the gospel to the islander population. It was the first mission of The Church of Jesus Christ of Latter-day Saints in which proselyting was systematically carried out in a language other than English. It was also the first mission outside North America to a non-European people.

From the beginning of the work in the Pacific, the elders felt they were dealing with the house of Israel. When challenged about the value of teaching the native population, George Q. Cannon, one of the original missionaries to Hawaii in 1850, replied, "The soul of a Sandwich Islander or a Lamanite is as precious in the sight of the Lord as the soul of a white man, whether born in America or Europe. Jesus died for one as much as the other."[16]

---

15. Pratt, *The Journals of Addison Pratt*, 114.
16. George Q. Cannon, *My First Mission* (Salt Lake City: Juvenile Instructor Office, 1879), 57.

From such modest beginnings, great things have come. Today, there are hundreds of thousands of Pacific Islander Latter-day Saints, and their faith is legendary in the Church. Samoa was the first country in the world to be completely covered by stakes, and before the recent surge in temple building, there were more temples per capita in the Pacific Islands than in any other area of the Church. Sixth-generation Latter-day Saints can be found in a number of places around the Pacific. Have you ever wondered why it is that the highest national percentages of Church membership today are found in the Pacific Islands or why the only branch of BYU located outside the Intermountain West is located in Hawaii? Is it because Church leaders were looking for a resort location where they and the students could enjoy sun and surf? Have you ever considered why it was that the first temple built outside western North America just happened to be located in the same place?

At first, the connection between Polynesians and the Book of Mormon may not seem obvious. Yet the link noted by Pacific Islanders is to Hagoth and the several boatloads of people who set sail and "were never heard of more" (see Alma 63:5–8). Over time, Hagoth's voyagers would come to be considered part of Polynesians' ancestry. In 1913 a group of Maori Saints made the long and arduous voyage from New Zealand to Utah to go through the temple. When they arrived on the West Coast, they telegraphed the First Presidency, "Who knows but that some of Hagoth's people have arrived, *pea*." Their leader, Stuart Meha, wrote, "I added the little word 'pea' (perhaps) not because of any element of doubt on my part but I wanted to raise comment which I succeeded in doing." Upon their arrival in Utah, leading Church authorities, including President Joseph F. Smith, held a reception for the Maori Saints. Among other things, President Smith said, "You brethren and sisters from New Zealand,

I want you to know that you are from the people of Hagoth and there is no 'pea' about it."[17]

Two years later, speaking at the October 1915 semiannual general conference, President Smith declared, "Away off in the Pacific Ocean are various groups of islands, from the Sandwich Islands down to Tahiti, Samoa, Tonga, and New Zealand. On them are thousands of good people . . . of the blood of Israel. When you carry the Gospel to them they receive it with open hearts. They need the same privileges . . . that we enjoy, but these are out of their power. They are poor, and they can't gather means to come up here to be endowed, and sealed for time and eternity, for their living and their dead, and to be baptized for their dead."[18] So he proposed that a temple be built for them, and a sustaining vote was called for. Interestingly, such a prospect had been entertained almost from the beginning of the work in the Pacific. In 1852, less than two years after the first contingent of missionaries arrived in Hawaii, they held a conference at which John Stillman Woodbury spoke in tongues. Elder Frances A. Hammond gave the interpretation, which he recorded in his journal: "The Lord is well pleased with the labors of his servants on the islands and angels of the Lord are near us, that the people we are laboring among are a remnant of the seed of Joseph, that they would be built up on these islands, and that a temple will be built in this land."[19]

---

17. Stuart Meha, "The Origin of the Maori," address delivered April 15, 1962, in *New Zealand: A Short Collection of Items of History*, ed. Glen L. Rudd (Salt Lake City: privately published, 1993), 4–5. Non-LDS support for this position is assessed in Jerry K. Loveland, "Hagoth and the Polynesian Tradition," *BYU Studies* 17 (Autumn 1976): 59–73.

18. Joseph F. Smith, in Conference Report, October 1915, 8.

19. Francis A. Hammond Journal, October 6, 1852, as cited in Joseph H. Spurrier, "The Hawaii Temple: A Special Place in a Special Land," *1986 Mormon Pacific Historical Society Conference Proceedings.*

Work in the Southern Hemisphere

A similar interest in the seed of Joseph motivated the beginning of the work in this hemisphere south of the United States. It was part of what led Elder Parley P. Pratt to sail to Chile in the 1850s, and it contributed to the early forays into Mexico several decades later. Politics and an entrenched cultural Catholicism made matters difficult in Latin America, but the legacy of Joseph Smith's concern for the children of Lehi persisted. By the twentieth century, other circumstances and motives would blend to expand the work to all peoples of the Americas. Nonetheless, though the initial and ostensible purpose of the first mission to South America was to work with the German immigrants around Buenos Aires and in southern Brazil, there was an early and aborted attempt to take the gospel to the Indians of northern Argentina.

That such people would eventually constitute the greater part of the Latin America harvest was the hope and faith of Elder Melvin J. Ballard, who inaugurated the work in South America. In 1931 he wrote an impassioned interpretation of the several revolutions that had taken place in South America. Recalling the interference the missionaries had received when attempting to reach the Chaco Indians and reflecting on the recent revolutions, Elder Ballard remarked: "Liberty must come before the Gospel message can be very effectively proclaimed among the millions of Indians who are descendants of Father Lehi and members of the House of Israel. The growing demand in all those South American republics for the separation of the church from the state is a very hopeful sign." Then referring to the Book of Mormon, he declared: "This record of America's ancient inhabitants was given to the Latter-day Saints, not essentially for themselves, but chiefly for the benefit of these descendants of Father Lehi, the American Indians. It must go to them, but it cannot go until God has prepared the way. This he is now doing. These numerous revolutions are steps towards that end. The Latter-day Saints do not, therefore, see disaster in these political disturbances, but rather progress, growth, and development."

The Book of Mormon predicts both the distress as well as the eventual deliverance of the Indian peoples. Elder Ballard found in the plight of the Indians fulfillment of Book of Mormon prophecies. "These predictions have been fulfilled to the letter," he declared. "No more cruel page in all history can be found than the story of the subjugation of the South American Indian."

Of course, he felt that the gospel would be the ultimate means of their redemption, but he also hoped that the future would bring what he called "the return of large landed estates to the government for redistribution to the common people." His Book of Mormon–based concern for millions of disempowered Latin American Indians profoundly influenced his assessment of current sociopolitical affairs as well as the nature of the Mormon mission to Latin America. "God speed every movement," he concluded, "that looks for the emancipation of the downtrodden and oppressed Indians of South America and prepare us [as Latter-day Saints] that we may discharge our sacred obligation to take the torch of light and truth to them, that they may begin to blossom as the rose and prepare for the return of their former blessings."[20] What a powerful articulation of the legacy of the Prophet Joseph Smith!

Though in the period following World War II, missionary outreach in Latin America was to all people, many who were taught and baptized traced some part of their ancestry to Father Lehi. Continued interest in the children of Lehi led to the building of secondary schools throughout Latin America and the Pacific. This the Church did in few other areas and never to the extent that it did in the lands of Lehi's descendants. From the first schools conducted by Caroline Crosby and Louisa Barnes Pratt in French Polynesia in the 1850s to the establishment of schools like Benemerito in Mexico or Lia-

---

20. Melvin J. Ballard, "Significance of South American Revolutions," *Improvement Era*, April 1931, 317–20.

hona High in Tonga in the twentieth century, Latter-day Saints have endeavored to live the legacy of nursing fathers and mothers. And that legacy continues today through the Perpetual Education Fund, though it serves all needy and qualified Saints.

Socioeconomic Oneness

The Prophet's vision of the Lamanites blossoming as a rose has always fit into an even grander vision of socioeconomic oneness for all God's children. In the same revelation that predicted that the Lamanites would blossom, the Lord warned that "it is not given that one man should possess that which is above another, wherefore, the world lieth in sin" (D&C 49:20). And elsewhere, with a particular eye to temporal affairs, revelation disclosed, "If ye are not one ye are not mine" (D&C 38:27). Joseph taught that the earth was the Lord's and that its human inhabitants, His children, were stewards who must act with proper regard for the rights of each other. In some of the strongest language in any of the revelations received by Joseph Smith, the Lord warned that "if any man shall take of the abundance which I have made, and impart not his portion . . . unto the poor and the needy, he shall, with the wicked, lift up his eyes in hell, being in torment" (D&C 104:18).

This vision has led generations of Saints to sympathize with the socioeconomic plight of Lehi's descendants. Land ownership, as Elder Ballard so poignantly pointed out, has always been at the heart of the tension between indigenous natives and colonizing settlers. Whether it was in reaction to the great *Mahele*, the land division that took place in Hawaii just two years before the arrival of Elder Cannon and companions, or to the 1840 Treaty of Waitangi in New Zealand, Latter-day Saint missionaries have demonstrated solidarity with their indigenous converts on this matter.

In Hawaii, by the end of the nineteenth century, ownership and control of the best agricultural land had shifted into the hands of white men. This was accompanied by the overthrow of the Hawaiian

Monarchy in 1893. However, in the final quarter of the twentieth century, Hawaiian Latter-day Saints themselves would play prominent roles in seeking redress of grievances. A young Hawaiian taxi driver, Sister Louise Rice, was profoundly touched by reading the memoirs of the Queen Liliuokalani. This Mormon mother organized ALOHA (Aboriginal Land of Hawaiian Ancestry) in an effort to improve the situation. ALOHA filed their grievances with the United States government. With the support of Senator Daniel K. Inouye of Hawaii, this led to a formal investigation of the overthrow of the monarchy and the illegal possession of Hawaiian lands.

In New Zealand in the late 1800s, mission president W. T. Stewart recorded in his diary the reaction of many a missionary to the plight of the Maori: "Read treaty between natives & English called Waitanga [sic] Treaty, made in 1840. It occurs to me that it is like most of the pacts made between whites & natives the world over, especially the aborigines of America, only monuments of deception and fraud."[21] In a letter to his wife, Alma Greenwood reported the reasons the Maori gave "for having their attention and interest directed to us and the cause we represent." Among other factors, "They say the churches . . . have been going up, and we have been going down on our own lands. . . . When the white man came here first, he brought the gun to shoot the man. Next he brought the Gospel to shoot the Maori and his land. But the Gospel which you bring shoots the kings, governors, ministers, churches and all."[22]

Through speech, action, and especially through scripture, Joseph Smith bequeathed to the Latter-day Saints an exalted view of the identity of indigenous peoples in the western hemisphere and in Polynesia, whom they understood to be the children of Lehi.

21. William Thomas Stewart Journal, September 14, 1883, Church Archives.
22. Alma Greenwood to F. M. Greenwood, May 14, 1884, Greenwood Scrapbook, Church Archives. A nearly identical version is found in Greenwood, "My New Zealand Mission," *Juvenile Instructor*, December 1, 1885, 258.

Such a legacy has made generations of Mormon missionaries noticeably more admiring of Native Americans and Pacific Islanders and more comfortable with their cultures than other people of European descent. As one would expect from Caucasians in the past, the Prophet's people were not immune from the racial assumptions of the age. Yet they wore the "white man's burden" more lightly than their Euro-American counterparts.

More than just a lessening of prejudice, however, Latter-day Saints have absorbed the Prophet's profound faith that the descendants of Lehi were in the Lord's hand in special ways. At a time when Church leaders had little positive to say about alleged visions and miracles among European Christians, Joseph F. Smith, then a counselor in the First Presidency, reflected his uncle's legacy in his reaction to Wovoka, the Paiute prophet associated with the Ghost Dance movement and the Wounded Knee Massacre. As to Wovoka's alleged visions, President Smith wrote, "It is in perfect harmony with the order of heaven for ministering spirits or messengers from God or Christ to visit the Lamanites or any other people, as Cornelius of old was visited, and as Christ visited Saul, and for the same purposes."

With regard to the Lamanites, President Smith spoke of God "hasten[ing] their enlightenment by means of dreams, visions, and heavenly manifestations." Smith also made it clear that "the object to be attained by such manifestations as the Lamanites claim to have had, admitting the same to be true and from God, can be no other than to begin the preparation of the Lamanites to receive a correct knowledge of God and of their fathers, and of the holy gospel already revealed and established among men, that they might believe, obey and be saved thereby."[23] From the Hopi to the Hawaiians, Church history in the Pacific and among Native Americans is replete with such accounts.

---

23. Joseph Fielding Smith, *Gospel Doctrine: Selections from the Sermons and Writings of Joseph F. Smith*, comp. John A. Widtsoe (Salt Lake: Deseret Book, 1939), 379, 381.

Time has permitted only the briefest glimpse of the Prophet's legacy in Latin America and the Pacific. Fully told, the story will fill volumes, for in one sense, every aspect of Church life and Latter-day Sainthood in these areas can be linked to Joseph's legacy. Yet behind it all was a vision, a vision of ennobling and enabling self-identity, a vision of covenant and promise that encouraged peoples too frequently demeaned and disregarded by technologically advantaged global neighbors to believe in themselves and, paraphrasing Elder David A. Bednar's words in the April 2005 general conference, choose the Lord so that their own longstanding chosennesss could be powerfully manifest in their lives. Today, literally millions of members of The Church of Jesus Christ of Latter-day Saints in Latin America and the Pacific trace some part of their ancestry to Father Lehi. This remarkable concentration fulfills another of Joseph's prophecies that the day would come "when the arm of the Lord shall be revealed in power in convincing . . . the house of Joseph, of the gospel of their salvation" and that it would "come to pass in a day, that every man shall hear the fulness of the gospel in his own tongue, and in his own language" (D&C 90:10–11). How fully we are witnessing the fulfillment of this prophecy in our day.

I, for one, am greatly inspired by, and profoundly grateful to, the Prophet Joseph Smith for doing something so wonderful for peoples who have so much to offer the human family. What a legacy of love, what a legacy of the power of human potential he has left us! That legacy invites us all to remember the Lord's words, "Inasmuch as ye have done it unto one of the least of these my brethren, ye have done it unto me" (Matthew 25:40).

Grant Underwood is a professor of history at Brigham Young University. This essay was presented at "Joseph Smith and the World," the International Society's sixteenth annual conference, April 2005, Brigham Young University, Provo, Utah.

Chapter 3

The Prophet's Impact on Europe, Then and Now

Elder Keith K. Hilbig

I AM INTRIGUED by Church history, especially with respect to Joseph Smith, the remarkable man and prophet who opened this dispensation. The impact of his work upon the world is significant. Upon reflection, I feel the title of my remarks may be a bit misleading, because the impact of his work (and that of his successors) has not necessarily been upon nation-states alone but also upon the individual inhabitants of those sovereign nations, which we collectively call Europe. His impact is not only upon a continent or a government; the impact is really upon people. For those European individuals who were exposed to and responded to the restored gospel, and for their progeny, the Prophet's impact upon them has been profound. And it remains profound. My approach shall not be one of details and academic analysis. Rather, since I am one of the progeny of that group, I want to speak with you on a personal level about experiences I have had in light of the larger issue, namely Joseph's impact upon Europe.

My wife also stems from the group who accepted the gospel in Europe in the early 1900s. Our children have become beneficiaries of those early labors, as have our grandchildren. So it will continue to reverberate through future generations. We have been blessed by the prophetic vision that Joseph had concerning the work in those foreign lands. Some results were apparent in his lifetime; others followed his martyrdom and continue into our time. Currently, nearly *all* the peoples of the European continent have been exposed to the gospel.

I have had the privilege of living, studying, working, and serving in a variety of settings throughout Western and Eastern Europe for about twelve years of my adult life. I desire to share with you some of the things that I personally experienced that reflect the impact of the Prophet, then and now.

In 1924, during the very chaotic decade following World War I in Germany and the prelude to what would become Hitler's rise in the following decade, two missionaries walked through the small town of Zwickau. It lies in the southeast corner of Germany, nestled up against the Erzgebirge, a mountain range that forms the border with Czechoslovakia. Those two missionaries brought the gospel to my grandmother and to my father, his brother, and two sisters. My father was baptized at age twelve. At sixteen, he was an orphan. He had just completed his three-year apprenticeship as a baker. I once asked him why he decided to become a baker. He answered, "It was the only way I could be assured of having something to eat."

At age sixteen, he and his seventeen-year-old brother, seeing no future in that environment and because of the gospel they had accepted as teenagers, came to the New World to begin a new life. Just one generation later, I had the privilege of earning a law degree. Such was one impact of Joseph, through those two missionaries in Zwickau, upon *my* life.

When my father landed at Ellis Island, they put a ribbon around his neck with a card attached, stating, "Send this person to Milwaukee." He and his brother walked out of the processing center, a taxi cab driver read the sign, and he took them to the correct train in New York City. They woke up a day and half later in Milwaukee, where their sister had gone earlier to live. The next day, a Sunday morning, they were up early. They went to Church in the small branch in Milwaukee, because the restored gospel was of such great importance to them.

At age twenty-one, some five years after his arrival, my father received a German-language triple combination from a friend. He suggested that my father consider serving a mission. My dad had been saving his money since he arrived in September 1929; he often said that he was perhaps responsible for the Great Depression, which began the next month. He was very cautious about preserving his limited funds. In 1937, some eight years after his arrival, he had saved enough money to request the opportunity to serve as a missionary. He was called at the height of the Depression, the very first missionary sent from the Chicago Illinois Stake. He took his triple combination with him during his service in the East German Mission, eventually proselyting in the town where he was born and where he was baptized.

My father was one of those German missionaries who escaped into Denmark the day before World War II began when all German borders were sealed. He always wanted to go back again and serve among the German-speaking Saints.

In 1962 he gave his German-language triple combination to me, as I left for my mission in Germany. When I came back, I returned it to him as he and my stepmother were called to serve as senior missionaries assigned to Austria-Yugoslavia. When they came back, I took it and used it during the three years our family served in Switzerland. Thereafter, I gave it to a son who was called to serve in Dresden, Germany, before the Berlin Wall came down, and later to another son who labored in the Germany Frankfurt Mission.

I am now holding this book in trust, against the day when (I am confident) the Lord will yet call one of my father's great-grandsons to again take this now eighty-year-old book into missionary service in Europe. I cannot comment on the impact of Joseph on European *governments*, but I do know about the impact of Joseph's labors upon European *individuals* and upon our family in particular.

To me, this German triple combination constitutes tangible evidence of the Prophet's impact upon Europe, then and now.

Now I should like to return to the time of the Prophet. We have heard of his worldview and of his world religion concept and of the results of his efforts in various parts of the world. Such a global vision in 1830 should not surprise us. It had to be (from the very beginning) a worldwide Church because the apostasy itself was worldwide—the cure would have to be at least as broad as the malady. Just as individual people were surrounded by a loss of truth for decades and centuries, so also would it be necessary that individual people be exposed to the fulness of truth.

This idea of establishing a world church was not Joseph's idea. We have spoken in terms of *his* decisions and *his* recommendations and *his* writings. In fact, that which he was teaching was of the Lord. The concept of the Church being worldwide, even at the outset, is to be found in the scriptures and the revelations. For example, if you will open the Book of Mormon and read the testimony of the Three Witnesses, the first line states, "Be it known unto all nations, kindreds, tongues and people, unto whom this work shall come: That we, through the grace of God the Father, . . . have seen the plates" (Book of Mormon, Testimony of Three Witnesses). Exactly the same opening line is contained in the testimony of the Eight Witnesses. Those experiences were in June of 1829, many months before the Church was even organized.

In section 58 of the Doctrine and Covenants, Joseph is in Jackson County, Missouri. This revelation is given to him in August 1831. In verse 45 (speaking of the missionaries) we read: "For, behold, they [the elders of the Church] shall push the people together from the ends of the earth." Now in that day the "pushing together" was going to be manifested in the creation of Zion, the *gathering of Zion*. Nowadays we seek to "push the people together" in *stakes of Zion*, where they are equally finding a refuge. But the central concept was to "push the people together from the ends of the earth" into Zion. And then just a few lines further, in verse 64, we read: "For, verily, the

sound [meaning the gospel message] must go forth from this place
[meaning Jackson County] into all the world, and unto the uttermost
parts of the earth." No question that this was intended to be an international effort. Three months later, Joseph received the revelation
that would become the preface to the Doctrine and Covenants. Now
from section 1, verses 1–2 and 4–5:

> Hearken, O ye people of my church, saith the voice of him who
> dwells on high, and whose eyes are upon all men; yea, verily
> I say: Hearken ye people from afar; and ye that are upon the
> islands of the sea, listen together.
>
> For verily the voice of the Lord is unto all men, and there
> is none to escape; and there is no eye that shall not see, neither
> ear that shall not hear, neither heart that shall not be pene-
> trated. . . .
>
> And the voice of warning shall be unto all people, by
> the mouths of my disciples, whom I have chosen in these last
> days.
>
> And they shall go forth and none shall stay them, for I the
> Lord have commanded them.

In the October 2003 general conference, President Gordon B.
Hinckley quoted those verses, and then he added these words: "There
can be no doubt concerning our responsibility to the peoples of the
earth. There can be no doubt that we are moving forward in pursuing
that responsibility."[1] The task outlined to the Prophet Joseph has now
been transferred to our shoulders by President Hinckley. May our
efforts have the same impact as was experienced in Joseph's day!

We have heard passages from the Wentworth Letter, including the "standard of truth" language, how it would go forth boldly
and nobly. We also have heard of Joseph's prophecy (as recorded by
Wilford Woodruff and recounted by him in general conference in
1898) about how the word, the Church, would fill North and South
America. I want to read a further portion of Joseph's prophetic text,

---

1. Gordon B. Hinckley, "The State of the Church," *Ensign*, November
    2003, 4.

because we usually stop at the "filling of the Americas." Joseph stated as follows: "It is only a little handful of Priesthood you see here tonight, but this Church will fill North and South America, it will fill the world. . . . This people will go into the Rocky Mountains; they will build temples to the Most High. They will raise up a posterity there."[2]

Part of the posterity that would be raised in that setting of the Rocky Mountains, I submit, would be the progeny of those who were gathered in Europe and ultimately landed in the Utah valleys. A generation later they would be sending their offspring back to Europe, the lands of their heritage. It was not only Joseph who thought in those terms. Sidney Rigdon reminisced once about a visit to the Peter Whitmer Sr. cabin in Waterloo, New York. He gave a talk in April of 1844, saying: "I recollect in the year 1830, I met the whole church of Christ in a little old log house just about 20 feet square . . . and we began to talk about the kingdom of God as if we had the world at our command; we talked with great confidence, and we talked big things, although we were not many people, we had big feelings; . . . we looked upon the men of the earth as grasshoppers . . . we talked about the people coming as doves to the windows, that all nations should flock unto it."[3] Now talk about self-confidence and the ability to carry out that obligation; they had it!

About six weeks before his martyrdom, Joseph stated, "I calculate to be one of the instruments of setting up the kingdom of Daniel by the word of the Lord, and I intend to lay a foundation that will revolutionize the whole world."[4] We can only speculate as to what would have happened if that martyrdom had been avoided or, at least, delayed, but it was not the plan.

---

2. Joseph Smith, as quoted by Wilford Woodruff, in Conference Report, April 1898, 57.
3. "Conference Minutes," *Times and Seasons*, May 1, 1844, 522–23.
4. Joseph Smith, *Teachings of the Prophet Joseph Smith*, comp. Joseph Fielding Smith (Salt Lake City: Deseret Book, 1976), 366.

In addition to Sidney Rigdon, Parley P. Pratt made this insightful statement referring to Joseph: "He has organized the kingdom of God.—*We* will extend its dominion. He has restored the fulness of the Gospel.—*We* will spread it abroad."[5] Again, an abiding sense of certainty and self-assurance is evidenced by the early Saints. Joseph grasped the big picture. He had the vision. But he needed strong men and strong women to realize that vision. The attitude of Parley P. Pratt reflects the kind of people whom the Lord raised up at the opening of this dispensation, people who would make it work. Joseph's boldness in pronouncements and expectations were, I suggest, born of his experiences with the Savior and other heavenly tutors. This was not Joseph's personal plan. He was the spokesman for what the Lord had in mind.

By January 1841, the Saints are, of course, in Nauvoo. Section 124 is given, continuing instructions to the Prophet Joseph Smith. I shall read from the middle of verse 2: "I say unto you [the Lord speaking to Joseph], that you are now called immediately to make a solemn proclamation of my gospel, and of this stake which I have planted to be a cornerstone of Zion, which shall be polished with the refinement which is after the similitude of a palace." In verse 3 the Lord stated: "This proclamation shall be made to all the kings of the world, to the four corners thereof, to the honorable president-elect, and the high-minded governors of the nation in which you live, and to all the nations of the earth scattered abroad."

Note that the proclamation that Joseph was commanded to prepare "immediately" was to be made to "all kings of the world, to the four corners thereof, to the honorable president-elect, and the high minded governors of the nation in which you live, and to all the nations of the earth scattered abroad."

In Doctrine and Covenants 124:12, the Lord said further, "And again, verily I say unto you, let my servant Robert B. Thompson help

---

5.   Parley P. Pratt, "Proclamation to the Church of Jesus Christ of Latter-day Saints: Greeting," *Millennial Star*, March 1845, 151; emphasis added.

you to write this proclamation." The proclamation was not produced in a timely manner. It was not until the martyrdom approached that they responded to the direction of the Lord. In April 1845 that four-year-old commandment was finally realized. It was, however, not written by Brother Robert B. Thompson (who probably fainted at the assignment). Rather, Wilford Woodruff picked up the pen. He wrote this "Proclamation to the World" in behalf of the Twelve. They approved his text, and it was printed and subsequently distributed by the missionaries throughout the world.

I shall read just a few excerpts to give you a flavor of the confident attitude of these pioneers. The proclamation was directed to all the various important people of the earth, as instructed by Doctrine and Covenants 124:3. The actual proclamation includes this bold language: "Know ye that the kingdom of God has come as has been predicted by ancient prophets and prayed for in all ages. Even that kingdom that shall fill the whole earth and shall stand forever." Being very conscious of Daniel's prophecy, the authors continue: "We say to all people, Repent, and be baptized in the name of Jesus Christ, for remission of sins; and you shall receive the Holy Spirit, and shall know the truth, and be numbered with the House of Israel." After fourteen pages of text, the proclamation concludes with a bold invitation and with a stirring promise of blessings:

> And we once more invite all the kings, presidents, governors, rulers, judges, and people of the earth, to aid us, the Latter-day Saints; and also, the Jews, and all the remnants of Israel, by your influence and protection, and by your silver and gold, that we may build the cities of Zion and Jerusalem, and the temples and sanctuaries of our God; and may accomplish the great restoration of all things, and bring in latter-day glory.
>
> That knowledge, truth, light, love, peace, union, honor, glory, and power, may fill the earth with eternal life and joy. That death, bondage, oppression, war, mourning, sorrow, and

pain, may be done away with for ever, and all tears be wiped from every eye.[6]

What lofty aspirations! But it wasn't only talk; they did try to go out and actually do it.

Early Gathering Efforts

If I am going to be true to my topic, I had better start now talking about Europe a bit. We are all aware that Europe was the initial source of the gathering to Zion. It would provide strength to Nauvoo. It would populate the Great Basin. It would establish the Church. And thereafter, the European immigrants would be sending out generation after generation to return to the lands of Europe as missionaries.

The very first foreign mission was, of course, Canada. However, the first overseas mission did not occur until much later. That effort commenced on Sunday, June 4, 1837, in the Kirtland Temple. Heber C. Kimball was attending Church services there. Following the meeting, the Prophet said to Heber, in effect, "I want to talk to you." He then issued the call for Heber C. Kimball to lead the overseas missionary effort, which was to commence in Great Britain.

Heber wrote in his journal that he was informed by "Brother Hyrum Smith of the Presidency of the Church," who said that he (Heber) had "been designed by the Spirit" and was now appointed to take charge of the mission for the kingdom of Great Britain. Heber C. Kimball was hesitant. He felt inadequate. He was concerned for the welfare of his family, but consider what Heber wrote in his journal: "The moment I understood the will of my Heavenly Father, I felt a determination to go at all hazards, believing that He would . . .

---

6. "Proclamation of the Twelve Apostles of the Church of Jesus Christ of Latter-day Saints," as quoted in James R. Clark, comp., *Messages of the First Presidency* (Salt Lake City: Bookcraft, 1965), 1:264.

endow me with every qualification I needed."[7] The men who would carry out the Prophet's vision operated with that mindset.

Seven brethren went. Heber was the leader, but with him came Orson Hyde, Willard Richards, Joseph Fielding, and then John Goodson, Isaac Russell, and John Snyder. This call came on June 4. By June 13 they were on their way to the East Coast, a mere nine days after the call. We do not know what Sister Kimball had to say, but Heber was gone by June 13. The missionaries landed in Liverpool on July 20. Ten days later, at the end of July 1837, the first baptisms occurred. The city of Preston, where a temple has now been built, is where the Church began in Great Britain.

The seven intrepid missionaries departed after nine months. It was a relatively short period, but when they left, some fifteen hundred baptisms had been performed. In 1838 six returned to America, while Willard Richards remained in England. In 1840 the second group was sent out: Brigham Young, Parley P. Pratt, Orson Pratt, John Taylor, Wilford Woodruff, and George A. Smith. Heber C. Kimball went along for his second tour of duty, and Willard Richards rejoined the arriving group to begin his second mission. Upon landing, Orson Pratt was assigned to Scotland. John Taylor was assigned to Ireland. Wilford Woodruff, George A. Smith, and Heber C. Kimball went into London to deal with the metropolis head on. There was great harvesting in all of those settings.

The success of this missionary effort must be measured not only in the number of baptisms but also by the effect it had upon the Quorum of the Twelve. In Kirtland the Quorum members had experienced some problems, but in Great Britain they labored together effectively. A relationship was forged; they solidified as a body; they were being prepared for what would follow once they returned to their homes.

---

7.   Heber C. Kimball, *Journal of Heber Kimball* (Salt Lake City: Juvenile Instructor Office, 1882), 10–11.

The baptismal successes generated hundreds of immigrants. The numbers of people leaving England because of the Church became somewhat of a topic in Great Britain. Charles Dickens wrote about the phenomenon in a book called the *Uncommercial Traveler.* He described a man (which was Dickens himself) who liked to travel about, observing events. Let me read from Dickens's novel: "I . . . had come aboard this Emigrant Ship to see what Eight hundred Latter-day Saints were like, and I found them (to the rout and overthrow of all my expectations) like what I will now describe with scrupulous exactness." What he saw surprised him (he had anticipated a coarse group, as he had seen on other immigrant ships). After confirming with the shipping agent that the people really were Mormons, Dickens's character says to the agent: "These are a very fine set of people you have brought together here. . . . Indeed, I think it would be difficult to find eight hundred people together anywhere else, and find so much beauty and so much strength and capacity for work among them." The agent responds saying, "I think so! We sent out about a thousand more, yes'day, from Liverpool."[8]

There was clearly something about those converts that impressed even a jaded Charles Dickens. He wrote that their "universal cheerfulness was amazing." He saluted the impressive Mormon convert immigrants as follows: "I should have said they were in their degree the pick and flower of England."[9]

By the way, that phrase became the title of a 1987 book that commemorated the first century and a half of the Church in England. They *were* indeed the pick and flower of England, being "pushed together" for the establishment of the Church. The European missionary work had been effective; these converts were changing their

8. Charles Dickens, *The Uncommercial Traveler,* [1863], 445–49.
9. Dickens, *The Uncommercial Traveler,* 445–49. Brigham Young, as quoted in "To the Editor of the Millennial Star," *Millennial Star,* February 1, 1846, 39.

lives. It was a palpable change, as Dickens's characterization of the Mormon convert immigrants confirms.

The second group of missionaries had spent a year in Great Britain and returned to Nauvoo in 1841. In 1846, Parley P. Pratt and John Taylor went back to England, some others having been sent in the intervening years. But Joseph was interested not only in Great Britain but also in the continent. Indeed, in 1843, he had assigned Orson Hyde and James Adams to go to St. Petersburg, Russia. I do not know what happened to them, but it would not be until 1989 that Mormon missionaries appeared in St. Petersburg, Russia.

Joseph's martyrdom occurred in 1844, and Brigham Young was confronted with many challenges. Yet Joseph's vision still had to be responded to. In 1849, Brigham sent John Taylor to France, and John Taylor went on to Germany as well. He translated the Book of Mormon into French, arranged for its printing, and then went up to Hamburg to work on the German translation of the Book of Mormon in 1851.

Germany in those days was not the Germany of today. There were thirty-one independent states comprising German territory. No central government existed. In 1840 a British convert had gone into Hamburg to try to preach and was immediately arrested. In 1841 Orson Hyde stopped in Germany on his way to the Holy Land; he was promptly detained by the authorities and thrown out. In 1843 a branch was finally established just south of Frankfurt, but the missionaries were imprisoned and banished from that particular land. In 1853 missionaries had tried to get back into Berlin, which was then Prussia. They were ordered to leave immediately.

There were, however, some successes, interestingly enough in East Germany. In 1855, Karl G. Maeser was baptized in Dresden. It was such a significant event that Franklin D. Richards, then the European Mission president based in England, crossed the channel to discover who this Karl G. Maeser really was. Within a year, Brother Maeser and his family had left Dresden, immigrating to Utah. The rest is, as they say, history (especially on the BYU campus).

President Heber J. Grant once said, "If nothing more had ever been accomplished in Germany than the conversion of Karl G. Maeser, it would have been worth all the effort and money and time for that alone." So President Grant thought highly of him as well.

Interestingly, after World War I things were so chaotic in Germany that no one interfered with the missionaries. Thus, the gospel was widely preached throughout the land. It was two of those missionaries who, in 1924, baptized my father. Politically and economically, things began to fall apart in Germany between the world wars, but the missionary work was productive.

The success was so great that, before World War II, German was the second language of the Church. There were more German-speaking members than any other language save English. There were large branches in Germany before World War II, each with hundreds of members during that brief period between the two world wars.

In 1850, Lorenzo Snow went into Switzerland, and in 1853 he traveled into the Piedmont, the northern part of Italy, where he worked with Protestants rather than Catholics. However, given the governmental and cultural situations then prevailing, it would not be until 1966 that Mormon missionaries officially went back into Italy. I might parenthetically note that in May 2005, the first stake in Rome was formed. What a bookend to the initial experiences of Lorenzo Snow so many decades ago—a stake in the city of Rome itself!

Regarding Scandinavia, Erastus Snow arrived there in 1850 and tried to work in Sweden, Norway, and Denmark. A branch was established in Copenhagen with just fifty members. The first Book of Mormon translated from English was in Danish. By the time Erastus Snow left Scandinavia in 1852, many converts had immigrated to Zion. However, there were still some seven hundred people who had been baptized but remained in Scandinavia. By 1857 there were 3,400 members resident in Scandinavia. Over the course of the nineteenth century, the records show that 14,000 converts from Scandinavia came to Utah. So once again, the impact was not on governments, for they had the upper hand (a tale that does not change from century to century). Thus, the impact on the people was great, and the gathering work was clearly under way.

Just quickly, let me give a European overview: in 1861 missionaries entered Belgium, in 1864 the Netherlands Mission was opened, and in 1865 a mission was created in Austria. Finally, in 1875, the missionaries entered Finland. From 1850 to 1900, the records of the Church reflect that a total of 4,831 missionaries were sent to Europe. The areas included Great Britain, Scandinavia, the Netherlands, Switzerland, Germany, and Austria. Just under five thousand missionaries were sent to Europe during the last half of the nineteenth century. More than half of that missionary total went to Great Britain, where the work still continued to grow.

Some Saints in Utah wondered why so few missionaries were being sent to the United States, while so many were going abroad. President Brigham Young made this statement in response: "We don't owe this nation another gospel sermon, they are left to feel the wrath of an angry God." This was pre–Civil War. President Young chose to place the missionary forces where the greatest results would occur, largely in Europe. He did not lose any sleep over the United States.

Now, the real reasons for this limited missionary effort within the States were, first, the polygamy issue. Once that practice became public, it became the topic of conversation. Much animosity toward the Church was generated throughout all of the states. Second, there was a great deal of affection for Great Britain among the Twelve, because they themselves had labored there. They wanted missionaries to return and help more of those people. And third, they had much more success per missionary than would have been the case if those missionaries had been sent to the States.

The work in Great Britain also spread the gospel throughout the British Empire. Many who joined later found themselves in India or Australia and thereby became the vehicle for beginning the Church in those lands. There were, of course, missionaries sent to the

Pacific Islands, but actual emigration from the islands (the gathering to Zion) did not occur as frequently as in Europe.

The Impact Today

Allow me to scroll forward and tell you about the impact of Joseph in Europe *now*. The most recent substantial impact occurred in Eastern Europe, when the Soviet Union began to disintegrate. Estonia was one of fifteen republics in the USSR—Russia, of course, being the largest republic. The Church's experience in Estonia evidences the hand of the Lord in this work.

In 1987 a new Finland Helsinki Mission president, Steven Ray Mecham, was set apart by Elder Russell M. Nelson to begin his assignment. In the blessing Elder Nelson stated that President Mecham would open missionary work in the Baltic States and Russia. Remember, this was said in 1987. The Baltic States (Estonia, Latvia, and Lithuania) were still part of the USSR. Elder Nelson, in effect, informed the president going to Finland, "You'll open up Eastern Europe." Now, Estonia was a tiny country, half the size of Utah, with a million and a half people; it did not like the Soviet system one bit.

Two years later, in October 1989, Elder Nelson attended a mission presidents' seminar for Europe. Sister Hilbig and I were at that seminar in Budapest, Hungary, and so was President Mecham. I learned afterward that Elder Nelson took him aside at that seminar and said, "President, the time has come for you to begin missionary work in Estonia and in Russia." President Mecham promptly sent two missionaries from Finland into Estonia on month-long visas. By December 1989 four Estonians had been baptized. They were the first citizens of the Soviet Union baptized in this era. Between December 1989 and April 1990, one hundred people had been baptized in Estonia.

In early 1990, Elder Nelson returned to Europe and formally dedicated the land of Estonia for the preaching of the gospel. I was touched by something we are not often able to read, namely that remarkable dedicatory prayer. I will read to you four sentences. Elder Nelson knelt down and offered these extraordinary words:

> We pray for a blessing upon the leaders of this land [remember, Estonia was still Soviet territory] that there may be peace and religious liberty that will enable the people of this land to come unto thee. Wilt thou grant unto them the privileges of freedom as a republic, an independent republic, not a part of the Soviet Union, and give unto them opportunity to be valiant unto thee. May these people become a beacon of faith to this part of the world that from this point the gospel shall roll forth to the nations to the East and south [which nations could only be their neighboring Baltics and then Ukraine] and to the neighboring areas even beyond. May that which is accomplished here be a great forerunner of the work in the Eastern part of Europe.[10]

This dedication of Estonia occurred just four months after the first baptisms in the land. Then, just sixteen months after this dedicatory prayer, Estonia declared its independence from the Soviet Union! It had begun to receive the wondrous blessings that had been pleaded for by an Apostle. From Estonia, the restored gospel did indeed go south into Latvia and then into Lithuania. Thereafter, it went east into Russia itself.

Now, if Joseph Smith had offered such a dedicatory prayer some 150 years ago, we possibly would now be saying, "Marvelous; it has finally come true." It is also marvelous when a modern Apostle, Elder Nelson, gave the prayer, and its realization was nearly instantaneous! The same hand has always been directing the Restoration, then and now. It was not much longer thereafter until the entire Soviet Union crumbled, and the gospel began to flourish in the lands of Eastern Europe. The world changed most rapidly. I could tell you a story about each one of the lands behind the iron curtain. Time will not permit today, but I will share one more.

While Sister Hilbig and I were still in Budapest at the seminar at which Elder Nelson presided, we looked out the window from the

---

10. Russell M. Nelson, Dedicatory Prayer of Estonia.

meeting hall and noticed that fire trucks were gathering in front of the parliament building. On that day in October 1989, the ladders went up—they were dismantling the Red Star on top of the parliament building in Budapest! (Just one year prior, Elder Nelson had dedicated the land of Hungary for the preaching of the gospel.) The people of Hungary had declared independence from the Soviet Bloc and obtained their freedom.

Later, as we were traveling with Elder Nelson, word came that Erich Honecker had just died. He was the Communist head of the East German government and the man who had finally, after years of effort allowed construction of a temple behind the iron curtain and missionaries to pierce that iron curtain. We asked Elder Nelson (who knew Honecker well), "What does this mean for the future?" His calm response still rings in my ears, "Whatever happens will work for the benefit of the Church." That's prophetic. In fact, just three weeks later, the Berlin Wall came down. It was all over. "Whatever happens will work for the benefit of the Church." And it was so.

Someday, perhaps we can talk about the twenty other stories I had prepared. They are essentially the same, each reminding us of the hand of the Lord in Eastern Europe. Joseph saw the future scope of the kingdom, but he had limited opportunity to implement it. There were, throughout the Soviet Empire, solid, committed, effective people who were willing to step in and do the implementation. In a very real sense, the fall of the Soviet Union and the opening up of the East is as much a pioneering effort as were the efforts in England a century and a half before. Both efforts contributed to the establishment of the Church. I find it interesting how much those two time periods and those two efforts have in common.

I am intrigued to consider what the *next* time period will bring. I am interested in history—both secular and Church—and the more I read of both, the more I come to appreciate that the Lord is directing the affairs of man. If we will, as members of His kingdom, do *our* part, the stone will indeed roll forth, and it will roll into the waiting lands that contain half the population of the earth: China, India, and the Muslim world. If the events of Eastern Europe have already miraculously come to pass, so also can governments and individuals respond to the plan of the Lord in the coming days, precipitating further miracles.

However, *we* must bring the same qualities, resolve, capacities, and commitment that made miracles possible a century and a half ago, indeed, fifteen years ago, for those attributes will certainly be required in the decades that lie ahead.

I leave with you my testimony that this is the work of the Lord. May the Lord bless us in our individual efforts and responsibilities against this great challenge of filling the earth and preparing for the Millennium, which work was commenced by the Prophet Joseph Smith and now rests upon our shoulders.

© by Intellectual Reserve, Inc.

Elder Keith K. Hilbig is a member of the First Quorum of the Seventy. This essay was presented at "Joseph Smith and the World," the International Society's sixteenth annual conference, April 2005, Brigham Young University, Provo, Utah.

Chapter 4

"A Babe upon Its Mother's Lap":
Church Development in a Developing World

Elder Robert S. Wood

IN A REAL sense, human societies, whether portrayed as developed or developing, are designated in the prefatory section of the Doctrine and Covenants simply as "Babylon the Great," whose fundamental tendency is to "seek not the Lord to establish his righteousness." At the same time, however, The Church of Jesus Christ of Latter-day Saints, called forth out of obscurity, has been commissioned to proclaim the fulness of the gospel, to establish the everlasting covenant in the hearts of the people, and to prepare them to "speak in the name of God the Lord, even the Savior of the world" (D&C 1:20).

In the first worldwide leadership training meeting on January 11, 2003, President Boyd K. Packer reminded us of an earlier such meeting, as reported by President Wilford Woodruff:

> [One] Sunday night [in 1834] the Prophet [Joseph Smith] called on all who held the Priesthood to gather into the little log school [in Kirtland, Ohio]. . . . It was a small house, perhaps 14 feet square. But it held the whole of the Priesthood of the Church of Jesus Christ of Latter-day Saints who were then in

the town of Kirtland, and who had gathered together to go off in Zion's camp. . . . The Prophet called upon the Elders of Israel with him to bear testimony of this work. . . . When they got through, the Prophet said, "Brethren, I have been very much edified and instructed in your testimonies here tonight, but I want to say to you before the Lord, that you know no more concerning the destinies of this Church and kingdom than a babe upon its mother's lap. You don't comprehend it. . . . It is only a little handful of Priesthood you see here tonight, but this Church will [grow until it will] fill North and South America— it will fill the world."[1]

Recalling the words of President Woodruff and speaking by satellite transmission to priesthood bearers around the world, President Packer underscored just how far the Church had developed since that Sunday evening in Kirtland. He cited the flock's diversity among whom the shepherds of Israel now labor. But he also cited the unity that transcends that diversity and the categories into which we sort people: "Although we differ," he said, "in language and custom and culture and in many ways, when we meet together we strengthen one another, and we become one. The language of the Church is the language of the Spirit."

Americans or Brazilians, French or Chinese, Europeans or Africans, developed or developing—there is a tie that steps over the limits of time, space, and tradition. As the Apostle Paul recognized in his own Mediterranean world, that bond makes us "no more strangers and foreigners, but fellowcitizens with the saints, and of the household of God." It is worth emphasizing that Paul recognized that this transcendent citizenship is founded upon "apostles and prophets, Jesus Christ himself being the chief corner stone" (Ephesians 2:19–20).

---

1. Wilford Woodruff, in Conference Report, April 1898, 57, punctuation modernized, as cited in Boyd K. Packer, worldwide leadership training meeting, January 11, 2003.

As it was in the first century, so it is today. With this vista before us, let us now together consider what is, in fact, developing in the developing world and how the Church's destiny, as foreseen by the Prophet Joseph Smith, is being realized in that segment of the Lord's vineyard.

Developmentalism and Multiculturalism

The very term *development* is weighted with much baggage and often intense controversy. As some of the terms of the debate are relevant to the discussion of the Church's role, particularly outside of Western Europe, Canada, and the United States, let me venture into these murky waters. The notion of the developing world preceded in various guises the contemporary world and may, in some sense, be seen as related to what the historian J. P. Bury called the "idea of progress" in Western history. So let me start where such things often begin—in ancient Greece.

Despite the strength of the ancient belief that human history is cyclical—or that, at best, humanity's finest moments lie behind it in some golden age—by the start of the fifth century before Christ, the Greek poet and philosopher Xenophanes (560–478 BC) wrote, "The gods did not reveal from the beginning all things to us; but in the course of time, through seeking, men find that which is better." Through human effort and striving, things may get better or, in other words, they develop.

Aristotle explicitly linked development with inherent potential and the fulfillment of that potential with human happiness. When each living thing is given proper external conditions and nurture, it tends toward some good or end. So it is with human beings and, by extension, human societies. In this view, individual and social development is not simply culturally determined—although favored or inhibited by the conditions of time and place—but is defined by the nature of human beings, their potential, and their proper end.

This philosophical stance was given a powerful boost with the industrial revolution's onset. Insight into how the material world works along with human inventiveness and invention reinforced both the notions of development as improvement and of the commonality of that development in all societies.

By the 1950s a whole literature on intellectual, scientific, technological, economic, social, and political development surfaced, but with it came controversy whether such an approach to those societies characterized as "developing" was just an imperial or colonial perspective, a mirror image of Western intellectual and social history.

Indeed, after the Second World War, policy makers and analysts alike divided the world in three parts, with two parts being defined by the Cold War divide and one part being the Third World that was not clearly associated with either side of that Cold War divide or was assertively nonaligned. A high percentage of those states were in the southern hemisphere and were characterized not only by their stance on the Cold War but also by their level of development. Development was explicitly defined by reference to key political, social, and economic traits of the American-led coalition, centered in North America (the United States and Canada), Western Europe, and Japan. Aside from the military containment of the Soviet Union and its partners, coalition members were increasingly defined by policy goals and processes that favored economically integrated, market-based, liberal democratic, and rule-coordinated communities.

With the Cold War's conclusion, containment—with its triadic view—gave way to another tripartite perspective, this time defined by the notion of globalization. The terms of reference were remarkably similar to those of the Cold War: vanguard societies networked together not only by the instruments of the information revolution but also by broader and deeper economic integration and commitment to democratic norms and practices. This vanguard is the center and the driver of global economic growth and increasing social equality. It centers as during the Cold War in Western Europe, North

America, and Japan and accounts for 70 percent of global gross domestic product (GDP), 80 percent of global foreign direct investments (FDIs), and 10 percent of global population.

If Western Europe, North America, and Japan are again the new First World core, what are, in this view, the other two worlds? The Second World refers to those societies who are going through the interlinked process of domestic political transformation and international economic integration, with all the social and cultural implications implied by such changes. This is seen as the true world of development and includes such diverse states as China, India, Argentina, Brazil, Chile, Mexico, a number of states in Southeast and Northeast Asia, and the states of Eastern and Central Europe associated with the European Union. Some states may be problematic as to whether or when they would enter into this world, but the key direction of progress is seen as integration with the First World.

Transitional disruptions in investment and employment patterns and social dislocations are assumed not only in the Second World but in the First World as well, but the expectation is that sustained economic growth, democratization, and social betterment will result. And what of those states who seem marginalized in this process, notably in the Middle East and Africa? They are clearly the newly defined Third World denizens and a breeding ground of resentment, anger, and violence.

Whether from a Cold War or a globalization perspective, this is, of course, an idealized version of the *worlds* since the Second World War. It does sustain the argument of those who see the very notion of development as stemming from a particular Western vantage point and being reflective of the political economies and the policies of key Western countries.

If there is, however, a powerful tendency in the literature of development to see certain common elements of intellectual, economic, or political evolution—indeed, progress—in both Western and non-Western societies, so there has arisen a comparably powerful school of thought that emphasizes the cultural distinctiveness and hence incommensurate evolution of different societies—with the possible exception of technological inventions. This latter exception could, however, be quite troublesome in the argument if we hold that technological development itself—and the science that undergirds it—decisively shapes other areas of human endeavor. In any case, we can discern two distinctive approaches to the course of social evolution—what I would call the *development school* and the *multicultural school*.

How might these perspectives bear upon the subject at hand? In the first place, if there is a common human nature and good—destiny, if you will—transcendent of history, then the touchstone by which to evaluate development in all cultures and societies must be that common nature and good. Gross domestic product, economic arrangements, political decision making, social relations, customs—all the items we use to pronounce a society as *developed* or *developing* may be consequential only to the degree that they nurture the good man or woman. If this is so, it may well be that literacy, political democracy, economic growth, free markets, and greater social equality are intimately connected to human potential and that the Western experience is universal in its implications and not simply the imperial and mirror-gazing fantasies of Western economists and politicians.

Second, it may also be that some practices that we too quickly dismiss as the Wasatch Front's quaint customs are intimately connected to the kingdom's doctrinal foundations. Zion is not only the pure in heart but also a society of the pure in heart. Israel, the kingdom of God, Zion—these are all social concepts. When the restored gospel enters into any country or society, the kingdom of God accompanies it. Being no more strangers and foreigners but fellow citizens is a weighty idea. A developing church in a developing world carries breathtaking implications.

It Will Fill the World

Whatever the vantage point, what finally defines the developing world? In the first instance, it is defined by what it lacks. Secondly, and more controversially, it is defined by whither it tends. In general, the developing world is deficient in sustained economic growth and social equality; it is lacking in constitutionally delimited democracy and honest bureaucratic structures; its market system is typically rudimentary and its modern infrastructure fragmented and unreliable; it is characterized more by oligarchy and personal favoritism than independent legal and institutional norms; its population is young, but its mortality rates are often high; personal and group security is fragile and violence more typical than peaceful resolution of disputes; and the hopes of its people, stimulated by a global media and market system, are often shattered by the realities of social barriers, corruption, and political incompetence.

However, these societies so characterized are really on a spectrum both in terms of the relationship between their past and their present and among each other. Development means not only movement away from the things described above but movement toward norms, institutions, practices, and global engagements that can only be described as Western in origin, empowered by a science and technology that reached its apogee in the West.

On the other hand, in many of these developing societies, particularly in the southern hemisphere, there is an important cultural gap between them and some of the most advanced Western-based communities—the spirit of faith. Unlike Europe, west *and* east, which has once again embraced paganism with a rapidity that few would have suspected, many of the peoples in the developing world retain a strong spiritual sense. As many commentators have noted, they are open as perhaps never before to the teachings of theistic religion in general and Christianity in particular. Indeed, it is in these areas that the Church's growth is most visible as it is among immigrants coming to the United States, Canada, and Europe from these developing regions.

In one sense, the establishment and deepening of the Church in these areas sustains the influence of Western modes of development, for the Church's culture, like the culture of Christianity in general, is intimately connected with certain norms closely associated with the rise of the West. At the same time, however, critical elements of Church doctrine and social practice increasingly diverge from the secular trends so widespread in the West. Such doctrines and practices focus and refine the spiritual sense often found among the peoples of the developing world. I would signal three key elements that have prepared the Church for the preaching of the gospel and the establishment of the kingdom in the developing world—doctrinal, cultural, and institutional.

"By Sound Doctrine Both to Exhort and to Convince" (Titus 1:9)

I am not sure that the general membership of the Church has fully grasped the significance of the worldwide training meetings commenced in January 2003. The broadcasts are the apostolic voice to Church leadership in every country about the fundamental doctrines, principles, and practices that define the restored gospel's mission and roles. Since the opening of the heavens to the Prophet Joseph Smith that spring day in 1820, the Lord through His prophets has established the latter-day kingdom's fundamental canon. Beyond that canon, over the years, a tradition of religious exposition and teaching has evolved, as have programs to meet the needs of a growing church. As the Church's membership has grown beyond its North American core, the Brethren have sought to reinforce in the minds of all people that which is most fundamental to the Restoration and to emphasize the key role of the Spirit's guidance in the conduct of the Church in a diverse world.

The unity of the faith worldwide is founded on Christ and the guidance and teachings of the apostles and prophets. It is undergirded by the commission to the Saints and their leaders, not to be themselves instructed by the philosophies of the world but to "teach the children of men the things which I [the Lord have] put into your hands by the power of the Spirit; and ye are to be taught from on high." They are summoned to "sanctify yourselves and ye shall be endowed with power, that ye may give even as I have spoken" (D&C 43:15–16).

What have been the central themes of these worldwide training meetings? They include the doctrines of the Restoration as revealed to the Prophet Joseph Smith and his successors; the principles of revelation and priesthood authority; the critical importance of the redeeming ordinances as the instruments of the Atonement and the temple as the focus of our efforts; the standards of personal worthiness; the eternal nature of the family; the mandate to prepare missionaries and preach the gospel; the role of the stake, the bishops, and the auxiliaries; and the adaptability of organization and programs to the varying circumstances of our members. Running through all these presentations are doctrinal foundations, illustrations on how to fulfill the Church's mission and the roles of the priesthood and auxiliaries, and the need to seek and follow with all diligence the Spirit's guidance in the diverse opportunities and challenges facing the Saints.

In effect, the Church's response to the diversity of the circumstances of our members is an emphasis on the basic doctrinal and principled foundations that both transcend those circumstances and provide the key to the necessary adaptations in programs and organization. There has been a great deal of talk in recent years about reducing and simplifying. Although much of the inspiration for this may lie in the need to provide our families "space" within which to carry out their divine role, a major impetus is to provide a framework within which the Church can respond to the varying circumstances of our members, most particularly in the developing world.

"An Holy Nation" (Exodus 19:6)

When the gospel enters into a country, the kingdom goes with it—and hence a particular culture. The Church members are the products of different histories, languages, and civilizations, which bring a richness of experiences, perspective, and custom to the common enterprise to bring forth and establish the cause of Zion. Overarching and transcending this rich variety of customs is a gospel culture. Often this culture joins seamlessly with the local culture, but at times it requires a change of such local cultural perspectives and practices.

Some are uncomfortable with the notion of a distinctive Latter-day Saint culture for fear that it represents the customs of the Western Mormons. There are, indeed, customs that are parochial, but a number of practices are integral to the restored gospel and the drama of latter-day Israel.

Robert Louis Wilken, a professor of the history of Christianity at the University of Virginia, recently wrote concerning the special culture of Christianity in general and its abandonment in European and American culture. Referring to T. S. Eliot's characterization of culture as the "total harvest of thinking and feeling," Wilken points to "the pattern of inherited meanings and sensibilities encoded in ritual, law, language, practice, and stories that can order, inspire, and guide the behavior, thoughts, and affections of a Christian people." Not only theological ideas but also actual historical experiences define the universal Christian community. As he concludes, "Christ does not simply infiltrate a culture; Christ creates culture by forming another city, another sovereignty with its own social and political life."[2]

What are some of the elements of the distinctive "pattern of inherited meanings and sensibilities" that characterize latter-day Israel? Some of those elements are grounded in basic doctrinal prin-

---

2. Robert Louis Wilken, "The Church as Culture," *First Things*, April 2004, 32.

ciples, as, for instance, the nature and role of the family, sexuality, dress and demeanor, the care of the body, the sanctity of speech, and certain forms of entertainment. The doctrine of eternal gender and the relationship between a man and woman, as well as the divinely mandated roles of mothers and fathers, are closely connected with standards of sexual behavior, modesty in dress and speech, and the inappropriateness of some recreational and lifestyle choices. The Word of Wisdom also does not simply define what should be taken into the body but separates Latter-day Saints from some of the cultural practices and associations often connected with such things as alcohol, smoking, drugs, coffee, and tea.

The concept of individual freedom is central to the plan of salvation and the Atonement and carries implications far beyond the theological realm. The organization of society and notions of rights and duties naturally flow from the teachings that life entails not only choice but also the ability to make choices and to be responsible for the consequences of our actions—in effect, personal accountability. The emphasis on both self-reliance and ties of community and charity are themselves shaped by the central doctrine of moral agency and personal freedom. These beliefs and norms give rise in turn to certain cultural expectations and patterns of behavior distinct from the broader society, whether it be in the highly secular society of the developed world or the more restrictive but spiritually open societies in much of the developing world.

If fundamental doctrine defines the broad culture, so too does the historical experience of the Latter-day Saints. As doctrine has shaped the "pattern of inherited meanings and sensibilities," so too has the history of the restored Church. To say that the events in upper-state New York, Kirtland, Zion's Camp, Missouri, Illinois, the westward trek, and the rise of the Mormon communities in the West are but parts of Americana or Western American history is to miss the universal significance of these shaping events in the latter-day kingdom's rise. It would be comparable to saying that the Passover, the forty years in the wilderness, the Babylonian captivity are but chapters in the history of Egypt, Canaan, and the ancient world. Not only was Israel defined by these epics but so too was the consciousness of Lehi's children and of Christianity itself.

The twenty-fourth of July celebration and the Mormons' settlements throughout the West are not of parochial concern but are the workings of God to prepare a people with a universal mission and readiness to receive the triumphant Lord upon His return. The spread of the gospel and the kingdom entails the incorporation of diverse peoples into this historical consciousness. It is part of the spiritual covenant that causes them to stand apart from their societies, even as the nineteenth-century Saints were separated from the diverse peoples from which they came. As Peter told the early-day Saints, harking back to the commission of Moses to the children of Israel, "Ye are a chosen generation, a royal priesthood, an holy nation, . . . which in time past were not a people, but are now the people of God." He also said, "As he which hath called you is holy, so be ye holy in all manner of conversation" (1 Peter 2:9–10; 1:15).

"Fitly Framed Together" (Ephesians 2:21)

As an eternal and universal doctrine and a transcendent culture have prepared the Church for its vocation in the developing world, so also has the inspired organization raised up by the Prophet Joseph Smith. One stands in awe at the simplicity and adaptability of the institutions established by the Prophet and their subsequent development to meet the needs of a growing and increasingly diverse church. Family focus; lay leadership; priesthood keys and quorums; inspired and hierarchically generated and congregationally sustained calls; geographically delimited local congregations; stakes as the fundamental defense, refuge, and gathering places of the Saints; gender-based, age, and special-needs groups organized as auxiliaries of the priesthood—these institutional building blocks can be introduced and adapted in remarkably different circumstances. Programs have and will change, but these fundamental institutional elements, like the doctrine, remain constant. Overarching these local organizations stands the apostolic direction. In many respects, it has been at the pinnacle of the Church where the most significant developments have occurred.

If we had to pick a date of most contemporary significance to the Church's growth in the developing world, we could probably do no better than June 9, 1978, subsequently followed by an official declaration of the First Presidency on September 30 in the same year. As the declaration stated, "In early June of this year, the First Presidency announced that a revelation had been received by President Spencer W. Kimball extending priesthood and temple blessings to all worthy male members of the Church" (Official Declaration–2). The implications of this removal of all restrictions on those of African descent were immense for the preaching of the gospel and establishing the Church in Africa, Brazil, and around the world. If one adds the global explosion of temple building, reaching its apogee under the direction of President Gordon B. Hinckley, the Church's whole relationship to areas once distant from Salt Lake City, not only physically but socially, was decisively altered from that June date onward.

Another key element in the developing Church is in the transformation and extension of the apostolic voice. In my own memory, the direct involvement of the Apostles, organized in the First Presidency and the Quorum of the Twelve, has been intense and extensive, not only in the policy but in the implementation arena. As one reads the Church's history, it is clear how necessary this extensive direction was. The spirit of the organization that the Prophet erected had to penetrate deeply into the consciousness of lay leaders coming from many backgrounds and cultures. Handbooks and manuals have been written to codify the objectives, standards, and practices of the Church organization, but, as has often been noted, there are intangible things that cannot be reduced to paper or computer programs. In a real sense, the Church is multigenerational not simply in the sense that it generates families of Latter-day Saints, but it is multigenerational in its organizational capacity. Simply, it often takes several generations to appreciate fully how we ought to lead and guide.

We can take nearly any country in which the Church has grown in recent years to appreciate how the strength of the Church organization depends on the transmission of the gospel through several generations. In Brazil, where I served in an Area Presidency for three years, I was struck by how developed the Church was in the south as compared to the north, where the Church's establishment was of later origins. Yet even there, the great strength came from a few families who had years earlier joined the Church, as well as those families who had moved into the area from the south. At the same time, I saw the foundation of families who will provide the inspiration and leadership of the Brazil North Area and of the Church as a whole in the years to come.

This process of development in Brazil is in fact comparable to what has occurred elsewhere, even in the United States. A number of families who came from the Rocky Mountain West moved to the west and east coasts and the north and south of the United States and provided the initial Church leadership, which has subsequently given way to "homegrown" families who have provided leaders not only in their localities but throughout the world.

It has sometimes been joked that the Church is guided by revelation, inspiration, and relation. Underlying this wry witticism lies a profound truth. The Church's rise depends not only on those who can read and understand the "rule books" but also on those whose very instincts and sentiments grasp the spirit that is at the heart of the institution. More, they grasp that it is the Spirit that must ultimately be the guide. As the Church's history demonstrates, this understanding can be seized by a single new convert. But it becomes rooted and is perpetuated in his or her own family.

To return to the original point, given the need for close guidance of a young and growing church, it is not surprising how involved the Apostles have been in the Church's daily administration. Yet, in recent years, as the Church spread into many cultures and climes and witnessed unparalleled growth, it became apparent that the key issue was how to ensure that the apostolic voice would continue to be heard. The worldwide leadership meetings, the reach of modern telecommunications, the active chairing of the Church's principal committees, and a travel schedule that remains breathtaking—these all will remain key elements in ensuring that the apostolic and prophetic foundations of the kingdom endure. At the same time, progressive steps in the evolution of the general organization have extended the apostolic voice.

In April 2004 it was announced that, beginning in the second half of the year, many stake conferences theretofore presided over by a General Authority or Area Seventy would be clustered together, and the First Presidency and members of the Quorum of the Twelve would meet with those stakes in their respective centers on the Sunday of conference by satellite transmission. The stake presidents would preside over the regular Saturday priesthood leadership and Saturday evening sessions. Moreover, the reorganization of stakes were to be henceforth done by the Quorum of the Twelve and the seven Presidents of the Seventy, assisted where needed by other General Authorities and Area Seventies.

Over the years the Apostles have organized and deployed various "arms" to share in the burdens of administration and by which they could reach throughout the world. Assistants to the Twelve, additional counselors in the First Presidency, regional representatives, area administrators, as well as the development of an extensive Church "civil service" in the temporal and programmatic areas, have all been employed to ensure the clarity, reach, and vigor of the apostolic guidance.

But one of the most significant developments has been in the extension of the role of the Seventy. The Lord declared in the Doctrine and Covenants the pattern whereby the Apostles may build up the Church and regulate all of its affairs:

> The Twelve are a Traveling Presiding High Council, to officiate
> in the name of the Lord, under the direction of the Presidency

of the Church, agreeable to the institution of heaven; to build
up the church, and regulate all the affairs of the same in all
nations, first unto the Gentiles and secondly unto the Jews.

The Seventy are to act in the name of the Lord, under the
direction of the Twelve or the traveling high council, in building up the church and regulating all the affairs of the same in
all nations, first unto the Gentiles and then to the Jews;

The Twelve being sent out, holding the keys, to open the
door by the proclamation of the gospel of Jesus Christ, and first
unto the Gentiles and then unto the Jews. . . .

It is the duty of the traveling high council to call upon the
Seventy, when they need assistance, to fill the several calls for
preaching and administering the gospel, instead of any others.
(D&C 107:33–35, 38)

In the same section the Lord called upon the Seventy to join
with the Twelve as "especial witnesses" of Christ and the restored
gospel "unto the Gentiles and in all the world—thus differing from
other officers in the church in the duties of their calling" (D&C
107:25).

Throughout much of Church history, this pattern was realized
by the organization of the seven-member First Council of the Seventy as General Authorities, with the body of the seventies called to
serve as full-time or stake missionaries. It is clear from the words of
section 107, however, that when the mission of the Church required,
the role of the Seventy could be considerably extended. In the early
1960s, in response to the Church growth, there began what President
Boyd K. Packer has called "a pattern of intense revelation."

First, in 1961, four members of the First Council of the Seventy
were ordained high priests and authorized to organize and reorga-
nize stakes and give assignments to stake presidents. The members
of the First Council of the Seventy were subsequently given the sealing power. After a gestation period in which regional representatives
were called and stake presidents were given increased authority, the
First Quorum of the Seventy, with provision for emeritus status, was
organized as General Authorities and called not only to assist in the
general administration at headquarters but also as Area Presidencies

to carry out the mandate to assist the Twelve to build up and regulate the Church in all nations. Subsequently, the stake seventies quorums were phased out, and the Second Quorum of the Seventy, with term appointments, was also called with its members designated as General Authorities with responsibilities comparable to the First Quorum.

Finally, in 1995, regional representatives gave way to Area Authorities, who were subsequently ordained Seventies and general officers of the Church. They were to serve in Church service comparable to bishops and stake presidents, continuing their professional lives, living in their places of residence, and given responsibility in the broad geographical areas in which the Church was organized. They were initially organized in the Third, Fourth, and Fifth Quorums and given extensive responsibilities in the organization and reorganization of stakes and general oversight responsibilities—some even serving in Area Presidencies. In April 2004 the First Presidency announced the division of the Fifth Quorum to create the Sixth Quorum.

It was further explained that the seven Presidents of the Seventy would be released as executive directors of six of the key headquarters departments and given responsibility for the eleven areas in Canada and the United States, hence dissolving the Area Presidencies in those areas. Other Seventies were called as executive directors of the several departments. Area Seventies, whose numbers grow, would continue to have area responsibilities. The international Area Presidencies would remain in place. Members of the Twelve, assisted by assigned members of the Presidency of the Seventy, serve as first contacts for these international Area Presidencies.

This is but an abbreviated sketch of recent organizational changes, but it points to two key developments. First, greater responsibilities devolved upon stake presidents, including the ordination of patriarchs and the setting apart of full-time missionaries. The responsibilities of stake presidents will be further heightened in the years to come. Second, the Seventies, under the direction of the

Quorum of the Twelve, were organized under the presidency of the seven Presidents of the Seventy, either as General Authorities or Area Seventies, to assist in the apostolic charge to build up and regulate the Church. The apostolic keys pertain only to the Apostles, but the apostolic authority may be exercised by the Seventy under the direction of the Apostles. Hence, the stakes as defenses, refuges, and gathering places have been built up under a strengthened local stake president, and apostolic oversight is universal and continuous, whatever the diversity of cultures and a world in commotion.

The Destiny of This Church and Kingdom

As President Hinckley has often noted, there was a great prologue to the Restoration of the Church—a development period, if you will. If all things are present with the Lord, it is clear that the preparation of ancient Israel, the ideas of ancient Greece, the rise of Christianity, the Renaissance, the Reformation, and the enlightenment ideas of the Age of Reason prepared the political, economic, and social soil for the implantation of the latter-day kingdom. The Church came "forth out of the wilderness of darkness, and shine[s] forth fair as the moon, clear as the sun, and terrible as an army with banners" (D&C 109:73).

If great secular developments prepared the way for the Restoration, it seems plausible that these same developments and others have converged together to prepare the way for the preaching of the gospel and the establishment of the Church throughout the world. Separate cultures may stand as barriers to the spread of the gospel kingdom, but the eroding and unifying forces of development begun in, but now no longer limited to, the West have cast down walls and opened doors. Many of the forces associated with political, economic, and social development are painful and even unjust. Some are morally corrupting. So too has it been in the history of Europe and America. But the power to weaken the "tradition of their fathers" (D&C 93:39) and to open doors and hearts must not be underestimated. What the Prophet Joseph Smith saw that Sunday night in 1834 was that the flowering of the Church and the sweep of history would ensure that "the truth of God will go forth boldly, nobly, and independent, till it has penetrated every continent, visited every clime, swept every country, and sounded in every ear, till the purposes of God shall be accomplished, and the Great Jehovah shall say the work is done."[3]

© by Intellectual Reserve, Inc.

Elder Robert S. Wood is a member of the Second Quorum of the Seventy. This essay was presented at "Church Development in the Developing World," the International Society's fifteenth annual conference, April 2004, Brigham Young University, Provo, Utah.

---

3. Joseph Smith, *History of the Church of Jesus Christ of Latter-day Saints*, ed. B. H. Roberts, 2nd ed. rev. (Salt Lake City: Deseret Book, 1957), 4:540.

Part II

Missionary Work in
a Global Village

Chapter 5

Sharing the Gospel in a Global Setting

Elder Lance B. Wickman

Come and see" (John 1:39). This gentle admonition of the Savior was uttered to two of John the Baptist's disciples. They had heard the Baptist declare that Jesus was the Lamb of God, indeed the very Son of God. "And the two disciples heard him speak, and they followed Jesus. Then Jesus turned, and saw them following, and saith unto them, What seek ye? They said unto him, Rabbi, (which is to say, being interpreted, Master) where dwelleth thou? He saith unto them, Come and see. . . . One of the two which heard John speak, and followed him, was Andrew, Simon Peter's brother. He first findeth his own brother Simon, and saith unto him, We have found the Messias, which is, being interpreted, the Christ" (John 1:37–41).

"Come and see." These words of soft invitation have a profound significance for the missionary work of The Church of Jesus Christ of Latter-day Saints. Indeed, they are the very lodestar of that work. They have dual significance. They were spoken by the Savior Himself, raising the curtain on the great work of bringing souls to Christ. This work began in the meridian of time and continues with an unparalleled scope and dynamism in these present and last days.

"Come and see." The words also capture the tone of that work. John and Andrew had found truth in the teachings of John the Baptist. But then came a mightier one, even Jesus of Nazareth. He did not belittle the truth they had already received. He only invited them to receive more, even a fulness of truth. "Come and see." Touched in their hearts as well as in their minds by His doctrines, their previous understanding was added upon, enabling them to declare to others, "We have found the Messias, which is . . . the Christ." And so it is today. Messengers of truth go forth from within the shadows of these hills to the very corners of the earth. They seek not to tear down but to build up; not to obscure truth but to sharpen it, to focus it, to add to it. And they do so not by strident argumentation, contention, or coercion but with a gentle beckoning—the same employed by the Master Himself so many centuries ago—"Come and see."

The Law and Religion Project is an endeavor of Emory University School of Law in Atlanta, Georgia. As its name suggests, this endeavor seeks to explore the interaction between religion and the religious on the one hand, and the operations of law and government on the other hand. Every few years, Emory University publishes a volume with the results of its research, relying heavily on contributions of legal scholars and religious clerics in a host of faiths and denominations. The readership for these books is largely government officials charged with responsibility for overseeing and regulating religious activity in their various nations and those in the academic and intellectual community that surround the government. These volumes have proven to have an important effect in the development of the law respecting religion in many nations.

Encouraging the development of principles of righteous government and religious liberty in every land is of prime importance to the Church. Indeed, the Lord has repeatedly so stated in modern revelation. In Doctrine and Covenants 44:3–5, He has said: "And it shall come to pass that they [the elders of the Church] shall go forth into the regions round about, and preach repentance unto the people. And many shall be converted, insomuch that *ye shall obtain power to organize yourselves according to the laws of man; that your enemies may not have power over you; that you may be preserved in all things; that you may be enabled to keep my laws; that every bond may be broken wherewith the enemy seeketh to destroy my people"* (emphasis added).

And not just any government: "And now, verily I say unto you concerning the laws of the land, it is my will that my people should observe to do all things whatsoever I command them. *And that law of the land which is constitutional, supporting that principle of freedom in maintaining rights and privileges, belongs to all mankind, and is justifiable before me.* Therefore, I, the Lord, justify you, and your brethren of my church, in befriending that law which is the constitutional law of the land; and as pertaining to law of man, whatsoever is more or less than this, cometh of evil" (D&C 98:4–6; emphasis added).

And so it was that some two and one-half years ago, Elder Dallin H. Oaks of the Quorum of the Twelve Apostles was interested when he was invited by Emory University to author a chapter on a forthcoming book about the challenges of religious proselytism in today's world. The First Presidency approved the project. He then invited me to assist him. Working together over a period of months, we produced a lengthy article, which we entitled "The Missionary Work of The Church of Jesus Christ of Latter-day Saints."[1]

We believe that in some respects this article is a unique piece—not in its doctrine, but in its scope. It explores every aspect of the missionary activity of the Church, from the underlying revelations and doctrine that motivate Latter-day Saints to proclaim the gospel "among all nations, kindreds, tongues, and people" (D&C 112:1), to the missionary culture of the Church, which begins with Primary songs like "I Hope They Call Me on a Mission," to the manner of calls of missionaries and mission presidents, to the modus operandi

---

1.   Dallin H. Oaks and Lance B. Wickman, "The Missionary Work of The Church of Jesus Christ of Latter-day Saints," in *Sharing the Book: Religious Perspectives on the Rights and Wrongs of Proselytism*, ed. John Witte Jr. and Richard C. Martin (Maryknoll, NY: Orbis Books, 1999), 247–75.

of missions, and to the collateral humanitarian and welfare activities of the Church.

The article then proceeds from an explication of these internal doctrines and programs of the Church to a discussion of what governments and the Church have a right to expect from one another. And therein, of course, is where the proverbial rubber meets the road in today's world. This is the issue that Emory University seeks to explore. This is the issue that is of critical importance to the Church as it moves forward under its divine mandate to "go ye therefore, and teach all nations, baptizing them in the name of the Father, and of the Son, and of the Holy Ghost" (Matthew 28:19).

It is my desire to attempt at least to touch on the vast dimensions of the "widescreen" magnificence and power of the missionary activity of the Church. For Latter-day Saints, proclaiming the gospel is more than a program. It is more even than just a teaching or doctrine of the Church. *Sharing the gospel is who and what we are as a people!* It is woven into the very fabric of our lives. Saith the Lord, "It becometh every man who hath been warned to warn his neighbor" (D&C 88:81). That mandate is the warp and woof of our lives.

Hence, it is vital that governments understand this reality. Attempts to regulate or restrict the preaching of the gospel by member missionaries is not just a limitation upon some auxiliary activity of Latter-day Saints. It is a material infringement on our religious freedom. And we are not the only Christian denomination for whom witnessing of Jesus Christ is a vital doctrine and activity. The legal scholars at Emory University have expressed concern about the implications of this basic fact. These scholars have wondered whether there is a tension between the fundamental Christian notion of community—namely, loving one's neighbor as oneself—and this great commission to witness. This is more than an academic inquiry. It has important philosophical ramifications for the laws adopted by nations. If the basic purpose of law is to ensure a peaceful community, then might it be asked, are the demands of religious freedom antithetical to that purpose?

Happily, our article declares that they are not. Indeed, the central teaching of the article is that for Latter-day Saints there is no tension between the Golden Rule and the so-called Great Commission. *To the contrary, we share the gospel because we want to be good neighbors!* But all is premised on the Savior's gentle invitation, "Come and see." Unfortunately, as virtually each day's newspaper reflects, that moderate entreaty is easily drowned in the powerful political currents and cross-currents of contemporary society.

On the positive side, there is no question that in the last decade particularly there has been an ascendancy of principles of religious freedom codified in the law of many lands that is nothing short of breathtaking, even miraculous. Where just a decade ago the Soviet empire stood implacably in the way of religious freedom across a wide expanse of Europe and Asia, there are now a host of fledgling democracies and nearly a dozen missions of the Church with thousands of members. Temples have even been announced. I remember as a stake president in California in the mid-1980s teasing prospective missionaries about recommending them for Siberia. Such teasing has been rendered obsolete by these dramatic events. We now have missionaries in Siberia!

And the progress is not limited to Central and Eastern Europe. Throughout Asia and Africa, nation after nation has liberalized its laws and opened its doors to the missionaries of the Church. I attended the Summer 1999 graduation ceremonies for BYU's College of Humanities. Dean Van Gessel shared with the graduates some remarkable statistics reflecting BYU's preeminence in conferring degrees in a host of languages. I could not help but think of the missionaries represented in the graduating classes at the Y and that this statistic is merely a reflection of this marvelous phenomenon— predicted by prophets ancient and modern—of the gospel going to every nation, kindred, and tongue.

But sadly all is not positive. There are forces at work that challenge our efforts to proclaim the gospel to the ends of the world. Some of these forces stem from excesses and atrocities perpetrated in the name of religion. One need only mention places such as Northern Ireland, the Balkans, the Middle East, and the Indian subcontinent to have instant recall of ongoing conflict and tragedy rooted in religious differences. Samuel P. Huntington of Harvard University has referred to these places as "fault lines."[2] These fault lines separate Catholics from Protestants, Christians from Muslims, and Muslims from Hindus. Commenting on Dr. Huntington's phrasing, another noted scholar, Paul Marshall, has stated:

> [The] chronic armed conflict is concentrated on the margins of the traditional religions, especially along the boundaries of the Islamic world. The Middle East, the southern Sahara, the Balkans, the Caucasus, Central Asia, and Southern Asia are where Islam, Christianity, Judaism, Buddhism, and Hinduism intersect. It is also where most wars have broken out in the last fifty years.
>
> These are not explicitly religious wars. But since religion shapes cultures, people in these regions have different histories and different views of human life. Regardless of the triggers for conflict, they are living in unstable areas where conflict is likely to occur—in religious fault zones that are prone to political earthquakes.[3]

To fulfill the Lord's mandate, the gospel must be preached in *every* nation—even those where there is conflict. Moreover, such conflicts also have a way of spilling over into other places. The specter of international terrorism—much of it in the name of religion—is a concern of government in every nation. As a consequence, many governments are engaged in the process of studying and classifying religions, seeking to determine those that are acceptable to the government and those that are disfavored.

---

2. Samuel P. Huntington, "Civilizations at Odds," *At Century's End: Great Minds Reflect on Our Times*, ed. Nathan P. Gardels (La Jolla, CA: ALTI Publishing, 1995), 59–67.

3. Paul Marshall, "Keeping the Faith: Religion, Freedom, and International Affairs," *Imprimis* 28, no. 3 (March 1999): 3.

The challenge presented by this international cauldron is further exacerbated by what Marshall refers to as a "secular myopia" that afflicts many government officials, policy makers, and the intellectual community that surrounds them. He describes this myopia as "an introverted, parochial inability even to see, much less understand, the role of religion in human life."[4]

Indeed, in Western nations particularly, "opinion makers and policy makers consider themselves the heirs of the 'Enlightenment.' . . . To them, all contemporary peoples, events, and issues fall into Enlightenment categories, which are most often political or ideological. . . . If what believers believe does not easily fall into an Enlightenment category, then it is assumed that they must be 'irrational.' Thus, [the term] 'fundamentalist' is now merely shorthand for 'religious fanatic'—for someone who is to be categorized rather than heard, observed rather than comprehended, dismissed rather than respected."[5]

As if these weren't complications enough, in many nations there are entrenched interests, usually a dominant or a state religion, which views with hostility the encroachments in terms of converts made by other sects and denominations on what these interests view as their own private preserve. Often these established religions seek to use their influence with government officials and rule makers to impede, if not to block altogether, inroads by the newcomers.

It is important to realize that fundamentally these phenomena are not targeted against Latter-day Saints. These are political and cultural circumstances that exist quite independently of the Church and its missionary endeavors. But with a missionary force of approximately sixty thousand young men and women serving in some 125 nations, the Church inevitably is bound to encounter legal and political predicaments created by these phenomena. As a result,

---

4. Marshall, "Keeping the Faith," 2.
5. Marshall, "Keeping the Faith," 3.

the Church is constantly at work to foster warm and cordial relationships with the agents and institutions of government.

All these efforts are forged on the anvil of the one central premise of Church missionary activity: the "come and see" principle. That principle is itself a reflection of one of the most fundamental of all Church doctrines—moral agency—a profound respect for the right of each individual to hear and to decide for himself. The Emory University article contains a section devoted to this doctrinal principle. To quote just an excerpt: "Earth was created as a proving ground for the spiritual children of God, to give them an opportunity to demonstrate by *individual choice* their faithfulness to God's commandments. Those who do so . . . will have 'glory added upon their heads for ever and ever.' Redemption for earthly sins and mistakes is made by Jesus Christ for those *choosing to follow him.*"[6]

Hence, the message of the restored gospel is basically one of *choice*. Such a message cannot be proclaimed in any other way than that which allows such choice to operate. This is the very essence of the expression "come and see." No hard sell, the gospel presented by the missionaries is a stunning display of eternal truths that glitter in their own right. These truths testify of themselves; our task is but to unveil them in an atmosphere that enables the investigator to accept or reject them at will. Hence, for Latter-day Saints there really is no tension between the Golden Rule and the Great Commission. Because we love our neighbor, we offer to share what we have, but we do so out of complete respect for his right to refuse to listen, much less embrace.

Our proclamations are no threat to the peace and tranquillity of the state. Indeed, embracing the gospel makes a person a better citizen. We believe that wise governments present no official impediments to Church representatives. To do otherwise, we believe, takes

---

6. Oaks and Wickman, "Missionary Work of The Church of Jesus Christ of Latter-day Saints," 251; emphasis added.

government beyond its rightful sphere. What follows is taken from the actual text of the article:

> In a letter dated March 1, 1842, the Prophet Joseph Smith responded to a request from Mr. John Wentworth, the editor and proprietor of the *Chicago Democrat*, for a written "sketch of the rise, progress, persecution, and faith of the Latter-day Saints". After giving the requested historical information, the Prophet's response, the "Wentworth Letter," concludes with thirteen short declarative statements summarizing the central doctrines of the church. These have since been extracted and canonized in a doctrinal statement known as the Articles of Faith. Two of these Articles of Faith are directly pertinent in describing the church's attitude toward governments and their rightful place in the religious affairs of men. . . .
>
> The Twelfth Article of Faith states: "We believe in being subject to kings, presidents, rulers, and magistrates, in obeying, honoring, and sustaining the law" (Articles of Faith, Pearl of Great Price). Events occurring shortly after this declaration illustrate the seriousness of the Latter-day Saints' commitment to this principle.
>
> The early history of the church was marred by intense persecution. Some of this was in response to Joseph Smith's claim that he had seen and conversed with God the Father, his son Jesus Christ, and other heavenly beings. Some of it was spawned by economic and political jealousies in the developing communities along the remote western frontier where the church had its origins. Whatever its causes, the effect of the persecution was to force the Mormons to move repeatedly. Initially organized in upstate New York, the main body of the Church moved to Kirtland, Ohio, and then in succession to Jackson County, Missouri; Daviess and Caldwell Counties, Missouri; Nauvoo, Illinois; and ultimately to the Great Basin. In each frontier community, law enforcement was either impotent or in league with those conspiring against the Mormons. Repeated appeals to state officials in Ohio, Missouri, Illinois, and even to the United States government elicited no protection.

Then, in June 1844, Joseph Smith and his brother, Hyrum, were assassinated by a mob while incarcerated in Carthage, Illinois. By February 1846 mob persecution around Nauvoo, Illinois, where most church members were then congregated, became so intense that the Mormon people were forced to commence their withdrawal from Illinois. Though it was the dead of winter, many Mormons under the leadership of Brigham Young, loaded what belongings they could into wagons and, abandoning their comfortable homes, crossed the frozen Mississippi River and headed west across Iowa. Within eight months virtually all had left Nauvoo—the last group at gunpoint! The privation and suffering of the Saints as they struggled across Iowa, destitute and mired in a seemingly endless sea of mud, was heartrending. They were homeless, with only the great wilderness before them. With the Rocky Mountains their destination, they were leaving the United States.

Into that desperate situation in late June 1846, Captain James Allen of the 1st U.S. Dragoons rode with an urgent appeal to the Mormons from the United States Government. The United States had declared war on Mexico, and President James K. Polk asked the Mormons to raise a battalion of 500 men to march to Santa Fe as part of General Stephen Kearny's Army of the West. To rank-and-file Mormons, this appeal was stupefying. Not only would their indigent families be left without able-bodied men, but this appeal was coming from the very government that had stood by disinterestedly time and again while mobs forced their depredations upon the Mormons, sometimes under color of state law. In the minds of some, they had every right to ignore the appeal and to turn their backs on the United States.

President Brigham Young, their leader, saw it differently. For one thing, the Saints could use the soldiers' wages to buy needed equipment and supplies for the trek west to the Great Basin. More fundamentally, their country was in need, and their government had called. President Young decided: the Saints would respond to the call. At his personal appeal, the Mormon Battalion was organized, literally overnight. Its 497 men marched away leaving wives and mothers, sisters and daughters to provide and care for their needy families. Their country had called, and the Mormons responded.

Suffering tremendous hardships, the Mormon Battalion ultimately pioneered a road across the Great American Desert to San Diego on the shores of the Pacific Ocean, a road that would later be followed by many thousands seeking their fortunes in California. The Mormon Battalion's march of more than two thousand miles was to be the longest foot march of infantry in the nation's history. Their courage and fortitude is a storied chapter in the history of the United States. It stands as a monument to church members' deep commitment to their Twelfth Article of Faith.

Latter-day Saints are law-abiding and loyal citizens. They obey the law, participate in the affairs of government at all levels, vote in elections, and serve in the armed forces of their respective nations. No government need ever view with suspicion the Latter-day Saint congregations within its borders. To the contrary, it can take comfort in the assurance that none of its citizens is more committed to "obeying, honoring, and sustaining the law" than its Mormon citizens.

In a revelation given to Joseph Smith in 1831, the Lord said, "Let no man break the laws of the land, for he that keepeth the laws of God hath no need to break the laws of the land" (Doctrine and Covenants 58:21). Accordingly, Latter-day Saints take seriously the Savior's admonition: "Render therefore unto Caesar the things which are Caesar's; and unto God the things which are God's" (Mt 22:21). This philosophy is manifest in the church's missionary program.

Most nations have specific legal requirements governing religion and religious representatives. While there are many similarities, each country has its own different requirements. Most require churches to register with the national government; many also require registration at the regional and/or local level as a condition of holding meetings, acquiring real property, opening bank accounts, and engaging in missionary activity. In some countries foreign religious representatives may need visas.

The church strives to identify and to comply with all legal requirements. It approaches every nation through the "front door" (that is, by complying with legal requirements). It expects its missionaries to abide by the law of the jurisdiction where they are serving and to respect local customs and culture. . . .

Latter-day Saints, who believe in "rendering unto Caesar" that which is properly Caesar's, also believe that governments have a responsibility to distinguish between "the things which are Caesar's" and "the things which are God's" and to guarantee religious freedom for the latter.

The church's Eleventh Article of Faith states: "We claim the privilege of worshiping Almighty God according to the dictates of our own conscience, and allow all men the same privilege, let them worship how, where, or what they may" (Articles of Faith, Pearl of Great Price).

In furtherance of the God-given right of moral agency, including the right to hear and to choose between competing philosophies, doctrines, and religions, Latter-day Saints believe that governments have a solemn duty to protect and preserve that agency to every person within the reach of their jurisdictions. The church's declaration of belief states:

> We believe that no government can exist in peace, except such laws are framed and held inviolate as will secure to each individual the free exercise of conscience, the right and control of property, and the protection of life (Doctrine and Covenants 134:2).

No government can long endure that does not secure these basic freedoms to its citizens. The scrap heap of history is strewn with the tattered remnants of regimes that behaved otherwise. . . .

The chronicles of God, as with the chronicles of history, teach that every man recognizes in his heart the God-given gift of freedom, or agency. Truly, "no government *can* exist in peace" that does not guarantee this to its citizens.

In no aspect of life are these fundamental freedoms more important than as they relate to every man's freedom of worship—his moral agency. Mormons believe that "[i]t is [not] just to mingle religious influence with civil government" (Doctrine and Covenants 134:9). This means that "religious societ[ies] [do not have] authority to try men on the right of property or life . . ." (ibid., 10) But government also has a duty to preserve moral agency. The Latter-day Saint declaration of belief states:

> We believe that religion is instituted of God; and that men are amenable to him, and to him only, for the exercise of it unless their religious opinions prompt them to infringe upon the rights and liberties of others; but we do not believe that human law has a right to interfere in prescribing rules of worship to bind the consciences of men, nor dictate forms for public or private devotions; that the civil magistrate should restrain crime, but never control conscience; should punish guilt, but never suppress the freedom of the soul (Doctrine and Covenants 134:4).

Within broad limits relating to legitimate concerns for health and safety, government has no place in directly or indirectly regulating matters of conscience, including religious opinion, expression, and exercise. Every person should be free in choosing who, where, and how he worships and his "forms for public or private devotions." The church believes that it is beyond the legitimate powers of government to compel membership or participation in one church while preventing or restricting them in another. . . .

Mormons believe deeply that one of government's most fundamental duties is to preserve "an equality among all men" when it comes to matters of religion and conscience. Every person is entitled to the right to speak his or her mind on such matters, and everyone else has the right to listen, or not. Every person is entitled to exercise the right to worship where, how, and as he or she pleases.

And every citizen, while exercising his own rights, has the duty to respect those same rights in others. Government has no stake in any point of view. Its only legitimate role between its citizens on such matters is to maintain their individual rights:

> We believe that . . . governments have a right, and are bound to enact laws for the protection of all citizens in the free exercise of their religious belief; but we do not believe that they have a right in justice to deprive citizens of this privilege, or proscribe them in their opinions, so long as a regard and reverence are shown

to the laws and such religious opinions do not justify sedition nor conspiracy (Doctrine and Covenants 134:7).

Hence, while some may assert that there is an inherent conflict between a religionist's exercise of his religion, including his need to express his convictions, and the right of others not to suffer the imposition of his exercise, for Latter-day Saints there is no tension between the so-called Great Commission and the Golden Rule. Latter-day Saints desire the opportunity to proclaim the gospel of Jesus Christ as they understand it to any and all who wish to listen, they accord every other man that same right, and they acknowledge that all have the right not to listen. They pledge to honor such principles and ask only that government guarantee them that right and protect them in its exercise.

What does the Church expect from government in practical terms? Simply put, the church asks for room to perform its divine mission to preach the gospel to all men and women, who have a right to *hear* it and *choose* for themselves whether to embrace it. As a minimum, this means the following:

1. *The right to worship.* Church members should have the right to practice their religion without interference by the agencies of government.
2. *The right to meet together.* Church members should have the right to meet together in public and in private in adequate facilities and without government scrutiny. The right of assembly is basic to religious freedom.
3. *The right to self-governance.* The church claims the right to non-interference by government in its internal affairs. Church doctrines and practices should be free from government regulation. The church has the right to determine who will serve as its officers, how long they will serve, and how the affairs of the church will be conducted.
4. *The right to communicate with church members.* Church members should have the right to regular communication with church leaders and other members, whether in person, in writing, or elec-

tronically. Such communications should not be prohibited, impeded, monitored, or otherwise interfered with.

5. *The right to legal entity status and action.* While the church respects the right of government to establish reasonable requirements for churches to become recognized as a legal entity, it asserts that it has a right to legal recognition upon reasonable conditions. Thus recognized, the church should be able to acquire, hold, and dispose of property, to open bank accounts, and to transact business necessary to church operations.

6. *The right to publicly declare beliefs.* Church missionaries should have the right to proclaim the gospel individually or before assemblies of people. This should include the right to print and distribute literature explaining the teachings and doctrines of the church, the right to display videos, tape recordings, and other electronic or graphic presentations concerning the church and its beliefs, and the right of reasonable access to the public press, radio, and television to disseminate messages and information concerning the church and its teachings.

7. *The right to travel freely.* Church members should have the right to travel freely to attend Church meetings and activities and to visit with other members. Similarly, full-time missionaries and other church representatives, even if citizens of another nation, should have the right, consistent with reasonable government regulations, to enter the government's jurisdiction and to proclaim the gospel and participate in church meetings and activities.

On its part, the church reaffirms its commitment to obey the law and to respect the rights of all persons. As previously mentioned, high pressure salesmanship, coercion, and inducement are not part of the church's program or approach. Consistent with the "come and see" principle, missionaries and other church representatives fulfill their callings by inviting those whom they meet to learn more. Courtesy and good will are the hallmarks of the approach of church representatives and members to non-members. They see their duty to "witness" in the first instance as extending an invitation and subsequently to explain gospel principles to those who wish to learn them. . . .

A genuine courtesy for others and respect for their beliefs is a hallmark of Latter-day Saints' relationship with others. Rather than attempting to challenge others' beliefs, they merely proffer the additional truths of the restored gospel to augment truths already possessed. Hence, Mormons manifest a sincere goodwill for other churches and for those with differing beliefs. This neighborliness and respect are an application of Mormon doctrine.

As a matter of principle, the Mormons are law-abiding and good citizens, and they conscientiously seek the good will of governments. But they also expect that governments and their representatives will reciprocate that same respect, goodwill, and cooperation. The right to worship, to hold meetings without governmental interference, to enjoy unfettered self-governance, to receive legal recognition, and to communicate among themselves as well as with others are among the rights they believe governments should guarantee to them and to all churches.

Mormon missionaries go about their work in accordance with these commitments and expectations. Serving for two years in the midst of the people, they master their language and embrace their culture. Traveling in pairs and observing a strict code of moral rectitude and comely appearance, these young men and women strive to reflect in their lives the precepts of the gospel truths they are teaching.

The driving force behind the work of missionaries and members of the church is their strongly-felt spiritual duty to witness of Jesus Christ and his restored gospel to every nation and people. Their history has abundant evidence of the sincerity of their missionary efforts and their willingness to sacrifice for them. Their record of rapid growth for over 150 years, culminating in a present worldwide membership of over 10 million, shows that their message is meaningful to many.

In carrying out their duty to witness, Mormons have two external restraints. Since the observance of law is strictly required, they must comply with all legal requirements in seeking admission to nations and in delivering their message. And since moral agency—the right of every soul to choose what he or she will believe and practice—is a fundamental tenet of the faith, Mormons cannot seek converts by coercion or consideration but only by invitation and persuasion. The proofs of their message are found in the lives of the members and in the witness of the Spirit. Their invitation to all the world is "Come and see."[7]

© by Intellectual Reserve, Inc.

Elder Lance B. Wickman is a member of the First Quorum of the Seventy. This essay was presented at "The Challenge of Sharing Religious Beliefs in a Global Setting," the International Society's tenth annual conference, August 1999, Brigham Young University, Provo, Utah.

7.   Oaks and Wickman, "Missionary Work of The Church of Jesus Christ of Latter-day Saints," 268–75.

Chapter 6

Challenges from Religious Communities in Spreading the Gospel

Hugh M. Matheson

I HAVE SPENT six years in Africa but have not made any formal studies of the topic at hand, so my remarks will be more anecdotal than empirical. I recently finished four years as the Church's international legal counsel for Africa. For part of that time, I also served as the Church's Africa Area director of public affairs. Of course, I do not speak for the Church. With those disclaimers out of the way, we can turn to the assigned topic: the challenges of religious communities in spreading the gospel.

First, let us talk about the opportunities in religious communities. What if Joseph Smith had come on the scene prior to the Reformation, or what if he had lived among non-Christians? In Africa the people who have already been converted to Christianity, in some form or another, are often more likely to be ready to hear the gospel. So the existence of other religious communities, especially Christian religious communities, which are teaching basic moral codes and strengthening the family, is a good thing. They bring light into people's lives and make them more receptive to the full light of the restored gospel.

We are finding common ground with many of these people and groups as we work to promote positive values, including the defense of the family. I see great opportunities for the Church to build bridges with the Islamic community in Nigeria and other African countries as we work together in international forums about the family. So there are great opportunities for spreading the gospel and promoting shared values because religious communities exist.

Of course, religious communities also present challenges, not the least of which arise because of apparently competitive proselyting activities. For example, a good Protestant church sends missionaries to Africa and spends a lot of time, money, and effort to convert people from their traditional beliefs. Then Latter-day Saint missionaries are sometimes seen as coming along and stealing some of the best people. These perceptions can lead to mistrust and can foster a desire to push against the Church's missionary effort.

Many of these religious groups have ties with parent organizations in the U.S. or Europe. When they begin to notice our arrival and growth in African cities, they start checking with headquarters. They receive all the "anti–Latter-day Saint" stuff, and they start to spread it around through congregations and the media. Unfortunately, human nature has a tendency to believe the first thing it hears about a subject. The next person who comes along and tries to change someone's opinion about a subject has a huge burden of proof. That is certainly true with perceptions of the Church. Before missionaries get very far in a new place, the people have often heard some pretty wild things about us that take some time to dislodge.

Sometimes minor misunderstandings are easily corrected. In Nairobi, I met an educated woman, very active in her church, whose preacher had quoted the New Testament in warning against the "Mammons" and the "Book of Mammon." With the beautiful East African–British accent, the two words do sound remarkably similar: *Mormon* and *mammon*. She wondered how we could possibly be proclaiming this "Book of Mammon" when the New Testament clearly states, "Ye cannot serve God and mammon" (Matthew 6:24). This is a silly little thing, but it is an example of the preconceived notions that are created about what we are and what we stand for.

There are many more serious examples, such as the misinformation that led to the freeze of the Church's activities in Ghana in the 1980s. Many great stories of faith arose out of that episode, which I am sure are being chronicled elsewhere. The end result was that the Church and its relationships in Ghana are stronger for having passed through that. But it was a costly and distracting episode that we would not want to see repeated. Many examples of misinformation are out there and are being spread by some of these religious communities. We have a lot of work to do.

It was frustrating to see the Church being misrepresented by religious groups in an African country. At the same time, I knew that in Salt Lake City and around the world we were cooperating with some of the same groups in humanitarian work, defense of religious freedom, promotion of family-friendly policies, and other areas. We need more communication to get past that hurdle of the bad first impressions laid down by those who are unfriendly toward the Church.

But religious opposition is and always has been a fact of life for the restored gospel. Those of us who have been on missions know that. One of my mission presidents is President E. Dale LeBaron. He thought I needed some reforming, so he put me in Potchefstroom, South Africa, for seven months, and I used to say it was like being a Catholic missionary in Provo. The city was the heart of the South African Dutch Reformed Church. The local *dominee* would go and collect copies of the Book of Mormon that we had placed with investigators, and it was a great experience when we would go get them back from him. You could say we were pioneering in the area of interfaith relations.

The Church survives and actually thrives in the face of this kind of religious opposition. But it can impinge on our ability to even operate in a country where these groups have access to political levers. Many discuss secularization and the marginalization of religious groups from public-policy making in the Western world. In Africa the opposite case exists. Often religions can constitute very powerful political blocs. Most countries have a church or a group of churches that support the head of state, and others support the opposition. Despite our clearly stated and carefully protected political neutrality, we sometimes get caught in serious political crossfire.

In most of these countries, we are required by law to register with the government to begin operating, and that can be a lengthy process partly because of these political concerns and because of opposition from politically powerful religious groups. Of course, we always go through the front door and are very careful about doing everything by the book, even if we are the only ones following the rules. Sometimes we have to wait while government leaders walk the political tightrope involved in letting us come into their country despite the opposition of some religious groups.

Even after going through that process of registration, we can face misunderstandings with governments. We like to work quietly. After going through the front door of registration, we do not make much hoopla. We just want to preach the gospel to families and individuals. But governments who have learned to see churches as political activists can easily assume that if you are not with them, you are against them. Sometimes our quiet but rapid growth comes to the notice of the government. The whispering starts, and word goes to the head of state: "These people are here, and they are spending money on buildings and programs and missionaries from overseas, and they are stealing the best people from our churches." Then pretty soon the Church is suspect. That is the kind of thing that happens in Africa. But as Area President J. Richard Clarke used to say, "If you can not stand a little competition, you had better not be in Africa."

All these postindependence African constitutions have religious freedom provisions. I have asked legal scholars, Supreme Court justices, and law deans all over the African continent about religious freedom case law in their countries. Of course, in the U.S. the Church practically wrote much of the case law on religious freedom, some of it good and some of it not so good. African legal scholars are familiar with American constitutional law, but when I asked if anything like it exists in modern African law, they just looked at me like I was an idiot: "What case law? You do not sue the government. You would not dare to take the ministry of interior or the ministry of justice to court, trying to enforce the constitutional provision on freedom on religion. You would be mad to try such a thing."

African governments have great words on paper, but they are not the words they live by. The words they *do* live by have a lot more to do with political power bases and political reality, often far from the ideal. But U.S. citizens cannot get too cocky; it has taken us more than two centuries and one civil war to get where we are on some of these issues.

Africa seems to be a tricky environment, but it is really kind of a simple environment. After you have been there a while, you get into the flow of it, and you start to know when to take things at face value and when to look behind the words for the cultural, political, and legal meanings. Unfortunately, the undercurrents of corruption and self-dealing color much of what goes on.

In all this corruption, there are plenty of opportunities to do good, to find common ground with thoughtful, moral people. Earlier I referred to the human tendency to believe the first bit of information on a given subject and not to believe later contradictory information. This tendency operates in Africa, and people there can be swayed by first impressions. But I also noticed that many Africans, especially in the cities, are sophisticated consumers of rhetoric. During the colonial era and in the years of independence since, they have had plenty of paternalistic, self-serving propaganda thrown at them. Though the initial mass reaction to propoganda can be exaggerated and even hysterical, the more thoughtful people are quite adept at subjecting things to a smell test. They know that institutions, including the media and especially the official media, put a spin on things and even make outright fabrications. Eventually, even the less thoughtful folks who were initially led down the garden path will admit they were deceived. Africans can be quite skeptical, curious, and open-minded. They debate things. I have had many well-reasoned conversations with taxi drivers, game guides, attorneys, church colleagues, media workers, and even government officials in Africa on political, legal, and religious topics.

If these opportunities are approached wisely and with some cultural savvy, the Church can tell its own story and be a powerful force for good in these countries. Unlike Japan, for instance, where it seems it would be very difficult to ever penetrate the consciousness of even a significant minority of the people, Church representatives can go into a capital city in Africa and become carefully and appropriately acquainted with powerful elites, heads of the state, and radio, television, and newspaper editors. Those relationships can sometimes be two-edged swords, but I think they are worth developing. Humanitarian work and profamily policy initiatives can serve the basis for relationship building. So can the general topic of religious tolerance and interfaith civility.

Because somebody is going to be telling our story, it might as well be us. One great way to start is by building bridges of understanding with religious leaders, humanitarian donors, media editors, academia, and governments. Of course, much great work is already being done in those areas by representatives of the Church: Latter-day Saint Charities, Brigham Young University, the Thrasher Research Fund, World Family Policy Center, Bonneville Media, Church Hosting, the International Affairs office in Washington, and many private individuals.

I think this work should continue and be encouraged at the institutional and individual levels. My friends from the Public Affairs Department are doing great work in this area. I would say that they and all of us should do all we can to build relationships and improve public understanding so we can prepare the ground, avoid some of these silly misunderstandings, and inoculate against some of the more outlandish things that might be said about the Church.

You can never know what fruit a relationship will bear in the future. In a certain African country a few years ago, we were targeted by an official inquiry on the subject of devil worship. Because of these and other accusations, the Church was apparently facing imminently pending deregistration. A conscientious man who had studied in the U.S. thirty years earlier and was impressed with some Latter-day Saints he had met warned us of this. He had visited Temple Square and knew the Church's standing and reputation in the U.S. All these years later, he had a high position in the particular government ministry that was reviewing our case. He contacted us and quite appropriately gave us the opportunity to have some input into the process. I cannot talk about the details, but over the next months the Lord put the pieces together, and some gentle words went to the head of state over a period of time, and we remained legally registered in that country.

These kinds of challenges can be averted and even prevented as we continue to make wise use of public communications, public affairs, and government relations. As the Brethren continue to send wise, seasoned, capable, humble, and faithful mission presidents and missionaries to work in these countries, we can avoid such challenges. And most important, these problems can be avoided as the marvelous, faithful local members take advantage of opportunities to boldly and publicly tell the truth.

In closing, I will tell one story about the important role of local members and priesthood leaders. A situation arose in an African country where a visiting American, who happened to be a member of the Church, was accused of doing something very unusual. I could tell you some of what was reported, but the stories were pretty gruesome. We still do not know what really happened, but suffice it to say that it was a medical situation that ended up creating some wild stories. This story hit the tabloids, and even the more reliable newspapers could not refrain from picking up this sensational tale. And, of course, they related his alleged bizarre behavior to his Church membership.

We Westerners, sitting in the area office, talked about how the Church should and should not respond. We got some very helpful input from Brother Michael Otterson in Public Affairs on an immediate response strategy, which we relayed to the local leaders. Once past that immediate response, the local priesthood leaders followed the established order of the Church by convening a multistake public affairs council under the leadership of a stake president and comprising good, solid men and women who were members and friends of the Church. They took one or two days to counsel together and plan a response. They communicated with the Area President, who also invited some participation from me. We gave them our insights. Then President James O. Mason led us in prayer and simply left the matter in the Lord's hands as He might inspire that local public affairs council to act.

And what did the council do? Things we Westerners might never have done. They turned the publicity into a missionary event! They set up open house displays at a stake center. They had rooms dedicated to family home evening, the Relief Society, the Young Men, the Young Women, and so on. They led the reporters and camera crews through the open house and then began the press conference with an opening hymn and an opening prayer. The stake president got up and said he did not know what had happened in that particular unusual event, but if it was anything like what was reported, the Church was against it. "You know how stories get told in our country," he said, "so let's not judge the man too quickly." And then he explained the doctrines and programs of the Church and testified of the Savior.

They had a closing hymn, and the media personnel were singing along. Some of the reporters were seen with tears in their eyes. Thereafter ensued two or three weeks of the best coverage of the Church we have ever had in that country or any other country in Africa.

Now, would we do that at a press conference in the United States? It would be fun to try! The point is that the local members knew the local press, and they were inspired that this was the appropriate approach.

The reaction of the media in that situation demonstrates the African thoughtfulness I mentioned earlier. These people, some of whom can so quickly jump to the wrong conclusions, are ultimately likely to recognize this cultural tendency and then adjust and say, "Hold on, let's find out what is really going on here." For instance, many Church members in Ghana believe that our current strength there is a result of heightened interest in the Church because the government had chased us out in the 1980s.

I do not get too worried about challenges presented by religious groups or the governments who are sometimes swayed by them. The Lord is in charge, and He knows what He is doing. And despite our clumsiness and anxiety, He somehow makes it work. When the Lord states that the gospel will "be proclaimed by the weak and the simple" (D&C 1:23), I do not think that His words are limited to nineteen-year-olds. With His help, these challenges easily become opportunities.

I will never forget a statement President Hinckley made to the Saints in Johannesburg, South Africa, when he visited in February 1998. South Africa, of course, faces all manner of economic and security challenges that are consistent with those of all developing countries and exacerbated by decades of the inefficient and immoral apartheid political system. President Hinckley's advice to us was to "starve your problems and feed your opportunities"—good counsel for individuals and institutions everywhere.

Religious and political challenges make frequent appearances in the pages of Church history. But they have resulted in some of the Church's greatest strengths, whether the fierce opposition to early missionary work in the British Isles, the mob violence in Missouri and the march of Zion's Camp, or the hardships of the westward migration and settling in the barren Great Basin. We should not be surprised when these historical patterns are repeated in countries where the restored gospel is newly introduced. We anxiously do the best we can, and the Lord and good people on the ground always make things turn out for the best in the long run.

Hugh M. Matheson is the former legal counsel for the Church's Africa Area. This essay was presented at "The Challenge of Sharing Religious Beliefs in a Global Setting," the International Society's tenth annual conference, August 1999, Brigham Young University, Provo, Utah.

Chapter 7

The Impact of Secularization on Proselytism in Europe:

A Minority Religion Perspective

W. Cole Durham Jr.

WE LIVE IN a world that is an odd mixture of the worlds of Sherem (see Jacob 7) and Korihor (see Alma 30). For me, one of the remarkable things about the Book of Mormon is that it was abridged and edited by prophetic figures writing after the collapse of one civilization and very late in the course of their own who could speak to our time as if we were present (see Mormon 8:35), knowing that their words would reach our generation. They did not know exactly which types of anti-Christ we would meet or which would be most persuasive to us, but they knew we would encounter them. Accordingly, the Book of Mormon is filled with accounts and images that warn us of the varying hazards: Jerusalem and Babylon, the great and spacious building, Sherem and Korihor. Sherem is the figure who criticizes prophets and revelations concerning Christ on the basis of orthodox religious texts. At the other pole stands Korihor, the secular anti-Christ, who prefigures in his thought the great masters of suspicion of the nineteenth and twentieth centuries—Darwin, Marx, Nietzsche, and Freud. We live in a world populated with figures from both sides.

The secularization thesis, which has been the basis of much sociological theory for the past century, is basically the claim that in the struggles between Sherems and Korihors that have shaped modernity, Korihor is on the prevailing side. Stated in more secular terms, that thesis is that in the aftermath of the industrial revolution and the increasing importance it has attached to material goods and the division of labor, societies would become ever more secular, and religious institutions would wither away.

Over the past decade, this key premise of sociological theory has come under increasing attack.[1] The secularization thesis is flawed. The "opiate of the people" is not withering away. The secularization thesis is being subjected to increasing doubt because it cannot explain the residual and growing religious influence that is being felt in the United States and throughout the world.[2] In fact, at least in the United States, high levels of religious activity continue, and if anything, over the past two decades, there has been a strengthening of religious activity and particularly more conservative religious groups have shown increased vitality.[3] In the former communist bloc, forty to seventy years of the most intense and brutal secularization efforts imaginable did not suffice to extirpate religiosity. The communist era certainly had a marked effect. The spirituality of a generation of Russians and central Europeans has been repressed and, for many, extinguished. And yet the core religious values still come back.

---

1. See, for example, José Casanova, *Public Religions in the Modern World* (Chicago: University of Chicago Press, 1994); Jeffrey K. Hadden and Anson Shupe, eds., *Secularization and Fundamentalism Reconsidered* (New York: Aragon House, 1989); David Martin, *A General Theory of Secularization* (New York: Harper and Row, 1978).

2. For indications of the vitality and resurgence of religion throughout the world, whether in more extreme forms, or more commonly in the strength and fruitfulness of the variety of religious traditions around the world, we need only to leaf through studies such as the recent world report on freedom of religion and belief (see Kevin Boyle and Juliet Sheen, eds., *Freedom of Religion and Belief: A World Report* [London and New York: Routledge, 1997]).

3. See Robert Wuthnow, *The Restructuring of American Religion: Society and Faith since World War II* (Princeton, NJ: Princeton University Press, 1989).

In what follows, I will address some of the ways the pattern of secularization has an adverse impact on missionary work and some of the steps that can be taken to address these problems.

Secularization and Europe

In Europe, much more than in America, the classical picture of secularization remains more accurate. Particularly in Western Europe, the phenomenon of the *Vergreisung der Kirchen*—the aging of the churches—tells the tale. Churches are for the most part empty, with continuing activity coming substantially from the elderly population. Material success of the second half of the twentieth century has diverted people's attention from religious involvement. New forms of "secularized religiosity" in such forms as the commitment to human rights and environmental values, coupled with internalized spirituality, have largely supplanted older patterns of religious involvement.

There are, of course, variations from this pattern. One of the most moving experiences I had was in the spring of 1990, going to a church in Kraków, Poland, and for the first time in my life seeing a European church filled to overflowing. Unfortunately, in the decade since the euphoric early days after the fall of communism, religious attendance in places like Poland is declining. In part, this is because church participation in Poland was a form of social protest against communism, and the more secular elements in the protest movement have dropped out. However, some of the decline reflects alienation against excessive pressure from the Catholic Church to press its agenda in Polish society. In general, Europe is a very secularized place, and the situation is not getting any better.

Secularism and Proselytism

Secular outlooks increasingly shape popular responses to proselyting. Three aspects of the contemporary European response to religion underscore what I have in mind. The first factor has to do with relativism and scientism (or more accurately, pseudoscientism).

In the secularized setting, intense religiosity that becomes a central focus of life tends to be thought of as something dated or fanatical. A pervasive sense of relativism leads members of European society at large to assume that religion is essentially a matter of taste, that there are many paths to heaven, and that the concept of a true church is outmoded. The phenomenon of conversion is often regarded as an anomaly, to be explained by brainwashing. The assumption is that something as irrational as conversion, especially to a small, unknown religious group, could only be explained by some psychic distortion.

A second factor is the rise of privacy. In many ways, the European concern for privacy is even more intense than our own. Privacy legislation has substantially more clout in European societies, perhaps because European population densities are much higher than those in the United States, and people are more acutely conscious of the need for private space. One practical implication of this is the proliferation of electronic security systems in apartment complexes, making old door-to-door contacting systems much more difficult. At a deeper level, efforts to share religious beliefs are increasingly seen as an encroachment on privacy. If people on their own initiative want to search for a new religion, that is fine. But efforts to share religious beliefs are increasingly being viewed as aggressive, impolite, and wrongfully intruding on privacy. As societal norms shift in this area, even the fairly gentle "come and see" invitation associated with knocking on doors or standing at a street board comes to be sensed as an encroachment—as a kind of insensitivity. Over time, this will become a greater and greater problem.

Still a third factor is a peculiar blend of state paternalism and consumer protection. Over the past two or three years, anticult efforts in Europe have been accelerating to an extraordinary degree. Throughout Europe, there is a sense that states should protect consumers from dangerous religious groups in the same way that consumers are protected from other forms of consumer fraud. This is a very strange idea in countries committed to religious freedom and nonintervention in matters of religious belief, but its strength is growing. Formal inquiry commissions have been established in France, Belgium, Germany, Austria, and Switzerland. Reports issued by these commissions have been filled with biased, unscientific, and often rabid statements that tend to stereotype and demonize sects and cults. Austria has passed a law consigning many religious groups to second-class status for at least ten years. (Fortunately, we are not impacted by this law because we are a recognized church in Austria.) Unbelievably, the French government has adopted official policies that have literally declared war on the sects. At the Council of Europe, a resolution was passed in June 1999 calling, among other things, for the creation of information centers about sects throughout Europe. A recent U.S. State Department group that went to France to investigate what is happening met with some members of The Church of Jesus Christ of Latter-day Saints (as part of meetings with many groups) and determined that while Latter-day Saints are not formally on the French "sect list," they have already begun to be adversely affected by these initiatives. Note that these difficulties are not located in former socialist bloc countries that lack experience with new religious movements. Sect observatories or investigations have been established or carried out in France, Belgium, Germany, Austria, and Switzerland. These are the core nations of Western Europe. Some of the positions being taken are really unbelievable. There appear to be some in France who think that it is not clear whether a sect counts as a religion for purposes of religious freedom protections. For those of us accustomed to thinking of Western Europe as a bastion of human rights, these developments have been extremely unnerving.

There are some brighter signs: the ultimate German report concluded that worries about the dangers of sects were exaggerated, and a Swedish report in 1998 was quite critical of earlier sect commission reports from other countries. The initiative at the level of the Council of Europe was toned down somewhat, and there are efforts afoot to help increase the likelihood that sect observatories will be balanced sources of information and not merely centers of anticult propaganda. Credible Europeans maintain that Americans are simply getting overly distressed about these matters. Their view is that there is nothing wrong with providing more information about religious groups and that nothing malign is intended. The difficulty is the danger that such observatories tend to be captured by rabidly anticult personnel, which generally means rabidly anti–Latter-day Saint and anti–Jehovah's Witness as well. Moreover, even if those placed in charge of such observatories are objective and well intentioned, they can do significant damage by implicitly giving their stamp of approval to information that is in fact biased or misleading. In any event, militant anticult efforts continue, and the Church is generally a major target, because The Church of Jesus Christ of Latter-day Saints is larger and more effective than many other churches.

The Eastern Impact of Western Infractions

The problems in Western Europe compound the problems being faced in Eastern Europe. At least three reasons can be cited for this.

First, leading anticult figures in the West, some of whom hold paid government positions, are actively working to foment anticult sentiments throughout the former communist bloc. Anticult efforts appear to be well organized and well financed, making them all the more effective.

Second, the current cultural setting in those areas is conducive to scapegoating smaller religious groups for the more massive economic and social problems being experienced in those countries. This is one of the classic problems associated with anti-Semitism. It is all too easy for politicians to lay blame for various social ills at the door of small and unknown groups who are foreign, strange, and politically powerless. The result can be fairly devastating for all smaller religious groups, who are inevitably branded by association with overbroad stereotypes about "dangerous sects."

Third, the fact that government bodies in the West are holding inquiries and setting up sect observatories and, in some cases, passing laws to restrict their activities is exploited to legitimize parallel and typically much worse activities farther east. When one speaks as a human rights worker with officials in Eastern Europe about problematic legislation in their countries, one now finds them responding, "We're just doing what Austria has done," or, "We're just implementing a recommendation from the Council of Europe." These officials are basically saying that these are key democratic institutions, and what they do is legitimate, so we can do it too. Unfortunately, these justifications are used to rationalize encroachments on religious freedom that go much further than anything that would be allowed in the West, where there are traditions and social controls that help prevent the worst abuses.

This compounds a general pattern of backsliding in the former socialist bloc. At the beginning of the 1990s, there was euphoria everywhere, manifested as the rapid embrace of key Western values such as religious freedom. When people in the socialist bloc realized this was not a kind of magic wand that would transform them, Cinderellalike, into rich Westerners, a kind of disenchantment and demoralization began to set in. As a result, there is increasing willingness of governments to consider and pass legislation that puts tighter controls on smaller religious groups. Dominant religions in particular countries can more easily defuse claims that religious human rights require a more open, tolerant, and equalitarian society. Part of this is the result of the ongoing influence of secularization. Part has to do with nationalism (particularly where dominant religious traditions have historic ties with nationalist instincts). Part is a kind of resistance to worries about neocolonialism. Countries are sensitive to the onslaught of American culture in the form of McDonald's, Burger King, Pizza Hut, television, movies, music, youth culture, and so forth. All these things breed sentiments for tightening borders and resisting the influence of perceived bearers of foreign cultural influence.

Countertrends to Secularization

Having said all this, I would also like to emphasize that I think there are also signs that the secularization thesis will turn out to be as inaccurate for Europe as it is for the United States. One obvious counter to the secularization thesis is the survival of religion in the former communist bloc countries. The fact that religion has survived there and remained vigorous in that particularly hostile environment says much for the staying power of religion and its importance to human existence. A second point, and one I think suggests particular hope, is that there are signs that the younger generation throughout Europe is increasingly open to spiritual values. I have no comprehensive data but have been surprised by the number of younger scholars in the East and the West who are religious. My own sense is that just as we are seeing remarkable talent coming up within the Church, reflecting the fact that many chosen spirits have been preserved to come forth in the last days, so we are beginning to see similar individuals throughout the world who will be receptive to the gospel message. A third noteworthy fact is the proliferation of more intense religious groups. Sophisticated, secular, and world-weary groups in society tend to view such groups (including ours) with disdain, but the growing strength of such groups, albeit often only at the margins of society, is an indication of the hunger for deeper spiritual values.

The Perspective of Minority Religions on Proselyting

With these factors in mind, I would like to focus on ways that minority religious groups (including our own) see the right to engage in proselyting. For smaller groups, outreach is vital not only to growth but also to survival. All religious groups suffer attrition from the forces of secularization, and this is a particular problem for groups that have only small numbers of believers in the first place.

Representatives of larger religious groups typically do not see the issues from the same vantage point. I remember sitting a few years ago with a very distinguished set of experts on proselyting issues from several churches. The truly frightening thing for me was looking around and realizing that I was probably the only person there who had ever actually engaged in missionary work and, not surprisingly, was one of the few who had a positive view of proselyting. In general, our brothers and sisters in larger denominations think of missionary work in very negative ways.

On another occasion, I took a group of Russians to the headquarters of the National Council of Churches (NCC). This is, of course, a fairly liberal group, but I was still surprised by the message delivered by one of the top leaders of the organization. After welcoming the Russians to the NCC, she went on at some length to say how embarrassed she felt about the "problem of proselyting." She admitted that even some of the member churches of the NCC were engaged in proselyting. She apologized again and again for this unbecoming behavior. That is fairly representative of how things are in much of the world. The fact that proselytism is increasingly viewed in a negative light and that understanding for the importance and legitimacy of sharing religious views is fading means that religious liberty protections for sharing religious views are also at risk. In what follows, I hope to address some of the resulting concerns.

Returning to the perspective of smaller groups, it is necessary to stress that I cannot begin to address the full range of views that emerging and minority religions take toward proselyting. One of the things that is most clear about the religions of our planet is that they are extraordinarily diverse, and they have correspondingly diverse views about the ethics of sharing their views with others. What I will attempt to do, however, is identify some of the reasons why proselyting is so important to smaller religious communities, and more broadly why it is so vital that we pay particular attention to their sensitivities with respect to proselytism. In general, the real test of religious freedom is not how larger groups are treated. They generally have much greater access to political power and the powerful background institutions of culture than smaller groups and can accordingly fend for themselves. This is as true with respect to proselytism as it is with other matters. The fact that larger religions conclude that proselytism is not a preferred strategy for community building and maintenance should not necessarily guide the judgments of smaller religious groups, who are generally facing much more difficult problems precisely because they are often swimming against the stream of the dominant culture. Moreover, my sense is that smaller groups have a much more accurate perception of what is really involved as a practical matter in the phenomenon of proselyting. Their experience can give us a clearer picture of where the genuine problems with proselyting lie and can help us avoid broad descriptions of "improper" proselyting that might lead to correspondingly broad restrictions on legitimate religious activities.

Terminology

An example of the cultural power wielded by larger religious groups is evident in the negative charge associated with the term *proselyting* itself. It is only when I began entering into dialogue with individuals from larger religious traditions that I began to sense anything negative about the term. Within our tradition, the term *proselyting* is normally used to refer to legitimate religious persuasion—to the sharing of one's belief with others under genuinely noncoercive circumstances. It is only from the larger traditions that I have learned that *proselyting* is something suspect, something that might not be eligible for the normal protections of freedom of religion and freedom of expression.

We owe current formulations of the distinction between legitimate witnessing activities and improper proselytism to documents drawn up by larger denominations.[4] Unstated (perhaps not intended,

---

4. See, for example, *Common Witness and Proselytism*, reprinted in *Ecumenical Review* 9 (1971), a study document prepared in 1970 by a Joint Theological Commission between the Roman Catholic Church and the World Council of Churches.

but nonetheless felt by smaller groups) is an implicit message of con-
descension: a religious organization that feels the need to be actively
engaged in the process of community building is at best doing
something distasteful or uncouth and, more likely, is behaving in an
unethical manner. The very terminology we use is molded by wield-
ers of cultural power into a not-so-subtle tool of disparagement. I
do not want to make too much of this point because, as will become
evident, I believe the larger churches have in fact identified genuine
moral issues that need to be faced at the edges of legitimate religious
persuasion. But I am saddened that a once legitimate term has now
been so freighted with negative associations that the term has become
difficult to use. I agree with the definition offered in Tad Stahnke's
excellent article on proselytism, which provides that "'proselytism'
means expressive conduct undertaken with the purpose of trying to
change the religious beliefs, affiliation, or identity of another."[5] But
because of the negative charge that increasingly taints even "proper"
positivism, I will use the term *religious persuasion* in what follows
when I am referring to legitimate proselyting and *improper (or abusive) proselyting* when referring to illegitimate activity.

Shared Positive Attitudes regarding the Right to Engage in Religious Persuasion

Contrary to what some might think, there is in fact broad agreement among both the larger and the smaller religious groups I know
best about the conditions for religious persuasion. Everyone recognizes that at some level religious persuasion and teaching is vital to
the flourishing of religious life. While different traditions have different views about how actively beliefs should be shared, everyone
recognizes that all religious traditions have depended on fairly active
proselyting at least at some stages in their history. Moreover, every

---

5. Tad Stahnke, "Proselytism and the Freedom to Change Religion in
    International Human Rights Law," *Brigham Young University Law
    Review* 1999, no. 1 (1999): 255.

tradition believes that the power of teaching by example should be allowed. (We do not imprison people merely because they have done saintly acts that are admired even by people of other faiths.) It is further understood that, for many religions, active profession of faith is as central to religious practice as participating in sacramental rituals, such as the Eucharist.

Shared Understanding of Limiting Principles

There is also considerable consensus as to the basic governing principles of restrictions. As Monsignor Roland Minnerath formulates the point, legitimate religious persuasion "cannot be imposed from outside by means of psychological or physical constraint. In our present understanding of human rights this freedom is rooted in the very nature of human beings and must be recognized as a civil right protected by law."[6] The central point here is that persuasion accompanied by improper coercion is illegitimate. As the European Court of Human Rights recognized in the *Kokkinakis* case, there are several types of conduct that constitute improper proselytism: (1) physical force, (2) deception, (3) undue influence, and (4) inappropriate material incentives.[7] Each of these types of conduct have the result that a religious choice made under their influence is not genuine or authentic. Freedom in the most sensitive and sacred of all domains—in the realm of conscience—is violated.

Similarly, there is considerable consensus that discussions of religious differences should be respectful, honest, and civil. This does not mean that society, groups, or individuals should be shielded as a matter of law from robust and sometimes overzealous discussion, and it certainly does not mean that one group cannot question the validity or truth of the beliefs of another. But such respect needs

---

6. Roland Minnerath, *Proselytism: An Ethic[al] Perspective (Catholicism)*, 1, unpublished manuscript in author's possession.

7. *Kokkinakis v. Greece*, European Court of Human Rights, A 260-A (1993).

to go in two directions. Majority groups are all too prone to disparage smaller groups as sects and to engage in stereotypical thinking about them. My sense is that smaller groups suffer far more from such disparagement than larger groups. Moreover, smaller groups tend to be deterred from challenging such behavior emanating from larger groups because any effort to do so simply attracts intensified reactions and negative repercussions in return.

Proselytism and International Instruments

At this point there is an array of international instruments that address religious freedom issues and can be used as the basis for an expansive right to engage in religious persuasion. It is important that the legitimacy of these arguments not be undermined by the fact that the issue of proselytism is not more explicitly addressed. There is a history to the silence on these issues in the international instruments. The silence reflects compromise rather than principle. That is, the key international instruments were adopted in Cold War settings in which it was not possible to secure commitment to a full measure of religious freedom by socialist and Muslim countries. I suppose they could counter by arguing that they conceded too much to religious liberty claims. But we need to remember that we are dealing with human rights. That is, it is important to remember that human beings are entitled to religious freedom (including the right to engage in religious persuasion) simply because they are human. We do not hold these rights at the discretion of any state or any collection of states. We have achieved remarkable success in our time in articulating and codifying principles of religious freedom, but the fact that all states have not yet agreed on the full range of legitimate religious freedom does not mean that the right does not exist or that every effort should not be made to better achieve it.

Dealing with Sources of Admittedly Counterproductive Coercive Behavior

If anything, smaller religious groups tend to be more concerned with making certain that conversion is voluntary rather than the larger denominations are. Inauthentic conversion tends to become a drag on the smaller religious community. An individual who converts because of material inducements rather than for spiritual reasons is likely to constantly renew requests for additional material benefits, creating a drag on the overall resources of the group. Similarly, conversion by physical force creates needs for maintaining coercive pressures, which is not only costly but also demoralizing, and so forth.

Indeed, when we contemplate the disadvantages of coerced conversion to a religious group, we wonder why the phenomenon arises in the first place. One reason is excessive or misguided zeal. A second may be a desire for independent corroboration of the improper proselyter's own views (if someone else converts, my beliefs must be correct). A third reason may be that if one coerces outward conformity to religious beliefs, sincere belief may ultimately be induced, either later in the life of the target of coercion or later in the life of the target's children. This strategy demands extraordinary coercive pressure and probably cannot be accomplished without the active cooperation of the state. A fourth category of reasons has to do with administrative pressures. A mission leader needs to vindicate requests for ongoing funding or other forms of support, and the number of converts is a ready measure of success. Missionaries may feel a sense of competition with each other, which may create pressures for numbers. No doubt there are other institutional pressures that cause improper proselyting. This suggests that there may be value in refocusing discussions about improper proselyting. The controversy is not whether coercive conversion is good or bad as an ethical matter. The question is how we address the institutional or psychological pressures that lead to admittedly counterproductive excesses.

Invisible Sources of Coercion

Smaller groups tend to be acutely conscious of the subtle and somewhat invisible forms of coercion often exercised (whether consciously or unconsciously) by dominant groups. One of the early arguments for religious freedom was John Locke's claim that since religious beliefs could not be coerced, the state should not waste its efforts in trying to impose such beliefs. While it is true, in general, that the most one can hope to accomplish by coercion (at least in the short run) is inducing hypocrisy, Locke's theory overlooks the coercion that can be accomplished by maintaining ignorance. That is, coercion may not be very effective as a device for instilling sincerely religious beliefs, but it is extraordinarily effective in avoiding change of belief. It is extremely difficult to be converted to a belief of which one has never heard. In this connection, the Prophet Joseph Smith was the rarest of exceptions. Concerted efforts to filter the ideas to which believers are exposed or to tarnish ideas with negative stereotypes so that they are avoided are much more effective devices for conditioning belief than physical brainwashing.

In a parallel vein, just as material inducements may constitute an improper inducement to convert to a religion, so material disincentives may constitute impermissible inducements at the point of exit. My sense is that whatever material inducements proselyting groups may use to encourage conversion pale by comparison to the economic and social disincentives larger groups can mobilize to deter an individual from leaving a religion: disinheritance, reduced job and educational opportunities, social isolation, and so forth. To the extent that coercion in religious matters is impermissible, the coercive mechanisms used by larger groups may be as deserving of scrutiny as the techniques used by smaller groups. I use the term *scrutiny* advisedly here because I believe that, in general, state intervention in these areas should be minimized.

Truth, Exclusivity, and Danger

There is a tendency to believe that religious communities that take truth seriously, particularly when they make exclusive claims to truth, constitute a danger to society. The argument seems to be that exclusive truth claims are themselves inherently dangerous. As Monsignor Minnerath states the problem, "If you have an exclusive concept of truth then you need to convert everybody to your faith in order to save them. Then you are likely to indulge even in violent means, for the good of your victims."[8] The only way to avoid this risk, the argument continues, is to profess an inclusive concept of religious truth.

While there are certainly belief systems that exemplify such dangers, the argument is radically overstated in the context of the modern pluralistic world. At least two additional beliefs are needed to transform a belief system that makes exclusive claims to truth into a social danger. First, if the belief system includes internal beliefs that the dignity of other human beings should be respected, even if they hold erroneous religious beliefs, we cannot assume that this exclusive religious truth claim is a social danger. Second, if a religion does not believe it is entitled to use coercive force to convert, whether that force is in private or public hands, the risk also does not arise. Much of the progress in fields of religious liberty made over the past three decades has resulted from the dramatic events of the Second Vatican Council and the effective internalization of religious freedom norms within the Roman Catholic tradition. The most effective way to achieve religious freedom is to find ways to help strengthen the already existing norms within virtually all religious traditions that call for toleration and mutual respect.

Ecumenism and Dialogue

Ecumenical efforts and dialogue can also promote understanding. But it is important to remember that whether ecumenical

---

8. Minnerath, *Proslytism*, note 9.

approaches should be adopted is itself a matter of religious belief and sometimes of profound disagreement. For religious traditions that desire to engage in ecumenical processes, encouraging such processes is no doubt helpful. But to assume that it is somehow ethically incorrect to take a different stand simply misunderstands the nature of religious freedom. If a particular religious group holds as one of its beliefs that it should not compromise its doctrines or that it is not authorized to enter into joint ministry with individuals of other faiths, this is itself a matter of conscience protected by religious freedom. It is as incorrect to invoke state power in support of ecumenism as it is to invoke state power in favor of any particular group (whether participating in or rejecting ecumenical discourse).

As a practical matter, however, it is often possible to promote the same beneficial levels of tolerance and understanding by facilitating cooperation on projects of common concern. This can include cooperative charitable and humanitarian aid projects. It can also involve common efforts in support of religious freedom. This is an area where indirect approaches to promoting goodwill and mutual understanding may be more effective than direct approaches.

Beware of Self-defeating Arguments

I have worked extensively over the course of the past decade in Eastern Europe and have repeatedly confronted arguments against proselytism with the following form, typically made by Orthodox priests in various countries where the Orthodox tradition is dominant: our people are not as educated about religion as the citizens of the West. This means that whenever a foreign missionary confronts them with new religious ideas, they are being subject to undue influence. Their susceptibility and ignorance mean that the attempt at religious persuasion is inherently coercive, and thus the activity is automatically impermissible proselyting. The difficulty with this argument is that it is self-defeating. If true, it also means that it is impermissible proselyting for the Orthodox priest to try to convert his people (unless he concludes that he is insufficiently educated, too, but in that case he would have no claim to teach).

The Need to Avoid Overly Expansive Interpretations of Improper Proselytism

One of the passages from the European Court of Human Rights' *Kokkinakis* decision that I particularly enjoy reading with students is a paragraph from the opinion of Judge Valticos, the dissenting Greek judge in the case. It reads as follows:

> Let us look now at the facts of the case. On the one hand, we have a militant Jehovah's Witness, a hard-bitten adept of proselytism, a specialist in conversion, a martyr of the criminal courts whose earlier convictions have served only to harden him in his militancy, and, on the other hand, the ideal victim, a naive woman, the wife of a cantor in the Orthodox Church (if he manages to convert her, what a triumph!). He swoops on her, trumpets that he has good news for her (the play on words is obvious, but no doubt not to her), manages to get himself let in and, as an experienced commercial traveler and cunning purveyor of a faith he wants to spread, expounds to her his intellectual wares cunningly wrapped up in a mantle of universal peace and radiant happiness. Who, indeed, would not like peace and happiness? But is this the mere exposition of Mr. Kokkinakis's beliefs or is it not rather an attempt to beguile the simple soul of the cantor's wife? Does the Convention afford its protection to such undertakings? Certainly not.

Fortunately, the European Court recognized that the last sentence was wrong. Normal efforts to engage in religious persuasion—even fairly activist efforts such as those of Mr. Kokkinakis—are clearly protected by the European Convention, as well they should be.

What is interesting about this paragraph is that it exemplifies the need to be very cautious about overly expansive interpretations of the various subcategories of improper coercion. In Judge Valtico's view, simply going door to door (even if characterized as "swooping" and "getting himself let in") is misconstrued as illegitimate physical force. If there were ongoing harassment, intentional ignoring of requests not to approach a door, illegal trespassing, or the like, the matter might be different. But Kokkinakis's "militancy" is hardly a coerced conversion by the sword. The undue influence and naïveté argument also goes too far. I suspect Mrs. Kyriakis, the Greek woman whom Kokkinakis visited, was not exactly pleased with her husband's argument that she was a dimwit, and I suspect she was right to be outraged. One does not have to be a graduate theologian to be eligible to participate in religious discourse, and believers need not restrict their efforts to share their beliefs to persons with that level of training. Similarly, the fact that Kokkinakis claimed to have good news is obviously not fraud. Believers in minority religions face incredible burdens in overcoming stereotypes that undercut their credibility. It is natural that they maneuver to avoid such stereotypes long enough that genuine interpersonal dialogue can begin. The "wares cunningly wrapped" reminds one of worries about material inducements. There is an entire field to be wrestled with here: it is all well and good to proscribe conditioning access to material goods on conversion. But once conversion has occurred, particularly where every effort is made to confirm that the conversion is sincere, must a religious group discriminate against its own members in distribution of charitable and educational resources?

What all of this points to is the extraordinary need to be extremely cautious in expanding the *Kokkinakis* categories that are designed to identify improper proselyting. There are indeed situations in which efforts at religious persuasion veer into zones of impermissibly coercive behavior, but states should beware of drawing those boundaries in vague or broad ways because of the inevitable narrowing of first freedoms that otherwise results. The presumption in societies genuinely committed to human rights is that some tolerance for excessive and questionable zeal is a small price to pay to make certain that core rights of human dignity, expression, and freedom of religion are not compromised.

Conclusion

Let me conclude by going back to the Sherem-Korihor analogy I invoked at the beginning of this chapter. We will continue to face Sherems and Korihors in the days ahead. They will threaten not only core beliefs of the gospel and people's receptiveness to those core beliefs but also the canons of religious freedom as well. We are already seeing ways that the right to engage in religious persuasion is losing ground. It is thus vital that we do all that is possible to shore up understanding of this critical right. We need to learn to be as effective in teaching the truth of the eleventh article of faith as we are in teaching all the others. The eleventh article of faith is not just a bit of special pleading, thrown in to encourage others to leave us in peace so we can teach and practice all the other articles of faith: "We claim the privilege of worshiping Almighty God according to the dictates of our own conscience, and allow all men the same privilege, let them worship how, where, or what they may." This article of faith is a core gospel teaching. We need to be able to join with other forces for good in protecting it, in reminding others of its importance, in broadening the consensus that supports it, and in helping to implement it. We need to remind people that religious persuasion warrants, if anything, more, and certainly not less, than other forms of freedom of expression. We need to draw attention to the invisible infractions, as well as the more obvious ones. And in all of this, we need to be sure to do unto others as we would have them do unto us.

W. Cole Durham Jr. is a professor of law at Brigham Young University and is the director of Brigham Young University's International Center for Law and Religion Studies. This essay was presented at "The Challenge of Sharing Religious Beliefs in a Global Setting," the International Society's tenth annual conference, August 1999, Brigham Young University, Provo, Utah.

Chapter 8

Challenges to Establishing the Church in the Middle East

James A. Toronto

İт HAS BEEN my good fortune to have spent ten years living in the Middle East with my family in a variety of settings: Saudi Arabia, Egypt, and, more recently, Jordan, where I served as the director of The Church of Jesus Christ of Latter-day Saints' Center for Cultural and Educational Affairs. This chapter is based primarily on research and personal observations from the time I have spent living in the Islamic world.

When people ask me about the Middle East, it is usually with the idea in mind that the Church is making no headway at all there. The question is usually posed somewhat like this, what are we ever going to do about the Middle East? The good news, I reply, is that the Church is already doing quite a lot in the Middle East. We have established a presence there and built many positive relationships in government and academic circles. The not-so-good news, of course, is that we still have a long way to go, and that seems to be a theme for all the areas we have discussed in this book. Part of my response to that question is always to ask, which part of the Middle East or Islamic world are you referring to?

The Middle East, even though we tend to think of it as a monolithic, homogeneous bloc of nations, is in fact quite diverse in composition. It is therefore crucial to consider each area or each country individually in order to assess the prospects for the Church. That is what I have tried to do in my role during the past three years as adviser for Middle Eastern affairs to the Europe East Area President, Elder Charles Didier (and before him, Elder Dennis B. Neuenschwander). The theme I have emphasized over and over is that we must look at each country separately and avoid sweeping generalizations that prevent our having a clear picture of the legal, political, and religious realities in the region. In this chapter I will discuss the context, current activities, and prospects of the Church in the Middle East.

Historical, Political, and Religious Context

I would like to summarize some characteristics of the Middle East that have impacted the Church's ability to operate openly and to share its message. All the countries of the Middle East, with the exception of Israel, are Muslim. All are also Arab nations except for Turkey, Israel, Iran, Pakistan, and Afghanistan. The Muslim countries all share some aspects of religious law and practice but are extremely diverse in ethnic, linguistic, political, and legal orientation. The countries of the Middle East are developing countries economically and politically. Most of them are less than sixty years old with newly emerging legal and political systems. They have not had much time to develop their national institutions. Various systems of governance are represented. There are oligarchic monarchies: fiefdoms of ruling elites in countries of the Arabian Peninsula and Gulf area. There are also constitutional monarchies in Jordan and Morocco. Another category are the Middle-Eastern-style democracies that have the rough form and rhetoric of a democracy but not the substance of Western democracies with full human rights, freedom of speech and press, and political enfranchisement for all citizens. I include under this rubric Egypt, Turkey, Lebanon, Israel, Syria, Iraq, Tunisia, and Algeria.

All these countries are going through a transitional period in which they are trying to reconcile modern notions of religious pluralism and human rights with traditional legal and social systems. This creates a kind of hybrid system of law. Most of them have adopted a Western legal code dating from the colonial period to deal with constitutional and civil matters. At the same time, there exists a system of traditional tribal law and Islamic religious law, called *shari'a*, which governs criminal, personal, and family matters. These hybrid systems of legal thought and practice create tensions and ambiguities that make it difficult to define the relationship between church and state.

All countries in the Middle East, because of the tenuous nature of their fledgling political and economic systems, have an obsession with maintaining security and stability. Though most constitutions guarantee religious liberty and tolerance for religious minorities, including some sort of statement to that effect, issues of security and stability always supersede those of religious freedom.

Political turmoil and economic deprivation are other characteristics of these countries. Life is chaotic and unpredictable. Institutions are inefficient and unreliable, and therefore personal influence with authority figures (the term in Arabic for this is *wasta*) is a way of life. This is the informal but well-established norm for getting things done when institutional processes are unreliable. Protocols and procedures for obtaining basic human rights, if they exist at all, are often circumvented. Instead, nepotism, influence buying, and cronyism—all related to the norms of a kinship society that new political ideals have not yet supplanted—are widely practiced.

Another aspect of life in the Middle East is a spirit of rivalry and jealousy between the three monotheistic or Abrahamic religions. I am referring here to Islam, Judaism, and Christianity. These hostilities between the three great religions are widespread and deeply rooted historically. Moreover, there are internal tensions in each of these religious communities: competing ideologies, interpretations, and factions. For example, the differences between Shi'ite and Sunni over who should lead the Islamic community have led to conflict and bloodshed during the pilgrimage in Mecca. In Judaism, the struggle between the orthodox Jews and the secular Jews has also turned violent at times. Israeli prime minister Yitzhak Rabin was assassinated as a result of that conflict. There have been divisions and strife in the Christian community in Jerusalem over who controls the holy sites. At Easter time in 1999, fighting broke out between rival Christian sects at the Church of the Holy Sepulchre over who controls access to the sanctuary. Another dimension of this inter- and intrareligious conflict is the question of proselyting. Though not explicitly prohibited in most of the legal codes, proselyting by non-Muslims is nevertheless proscribed because of concerns about preserving political and social stability. Religious minorities are allowed to practice their religion and hold worship services as long as these activities are low key and do not involve proselyting among Muslims, the majority religious community.

The Church's status and prospects are influenced by the interplay of all these factors. Like other Christian groups in general, our presence and activities are limited because of social and sometimes legal restrictions against proselyting. The old, well-established, legally recognized churches have their roots in nineteenth-century missionary work, carried out under the relative tolerance of the Ottoman Empire. New religious groups, who came in after the post–World War II revolutions, have encountered great difficulty in achieving legal status. In other words, if a church was already present in a country when it was established and the new constitution was drawn up, then it was recognized by the government. On the other hand, if a church (such as The Church of Jesus Christ of Latter-day Saints) came in after the late 1940s or early '50s, then it generally encountered many obstacles to legal recognition.

The Church had missionaries and congregations in the nineteenth century, as did other Christian groups, in Turkey, Egypt, Syria, Lebanon, and Palestine (which today is Israel, the West Bank, and Gaza). Because of our doctrine of gathering, everyone migrated to

Utah and the congregations withered away, so we missed the wave. I will use that phrase coined by surfers because the metaphor captures the notion of historical waves of opportunity that come along from time to time in the Middle East. We missed the wave in the early post–World War II era that allowed Catholics, Greek Orthodox, Protestants, and Seventh-day Adventists to be recognized in Middle Eastern countries. I believe deeply in the doctrine of gathering, and I think it was divinely inspired and thus the right thing to do at the time. I am merely pointing out that there was a cost in terms of our presence in the Middle East today. If some of those congregations had managed to survive, we would likely be recognized along with the Catholics, the Seventh-day Adventists, and various Protestant groups.

Most of the opposition we have received in our efforts to achieve full legal standing has come from these old established Christian communities, not from the Muslims. In the Middle East, marriages, inheritance issues, and funeral rites are handled exclusively by religious communities, not the government or private sector. To have legal sanction to carry out these functions in society is vital for political and economic reasons, and the established churches are therefore loathe to relinquish any part of their traditional power base to newer churches. When new churches, like ours, cannot achieve full legal status, church members are forced to turn to non-LDS religious officials to handle their marriage, inheritance, and funeral issues. Non-recognition also makes it difficult, in some cases impossible, to hold religious services, purchase or lease real estate, and open bank accounts.

The Church's approach has been to do careful research in each country, identify the unique obstacles that each national system presents, and then work with representatives of government, academe, and business to systematically address these issues. This has required some flexibility and reordering of priorities for Church leadership. An example of this was something Elder Neuenschwander told me during a meeting in Frankfurt: "Our goal in the Middle East is not growth through traditional proselyting and conversion, but establishing a viable presence, building bridges of trust and friendship, and promoting goodwill." In other words, the Church is willing in some circumstances to use its resources to support humanitarian and academic activities rather than proselyting efforts. I think that is quite an extraordinary approach given the Church's historical and doctrinal emphasis on missionary work. Church leaders are saying that in areas where there are severe restrictions and obstacles we will go slow and seek to establish a presence without evangelization.

It was in response to the reality of these political, social, and legal constraints that the Church adopted a policy of not proselyting among Muslims. This policy, formulated during the early 1990s, prohibits teaching or baptizing Muslims who live in the United States or Europe but are planning to return to the Middle East. The premise for this policy is that Muslims who join the Church and go back to a Middle Eastern society find it almost impossible to honor their covenants and practice their religion.

Current Status of the Church in the Middle East

I would like to say a few things about the current situation in the Middle East and where we stand now. The following examples will illustrate how some of the general trends that I discussed above directly affect the Church's activities. In Middle Eastern countries, there is no legally defined procedure for church recognition, and this fact creates many ambiguities for us. The more religiously progressive governments like Jordan, Turkey, Lebanon, Syria, and Egypt advocate religious tolerance and pluralism, but they refuse to provide the legal and structural means to achieve that pluralism for fear of inciting militant religious groups or offending powerful religious elites, thereby destabilizing the country.

The challenge facing the Church in these circumstances is how to proceed toward establishing a legal presence when the process for accomplishing this is either poorly defined or nonexistent. There has been much discussion of President Gordon B. Hinckley's statement that the Church always goes through the front door when seeking to establish itself in a country. The question I often found myself asking in Middle Eastern countries is, where is the front door? What I found was that often there was no front door through which new churches could achieve legal status, or if there was one, I found that nobody ever used it because it led nowhere.

For instance, in Jordan the Church has permission from the government, based on a formal agreement signed in 1989, to sponsor cultural and educational activities. But we do not have permission to hold formal religious services. We were advised by our Jordanian attorneys that we probably should avoid holding any religious meetings until we could obtain a royal decree recognizing the Church. An appeal directly to His Majesty the King was the only viable approach, they said. Other Jordanian advisers assured us there were alternative doors through which legal recognition could be obtained, and they all had a friend or relative who would be glad to help us. In the meantime, the Church has grown slowly but steadily. We have three branches of the Church in Jordan, about one hundred members, many of whom are Arab Christians who joined the Church in Jordan after hearing about us by word of mouth from friends and relatives. We have four missionary couples who work with members but do not engage in proselyting. Legally, however, our position is tenuous. While we do not have formal permission to hold religious services, the royal family has created an atmosphere of religious tolerance and has on many occasions expressed support for non-Muslim religious groups holding meetings as long as they do not cause problems. So in Jordan the Church operates in kind of a gray area—a legal twilight zone in which we are not quite sure what our real status is or what the approach is to achieving full legal status.

I had the opportunity to accompany Elder Jeffrey R. Holland and Elder Charles Didier when they met with Crown Prince Hassan in the Royal Palace in Amman. They presented a petition to him from the First Presidency requesting formal recognition for the Church. This meeting was the culmination of much hard work and years of effort, and this was the big day. After Elder Holland explained the purpose of our visit, the crown prince replied with a puzzled look on his face, "But what is the problem? You are pushing on an open door. Everyone enjoys religious freedom here. What is it that you want that you don't already have?" Elder Holland turned to me and said, "Jim, please explain for us why, at the nuts-and-bolts level, the Church needs to have recognition." It was fascinating and a bit troubling to see that in Crown Prince Hassan's mind, religious freedom for minorities was not even an issue. I think this attitude is characteristic of many liberal Western-educated political elites not only in Jordan but in most countries in the Islamic Middle East. There is a naive sense that rhetorically supporting religious rights for all religious groups actually establishes those rights.

In Egypt political instability has been the primary force impeding our efforts for Church recognition. In 1981 the Church's petition for recognition was awaiting President Anwar Sadat's final approval when he was assassinated. For almost twenty years now, the matter has been in a state of limbo; no one has been able to figure out what to do next. When I went to Egypt to help out with this process, we were asked by the government to affiliate legally with one of the four recognized Christian groups, one of the old established churches. That led to a rather unusual situation in which I was going to the Catholic, Protestant, and Seventh-day Adventist communities in Cairo and saying, "We would like you to affirm our right to worship and allow us to affiliate with you legally." Most of the church leaders with whom I spoke were quite understanding, and the Seventh-day Adventists, in particular, were anxious to help us because of their strong advocacy of religious liberty in the international arena. In the end, Latter-day Saint leaders decided that pursuing legal recognition through diplomatic channels would be more beneficial in the long run than an awkward affiliation with another church.

Turkey is officially a secular country that fiercely promotes a Western-style separation of church and state. It is not illegal for non-Muslim groups to proselyte: the constitution states that as long as the public order is not disturbed, people can share their religious views with others. The question, though, is what does it mean not to disturb the public order? The situation in neighboring Greece is instructive in this regard. There, freedom of religion is also guaranteed, but when our missionaries go out door to door, people occasionally get upset and call the police, who put the missionaries in jail. Then the Church attorney comes and arranges their release because they are on solid ground legally and have violated no laws. I think the same dynamic is at play in Turkey. In other words, legally it is permissible to proselyte, but socially and culturally, at the street level, the presence of missionaries in a society dominated by one powerful religious tradition (Greek Orthodox in Greece; Islam in Turkey) stirs up trouble, at least for the first decade or so after a mission opens. It thus becomes an issue of trying to decide if we are willing to send young missionaries to face in Turkey what they have experienced in Greece, continual harassment and occasional imprisonment.

Israel is a fascinating example. It is illegal only to induce someone to convert to another religion by offering them money. The Church signed a strict nonproselyting agreement with the Israeli government to defuse tensions between secular Jews who supported building the BYU Jerusalem Center and religious Jews who insisted that the Jerusalem Center would promote a spiritual holocaust in Israel. We were swept up in a larger debate among Israelis over the place of religion in a state struggling to reconcile the tensions inherent in a political system that proclaims itself both secular-democratic and religious-Jewish in nature.

In Dubai (United Arab Emirates) the Church has gained recognition by fiat due mostly to the efforts of a great Latter-day Saint, Joseph Platt. His efforts are reminiscent of Ammon's work among the Lamanites characterized by a desire to live among, understand, and serve the people (see Alma 17–20). Brother Platt and his family lived in the Gulf and worked for many years with the royal family, who came to regard him as a trusted friend. When he raised the problem that the Latter-day Saint branch faced in holding meetings, the shaikh wrote a note on official letterhead granting permission to hold services and to have our own building.

Issues and Prospects

One critical issue at this point in the Church's development in the Middle East is the problem of missionary emigration. My intent here is not to criticize but to be realistic about a part of the world that is difficult for the Church and to help us gain deeper understanding of the challenges we must confront. The Church unintentionally encourages immigration into European and North American countries because of the current policy of calling missionaries from developing countries to serve in industrialized nations. We do not intend to attract "rice Christians,"[1] but sometimes this policy, in places like Jordan, Albania, Ukraine, and other developing countries, has that very effect. For example, during the past four years six missionaries have been called from Jordan to serve in the United States and England. Of these six, only one has returned to live permanently in Jordan. The others have stayed in or gone back to their mission countries to work illegally.

As a result, there are young men lining up in Jordan because they have seen previous missionaries leave and find jobs in the United States or England, thus fulfilling the dream of many Jordanians. Sometimes bishops in the U.S. have helped these young men and women find work, which is a violation of their tourist or missionary visas. To the bishops' credit, they usually are unaware of these legal problems with visas. Those of us who work with the members in the Middle East have suggested that perhaps missionaries could be called to places like Nigeria or the Philippines or other developing

---

1.   The traditional metaphor referring to those who convert from one religion to another primarily for economic reasons.

areas where economic conditions are similar to, or worse than, those in Jordan. Then when these elders and sisters arrive home after their missions, instead of being discontent and wistfully longing for the greener pastures they experienced in the mission field, they will have an attitude of, "I think I'll stay here. My country looks mighty good to me." They would come to view their home countries as comparatively pleasant and appealing and thus be more willing to stay in their native land and anchor the Church rather than migrate to the West. I also think that working as missionaries in smaller branches rather than in well-developed, smoothly functioning wards and stakes will prepare them more effectively to deal with the kinds of issues and problems they will encounter as leaders in their own branches after returning home.

My point is that this has become a pressing issue in strengthening our tenuous relationships in the Middle East. The Church is gaining a reputation among people in Jordan as a vehicle for emigration. As the Jordanian government and U.S. embassy take note of this, our efforts to establish a respected, legal, long-term presence in Jordan and surrounding Middle Eastern countries will be hampered.

I want to share one last comment about relations between religious communities in the Middle East and the implications for establishing a viable long-term presence. The influence of militant religious communities will wax and wane depending on changing political, economic, and social conditions. The current struggle in the Islamic world over church-state issues is similar to that which occurred in Europe from the seventeenth to the nineteenth century. Greater political participation, higher standards of living, and increased access to education will gradually erode government concerns about religious unrest and allow for greater religious pluralism and freedom of worship. That is why we must be present, in place, with a reservoir of goodwill, prepared as President Spencer W. Kimball said, having a thorough understanding of the peoples, cultures, and languages of the region. We need to be in place when conditions improve, and I am optimistic they will improve gradually over time throughout the Middle East. Opportunities to consolidate our presence will emerge, but we have to be ready to catch the wave whenever and wherever it comes by.

James A. Toronto is an associate professor of Arabic and Islamic Studies at Brigham Young University. This essay was presented at "The Challenge of Sharing Religious Beliefs in a Global Setting," the International Society's tenth annual conference, August 1999, Brigham Young University, Provo, Utah.

Part III

Humanitarian Outreach and the Latter-day Saints

Chapter 9

Humanitarian Aid:
The Challenge of Self-Reliance

Elder James O. Mason

THE STORY OF Peter and John's experience at the temple gate with the lame beggar serves as an introduction to my message:

> And a certain man lame from his mother's womb was carried, whom they laid daily at the gate of the temple which is called Beautiful, to ask alms of them that entered into the temple;
>
> Who seeing Peter and John about to go into the temple asked an alms.
>
> And Peter, fastening his eyes upon him with John, said, Look on us.
>
> And he gave heed unto them, expecting to receive something of them.
>
> Then Peter said, Silver and gold have I none; but such as I have give I thee: In the name of Jesus Christ of Nazareth rise up and walk. (Acts 3:2–6)

The man wanted a coin. A coin was not what he most needed. He needed to walk, to work, to earn his own coins. The gospel provides unfathomable riches and even eternal life to those who accept and live the Master's teachings. The gospel also provides a way out of spiritual and temporal poverty. Peter reached down, took the crippled man by the right hand, "and lifted him up: and immediately his feet and ankle bones received strength" (Acts 3:7).

Our responsibility is first to lift ourselves and then our brothers and sisters, those in and out of The Church of Jesus Christ of Latter-day Saints. To the extent we can, we must all stand on our own feet. In a revelation to the Church in 1831, the Lord explained: "Let every man esteem his brother as himself. . . . For what man among you having twelve sons, and is no respecter of them, and they serve him obediently, and he saith unto the one: Be thou clothed in robes and sit thou here; and to the other: Be thou clothed in rags and sit thou there—and looketh upon his sons and saith I am just?" (D&C 38:24, 26).

The goal is a sufficiency for all. However, the clause "and they serve him obediently" should be in bold type! It is a condition established by the Lord.

In 1832 the Lord presented the concept of independence to His newly established kingdom: "That through my providence, notwithstanding the tribulation which shall descend upon you, that the church may stand independent above all other creatures beneath the celestial world" (D&C 78:14).

Two years later, the Prophet Joseph Smith received a revelation on exactly how the Saints were to assist the poor and needy to become independent and self-reliant. Section 104 of the Doctrine and Covenants reflects the mind and will of the Lord. We could spend the next hour on these four verses of scripture:

> And it is my purpose to provide for my saints, for all things are mine.
>
> But it must needs be done in mine own way; and behold this is the way that I, the Lord, have decreed to provide for my saints, that the poor shall be exalted, in that the rich are made low.
>
> For the earth is full, and there is enough and to spare; yea, I prepared all things, and have given unto the children of men to be agents unto themselves.
>
> Therefore, if any man shall take of the abundance which I have made, and impart not his portion, according to the law of my gospel, unto the poor and the needy, he shall, with

the wicked, lift up his eyes in hell, being in torment. (D&C 104:15–18)

The Lord expects the rich to help exalt the poor. However, the Lord has much more in mind than just filling empty tummies and clothing people. Much more is to be done, and the rich are to be made low in the process. Who are the rich? They are individuals with money, with experience, with sound ideas, or with a combination of the above. The rich are humbled and experience true joy when they get involved in helping others. Someone said, "The main difference in men and boys is the tone of their voice and the price of their toys." Perhaps the rich are made low by giving up their time and some of their toys.

In providing humanitarian aid, we must be aware that no good turn goes unpunished. We must also be aware of the unbending, exacting law of unintended consequences wherein while attempting to help we may do harm. As a boy, I tried to help a hatching baby chicken out of the egg. I learned, to my sorrow, it must work its own way out. My well-intentioned help only left the chick weak. It soon died. The chicks left to struggle were slower in hatching, but they finally emerged from the shell strong and vigorous. Although this example has no direct application to people, the principle is applicable. President Brigham Young noted: "My experience has taught me, and it has become a principle with me, that it is never any benefit to give, out and out, to man or woman, money, food, clothing or anything else, if they are able-bodied, and can work and earn what they need, when there is anything on the earth, for them to do. This is my principle, and I try to act upon it. To pursue a contrary course would ruin any community in the world and make them idlers."[1]

During the Great Depression, the Lord spoke again to one of His prophets on the matter of the poor. In the 1936 October general conference, President Heber J. Grant said: "Our primary purpose

---

1.   Brigham Young, *Discourses of Brigham Young*, sel. and arr. John A. Widtsoe (Salt Lake City: Deseret Book, 1943), 274–75.

was to set up, in so far as it might be possible, a system under which the curse of idleness would be done away with, the evils of a dole abolished, and independence, industry, thrift and self-respect be once more established amongst our people. The aim of the Church is to help the people to help themselves. Work is to be re-enthroned as the ruling principle of the lives of our Church membership."[2]

Those principles guide us today. They apply to all Heavenly Father's children both in and out of the Church. They highlight the great truth that sacrifice and obedience, rather than convenience and comfort, bring forth the blessings of both earth and heaven.

The intent of Church Welfare Services is to bless both giver and receiver. Each member of the Church has a welfare service responsibility. All members are expected to do all they can to be self-reliant and independent and to help in caring for others who have needs (see D&C 78:13–14). President Spencer W. Kimball stated: "The responsibility for each person's social, emotional, spiritual, physical, or economic well-being rests first upon himself, second upon his family, and third upon the Church if he is a faithful member thereof. No true Latter-day Saint, while physically or emotionally able will voluntarily shift the burden of his own or his family's well-being to someone else. So long as he can, under the inspiration of the Lord and with his own labors, he will supply himself and his family with the spiritual and temporal necessities of life."[3]

The emphasis on strengthening the family was there from the beginning. Poverty and weak or disrupted families go hand in hand in all cultures. President David O. McKay, in sharing a missionary experience, observed that acceptance of truth is difficult when people were burdened by severe poverty:

> In 1897 when I was on my first mission, I found myself, one morning, distributing tracts in a little undesirable district in Sterling, Scotland. I approached one door and in answer to the knock a haggard woman stood before me, poorly dressed, with

---

2. Heber J. Grant, in Conference Report, October 1936, 3.
3. Spencer W. Kimball, in Conference Report, October 1977, 124.

sunken cheeks and unkempt hair. As she received the tract I offered, she said, in a rather harsh voice, "Will this buy me any bread?" and as I started to tell her that it would buy her not only bread but something far more precious, a man equally haggard and underfed came up and said, "What is it?" She handed the tract to the man and said, "Gospel vendor! Shut the door!" From that moment I had a deeper realization that the Church of Christ should be and is interested in the temporal salvation of man. I walked away from the door feeling that that couple, with the bitterness in their hearts toward man and God, were in no position to receive the message of the gospel. They were in need of temporal help.[4]

When the term *humanitarian aid* is used, we generally have in mind those who are not of our faith. It seems to me that the same principles the Lord revealed to exalt the Saints must be applied if our efforts with members of other faiths are to bear the fruits of self-reliance.

The Church does not play in a minor league when it comes to rendering global assistance to the suffering, the poor, and the needy. I am certain that many others can give us an idea of the significant magnitude of Church Humanitarian Services that have been extended to the nations of the earth. With the scope of these activities being so great, it is that much more important that the outcome and results of our efforts be meaningful.

Analyses of humanitarian aid provided by some governments indicate that there is indeed a law of unintended consequences. Good intentions, proper motives, sincere generosity, and kindness do not guarantee that benevolent services will foster self-reliance or make a long-term, positive difference in people's lives. Fortunately, the U.S. government welfare program, administered at state and community levels, has been recently restructured. The dole was its foundation principle. Although well-meaning, it had predictable and serious unintended consequences. Recipients were not required to do anything

4. David O. McKay, in a Church Welfare Meeting, Salt Lake Tabernacle, General Conference, April 5, 1941.

for what they received. They soon looked upon their largesse as an entitlement, and the program's perverse rules led to dissolution of the two-parent family. Intergenerational dependency, moral decay, and single parenthood were the unfortunate harvests.

Bad welfare, if I can use that term, drives away *good* welfare. When government welfare was enacted, most of the poor stopped participating in religious-based charities that required able-bodied recipients to participate in character-building chores, such as splitting wood. Religious-based programs discouraged behaviors that encouraged idleness and irresponsibility, such as the use of alcohol. They could not compete, however, with the government's dole-based program and went out of business or were forced to adopt similar tactics. The idle poor began to be looked upon as *victims* rather than individuals or families who could be assisted to get back on their feet.

In Africa we found it advisable, in responding to conditions of chronic poverty, to separate humanitarian aid intended for those not of our faith from aid intended for the missions, stakes, and wards. Only in responding to natural disaster and war, where all segments of the population are involved, did they act as one. The establishment of Latter-day Saint Charities allows the Church to bring humanitarian aid and the ecclesiastic Church together at the top while maintaining an arm's length distance at operating levels.

The reason for this separation, except in responding to disasters, is to minimize the risk of inappropriate incentives for baptism. We do not want proselyting missionaries involved in rendering humanitarian assistance or mentioning in their missionary work that the Church might provide food, clothing, or other material things, even though it does. We desire spiritual and doctrinal conversion.

In the early days of the Church in Africa, when priesthood leaders were involved in used clothing distribution, contention sometimes resulted because members felt that leaders kept the best for their own family and friends. Neighbors of members often asked where the nice clothing had come from. When "from the Church" was the answer, people became interested in the Church for the wrong reasons. We do not want to create a church of "rice Christians."

Does humanitarian aid foster self-reliance? When people are suffering and need food, shelter, and medicine because of war, drought, earthquake, or flood, sustaining life is of primary importance. Perhaps sustaining life is the foundation of self-reliance.

In the past, the availability of humanitarian assistance from the industrialized nations has encouraged despotic national presidents and coup-leading opportunists to make unwise decisions and take irresponsible actions. They came to expect that humanitarian organizations would show up promptly and bail out the adverse consequences of their actions. Poorly supervised humanitarian aid has fostered an environment of graft and corruption.

Food, clothing, and medicine often fail to get to specified needy populations. Those in power see that resources go first to family, friends, and cronies. Goods are siphoned off to the marketplace. We have seen used clothing and sacks of beans with Latter-day Saint identification being sold in African markets. People in power use diverted humanitarian assistance to gain lucrative contracts. Maybe this is not so bad. President Brigham Young noted:

> Suppose that in this community there are ten beggars who beg from door to door for something to eat, and that nine of them are imposters who beg to escape work, and with an evil heart practise imposition upon the generous and sympathetic, and that only one of the ten who visit your doors is worthy of your bounty; which is best, to give food to the ten, to make sure of helping the truly needy one, or to repulse the ten because you do not know which is the worthy one? You will all say, Administer charitable gifts to the ten, rather than turn away the only truly worthy and truly needy person among them. If you do this, it will make no difference in your blessings, whether you

administer to worthy or unworthy persons, inasmuch as you give alms with a single eye to assist the truly needy.[5]

However, in many Third World countries, following President Young's compassionate council could lead to twenty beggars, not ten, at your door the next day, and forty the next. Aid must address the root causes of poverty. It must undermine greed and corruption and build character and integrity. It must strongly embrace and require the work ethic. Doing for people what they can and ought to do for themselves is a dangerous experiment that will not work. The well-being of any people depends upon their own initiative. Whatever is done under the guise of philanthropy or social morality that in any way lessens initiative is a major tragedy. To give people that which they do not earn is to make them think less of themselves and of you.

The only way to help people is to give them an opportunity to help themselves. The only solution to the grinding, chronic poverty in Africa and other places is the gospel of Jesus Christ. President Ezra Taft Benson testified during the October 1985 general conference that the gospel changes the heart of men and women:

> When you choose to follow Christ, you choose to be changed.
> . . . Can human hearts be changed? Why, of course! It happens every day in the great missionary work of the Church. It is one of the most widespread of Christ's modern miracles. If it hasn't happened to you—it should. . . . The Lord works from the inside out. The world works from the outside in. The world would take people out of the slums. Christ takes the slums out of people, and then they take themselves out of the slums. The world would mold men by changing their environment. Christ changes men, who then change their environment. The world would shape human behavior, but Christ can change human nature.[6]

---

5.   Brigham Young, in *Journal of Discourses* (London: Latter-day Saints' Book Depot, 1854–86), 8:12.

6.   Ezra Taft Benson, in Conference Report, October 1985, 4–5.

It is easy and quick to give things away, and it is difficult and labor intensive to create or identify projects that put people to work. The old saying "Give a man a fish and you feed him for a day. Teach a man to fish and you feed him [and his family] for a lifetime" is precisely true but difficult to accomplish.

Humanitarian aid best helps build self-reliance in conditions of chronic poverty by helping to overcome idleness. It does this by teaching people how to fish; grow, harvest, and market crops; manufacture products; and attend school. It might provide venture capital to carefully selected entrepreneurs who will be enabled to employ others. Projects that create jobs are labor intensive for the sponsoring organization and require the provision of staff or volunteers for supervision and monitoring, in addition to money and supplies. This leads to two important questions: Can we find skilled people to assist? Are we willing to invest in supporting and sustaining them in the field?

Church Humanitarian Services can be proud of the accomplishments of their employment resource centers that have been established in many developing countries. They are worth their weight in gold. Many have been assisted to find employment, even in countries with high unemployment rates.

If humanitarian aid makes people feel only more comfortable in their poverty, it will prolong the status quo and build dependency. The industrialized nations must be careful about indiscriminate shipment of used clothing to areas of poverty. It is useful in times of disaster and helpful when small quantities of appropriate used clothing can be targeted at specific needy populations, such as shelters and orphanages. We must realize that except in disasters, used clothing does not attack root causes and may make local industry less viable. Some countries restrict importation of used clothing because much of it moves, one way or the other, into the marketplace, and it undermines local industry and reduces employment. Used clothing distribution by the many groups contributing clothing in Africa contributes little to self-reliance because it is handed out with nothing expected in return.

Rarely do organizations that provide humanitarian aid develop well-thought-out plans or strategies with defined goals and expectations. They generally respond to the squeaky wheel, rather than assemble sufficient information about a population to use time and resources where they will do the most good. Sometimes efforts are targeted to a village where opportunity for meaningful, lasting accomplishment is meager. We must seek out people and local organizations that have the highest potential to succeed and become good employers. This kind does not initiate contact with those providing aid. Some squeaky wheels in developing countries are not worth greasing! Would you choose to target your humanitarian investment in the men and women who sit day after day near Temple Square with placards advertising that they are unemployed or homeless? There are better places to begin.

This reminds me of a story told by Elder Russell M. Nelson about the gentleman farmer. One day a friend visited this farmer and found him with a large pig under his arm. He was holding the pig as high as he could while the pig ate apples directly from the branches of the tree.

The friend inquired, "What in the world are you doing?"

"I'm feeding my pig," he replied.

"What a peculiar way to feed a pig," he said. "Isn't that a time-consuming task holding a pig while he eats that way?"

The farmer replied, "What is time to a pig?"

Humanitarian aid is a scarce commodity; resources as well as time must be used wisely! Plans for humanitarian aid need to include an objective assessment strategy. We know over time what we have sent or spent but little about how much self-reliance has been generated. We tend to believe success stories and discount criticism or complaints. We pat ourselves on the back but rarely admit failure, poor decisions, or the adverse consequences of our efforts.

It is like the entrepreneur I met in rural Tennessee. On the door of his office in big letters was the sign, "Veterinarian and Taxidermist." Underneath, in letters so small you had to get close to read, it said, "Either way you get your pet back."

I began my remarks with Peter and John, the Apostles. I will conclude with the Savior, Jesus Christ. He provided the pattern for helping others gain self-reliance:

(1) He went personally among the people. He was there; He breathed the same air; and He knew and appreciated the circumstances and problems of the people.

(2) He involved the people in making desirable changes and decisions by using provocative questions, illustrative stories, and parables to turn their minds in directions formerly closed by ignorance and tradition.

(3) He provided unique services and used inexpensive technology.

(4) He did not hesitate to ask those He helped to sacrifice and work hard. Development of character was basic to success.

(5) He performed miracles according to the people's faith.

(6) He was motivated by love, not self-aggrandizement, in everything He did, and love became the motivating power of His disciples.

© by Intellectual Reserve, Inc.

Elder James O. Mason is a former member of the Second Quorum of the Seventy. This essay was presented at "Development Assistance and Humanitarian Aid: The LDS Perspective," the International Society's eleventh annual conference, August 2000, Brigham Young University, Provo, Utah.

Chapter 10

Panel on Church Welfare Initiatives

Harold C. Brown, A. Terry Oakes, and E. Kent Hinckley

Church Welfare: His Sheep Are Serving the World

Harold C. Brown

THE LORD SAID He would place His sheep on His right hand and the goats on His left. He then explained that those on His right side are they who helped someone in need: "For I was an hungred, and ye gave me meat: I was thirsty, and ye gave me drink: I was a stranger, and ye took me in: naked, and ye clothed me: I was sick, and ye visited me: I was in prison, and ye came unto me" (Matthew 25:35–36). One of the main factors in that final judgment will be how willing we were to help others during this life. And so that is the ultimate goal and spiritual end we hope comes from welfare and giving.

A quote by President Marion G. Romney explains the importance and value of giving, "The Lord says that the efficacy of our prayers depends upon our liberality to the poor."[1] If you want an interesting study, read it carefully. "The Lord has said that the effi-

---

1. Marion G. Romney, in Conference Report, April 1979, 135.

cacy of our prayers depends upon our liberality to the poor." Let us each increase our fast offerings and assist in inspiring the Saints in the Church to do likewise. Give enough so that you can give yourself into the kingdom of God through consecrating your means and your time. I promise every one of you who will do it that you will increase your own prosperity, both spiritually and temporally.

The directors who run the Presiding Bishopric's temporal affairs throughout the world were recently in for training, and we had time with them. We were talking about teaching the law of the fast to people around the world. One of the directors raised his hand and said, "How do you teach people to fast when they go every day without food?" An interesting question. Another director wisely responded with, "Being hungry and starving isn't fasting." The requirement is the same, that we set aside that period of time—miss those two meals—in order to give to the poor and needy. I am confident that if one thing could be done internationally in terms of spiritually affecting people temporally, it would be to get them to pay their tithing and fast offerings and to get them to fast. I believe that if they did that, the Lord would bless them in many ways. In the Bible Dictionary it says, "The honest payment of tithing sanctifies both the individual and the land on which he lives."[2] So when people pay their tithes and offerings the blessing will come not only to individuals but also to their country. But how does this relate to welfare? "But it is not given that one man should possess that which is above another, wherefore the world lieth in sin" (D&C 49:20). There is an obligation to give to, and for us to take care of, the poor and needy. "A man filled with the love of God, is not content with blessing his family alone, but ranges through the whole world, anxious to bless the whole human race."[3]

---

2. Bible Dictionary, s.v. "Tithe."
3. Joseph Smith, *History of the Church of Jesus Christ of Latter-day Saints*, ed. B. H. Roberts, 2nd ed. rev. (Salt Lake City: Deseret Book, 1957), 4:227.

I never cease to be amazed by the Prophet Joseph Smith's statements and vision in so many areas.

What needs to be in place around the world before welfare can be successful? The answer is the administrative structure, and, in my view, this means Area Presidencies. Having three General Authorities there to give direction and stability to the Church is the single most important thing that has aided Church welfare in moving throughout the world. Our directors watch over the temporal affairs of the Church under the direction and guidance of these Area Presidencies. We also have regional welfare committees around the world. All of the stake presidents, stake Relief Society presidents, and the chairmen of the stake bishops council meet on a regular basis to coordinate and handle welfare matters. We also have area welfare agents who are an administrative body to assist stake presidents assigned to every welfare operation. Wherever there is an employment center in the Church, there is a stake president assigned to watch over it. This is true with every welfare operation we have.

Well-trained leaders are essential, and I think we have a long way to go, but great progress has been made. The very important thing, in my view, is to have simple operations adapted for international locations. We have four individuals coming into headquarters later this month who have been hired as full-time, paid area welfare managers. Under the direction of the director for temporal affairs, these people will handle the welfare work in the area. We have not had paid people before. When they were coming for training, I said, "Should we really even let them go to Welfare Square?" I was concerned that they would go there and see all those beautiful operations and then wonder when we are going to transfer them out, and we are not. I think they need to see the basic principles and the basic operations, but in a simplified format.

We have a number of handbooks and instructions to take care of the operations in the United States and Canada, and those are our guidelines internationally. I hope they do not grow beyond it. They are very simple. They are about helping members with employment needs. The staff will have a few materials, of course, but that is it. That is what the employment centers do worldwide—provide food to those in need. We have some small storehouses and canneries in Mexico and other parts of the world. One sheet, that is it—very simplified. They have only a few items on the stock list instead of the large stock list that we have here. Helping members with food storage means the same thing—simple operations to supplement the more important priesthood operations.

We have four main priorities in our department. First and foremost, we need to be concerned with priesthood welfare, which includes fasting and fast offerings and caring for the poor and needy. There is nothing like ordained officers of the Church who work under inspiration to help people fast and pay fast offerings. It is a formidable task, but it will happen.

The second priority is employment. Once a man gets a job, you hardly need any other welfare operation. If everyone was employed and able to care for themselves through the employment services, you would not need a storehouse, cannery, and quite often, social services—people tend to fight less if they have their needs met.

The third priority involves food and the use of land. Here, we have a few good ideas we are working on, and in some areas of the world we have pilot projects.

The fourth priority involves humanitarian service, because it is a blessing to people around the world and is an opportunity for the Church to be viewed in a positive light in areas of great need. God bless the wonderful Saints who give so generously. I cannot tell you how I feel about it personally, and I know others feel the same way as well. The contributions that come in on your donation slips for humanitarian aid blesses people around the world in ways it is difficult to imagine.

Economic Salvation for Our Brothers and Sisters

A. Terry Oakes

THIS IS AN exciting time in the Church for welfare. I wanted to start out with a quote that I was not familiar with before I started in welfare: "A man out of work is of special moment to the Church because, deprived of his inheritance, he is on trial as Job was on trial—for his integrity. . . . Continued economic dependence breaks him. . . . He is threatened with spiritual ruin. . . . The Church cannot hope to save a man on Sunday if during the week it is a complacent witness to the crucifixion of his soul."[4] President Gordon B. Hinckley said that about forty years ago. I know he still believes it today.

I thought I would give you a little bit of information on employment. In 1850 the Church had a Church Public Works Department. It was officially created to provide employment through the construction of public buildings and manufacturing facilities. Then in 1896 they established an employment bureau, which was operated by the Presiding Bishopric. In the 1920s the Relief Society president and the Presiding Bishopric maintained employment bureaus and stressed that each ward would have an employment representative to help. During the 1930s and '40s, a Deseret Employment Bureau still existed in Salt Lake City, but it was mostly for ward employment committees to help individuals who were out of work. The Salt Lake Regional Employment office was set up March 1, 1948. That was probably when we officially began to have paid staff in our employment centers. Domestically, in the United States and Canada, we currently have approximately one hundred employment resource centers, eleven of

---

4. *Helping Others to Help Themselves: The Story of the Mormon Church Welfare Program*, Historical Department Archives, The Church of Jesus Christ of Latter-day Saints (1945), 4.

which have paid employees, and we are in the midst of trying to get quite a few more.

You will notice that Eastern Europe is pretty blank. About a year ago, we had couples do employment work in Moscow and Kiev. It proved really difficult because of the economy and the way the members are fairly spread out. Our emphasis in Eastern Europe right now is microenterprise or microcredit. We are working with a few of the larger microcredit organizations to see what we can do with our members. We are also putting employment and humanitarian work really close together. Many of our humanitarian missionaries also do employment work.

The challenge to the individual internationally is that most have inadequate employment. Over a million members of the Church are either unemployed or underemployed. There are many countries where 70 to 75 percent of our Church leaders are unemployed and that same percentage of returned missionaries is unemployed. So we look at our current and future leadership and see that they are struggling. They lack education, but we have found what they really lack is *information* about resources and how to access them. We have visited over three thousand organizations now and have found schools, employers, and microcredit systems. There are a lot of resources out there, but our members have no idea they exist. They also have limited career goals. Most of them are planning where to get the next meal that day, rather than what they are going to be doing in ten years or how to get an education. They develop hopelessness and get into a cycle of poverty. Welfare is service, but if you are in this situation you struggle to serve.

Our guiding purpose as employment resource services is that we support Church leaders in helping individuals become self-reliant in their careers, so they can serve or show others how they have done it. We do this in three key ways: seek, plan, place.

First, we incorporate "seek." We tell our priesthood leaders that they need to seek out those in need. Our volunteers and paid staff seek out resources. Then we help the individual develop a career plan and place themselves in employment. I think the hardest thing we struggle with is defining the line between helping and creating dependency. That is hard to do. We assign mentors. We try to help as much as we can, but it is their responsibility to find their own employment.

The first of the three resources we deal with internationally, as far as volunteer and paid staff are concerned, is jobs—where they are and where the employers are. We are working closely with BYU in identifying major employers that will hire our members. One of the key things we use is Job Search Training, a class that runs anywhere from a day to two weeks, depending on the country. Job Search Training teaches simple career-planning techniques, such as how to meet a manager, present themselves, write a résumé or curriculum vitae, look in the yellow pages (if there are yellow pages), and identify what they want to do. This may last up to two weeks, but the first afternoon of the first day they are out looking for jobs. We try to create an urgency and have had great success as far as job placements through this class.

The second thing we become expert on in a country is who we develop relationships with—third-party institutions. They are not Church-run schools, but we try to find the best schools we can. Typically, once we tell them who we are and that we have students, they give us between 30 and 50 percent reductions in tuition. We also try to identify government agencies or private institutions that will give our students scholarships. In Mexico we have had good success with that. Internationally, we are focusing more on private schools than on public schools. It is hard for some of our members to get into public school; private schools are easier to get into. So we try to work out discounts for them to get into those.

The third thing in self-employment we deal with is identifying other employment resource institutions. There are many of them: Enterprise Mentors, Finca, and so forth. We conduct group meetings. For example, we just had one in Monterrey, Mexico, where 120 of our members came to learn about microcredit. After the meeting, we had a number of organizations present there, but if members wanted to meet with them they had to go to their place of business. That was only about three weeks ago, and since then we have had twelve people who are in business for themselves sign up to get a small loan so they can increase their businesses.

It is our responsibility to link individuals with resources and let them make the decisions about what they want to do. As far as future activities, we want to increase the support of Church leaders in employment activities and establish a World Wide Web site for training and resource dissemination. We are working on that right now. We think that it is going to be a real blessing in the future, as far as linking the individual with resources. We want to continue to develop our employment, educational, vocational, and self-employment opportunities and monitor key activities. We have goals regarding the people we want to place, how many we want to place, and what our cost is per placement.

We try to get an individual, as we call it, a *stabilizing* job—just so they can get food on the table. Then we try to work with them, finding out what kind of education they need in order to get that stabilizing job. For example, we worked with BYU and went to Wal-Mart in Mexico. Wal-Mart said, "Send us your members, and we'll hire them." The first week, they requested four hundred jobs. We sent them twelve qualified people because we had only twelve who had graduated from high school. The next week they asked for about three hundred, and we did a little bit better: we got twenty-six. We learned that we have a bit of a challenge here. Our members need to get through high school in order to get some of these better jobs.

In closing, I thought I would share a story from Lima, Peru, that I received from our manager down there. He was sitting in his office one evening after closing when a stake president knocked at the door and asked if he could visit with him. He said:

> He's a wonderful, humble man who has been out of work for eight months. He and his wife have been able to support their family during this time doing odd jobs. His wife also sells

beauty products. This has provided about 100 U.S. dollars a month. It is sufficient to make ends meet but not sufficient or stable enough to provide the peace of mind needed by one in such a responsible leadership position [of stake president].

During the interview, various alternatives were discussed. The Spirit was very strong. It was apparent that this good man was determined not to let himself be overcome by adversity. The desire to serve and succeed in taking care of his family was very strong. We had been meeting together for over an hour. In the course of the interview, his countenance began to change from near tears to hope. He confided that he had wanted to come to the employment resource center since it had opened in February (it was June), but he could not afford the cost of transportation. That night he had borrowed the money needed for bus fare, because he felt it was important for him to come. As we were almost ready to end the interview, after having sketched out a preliminary plan, the telephone rang. It was the general manager of the American-English Language Institute, who had called a few days earlier, asking us to send him several people to interview for sales positions and a manager of marketing position. He told us that all the people we had sent were hired and had turned out to be very effective. He then indicated a need for a manager of sales to help train and supervise. Without a moment of doubt, I told him that sitting across the desk from me was a man with just the characteristics he was seeking. I told him he was a leader in the Church. I then described the leadership experience and functions of a stake president in business terms. I told him that I felt this was just the man who could help him achieve his business goals. He responded, "Please send him to my office tomorrow morning for an interview at 9:00." The stake president went the next morning and was hired. He had to hire thirty other salesmen, who were returned missionaries.

For most people it would be inexplicable why the employer would have called at that hour of the evening knowing that the employment resource center was closed. But something happened to prompt him to do so. We know the Lord works in mysterious ways His wonders to perform. This incident is one more testimony to us here that He is directing this work and that He is personally concerned about each of His children.

I think that accurately represents what has happened. I could read letters for another hour about what is happening internationally and the blessings members get when they obtain gainful employment.

International Welfare

E. Kent Hinckley

THE GUIDING PURPOSE of the Production and Distribution division of Welfare Services is to efficiently provide and distribute quality food to the poor and needy members of the Church as requested by bishops; support family home storage; and provide work and service opportunities. As part of this charge, Production and Distribution also provides food for the Church's humanitarian efforts and maintains food reserves for the Church's emergency response. All these activities are intended to build character and self-reliance.

Infrastructure that Facilitates International Response

Physical facilities. It is because of the infrastructure which has been developed in Welfare Services since the mid-1930s that we are able to respond as we do to international needs. A significant element of this infrastructure is our ability to grow, raise, process, and distribute food with a measure of independence from the world. The Production and Distribution division is responsible for the operation of welfare farms that grow a variety of crops, ranging from wheat and alfalfa to dry beans, potatoes, and peas. Several orchards and vineyards raise a variety of fruits. A turkey ranch, cattle ranches, and dairies round out our production capabilities. Food is processed into cans and bottles in twenty wet-pack canneries. Other products prepared for use worldwide include several flour products, pasta, gelatin, honey, various meat and dairy products, powdered milk, and other powdered drinks, bread, and various soap products.

A trucking company, Deseret Transportation, provides the means to transport raw and finished products and the ability to respond quickly to emergency situations domestically and internationally.

Food reserves. A second element of the infrastructure are the food reserves maintained by the Church. Once a decision is made to respond to a situation where food is needed, the items to be donated are already in inventory at the bishops' storehouses. There are no delays caused by lead times to raise money, purchase the food, and then ship it to a central location to be further prepared for shipping to the affected area. Sufficient inventories of life-sustaining food are maintained so that there is a measure of independence from the world.

Volunteer organization. A third critical element of the infrastructure that allows us to respond internationally is the organization and tradition of volunteers who play a major role in every step of the growing, processing, and distribution of commodities. President J. Reuben Clark Jr. said, "The real long-term objective of the welfare plan is the building of character in the members of the Church, givers and receivers."[5] The scriptures also have numerous references to our obligation to assist the poor and needy.

The Production and Distribution division designs and utilizes facilities and processes in such a way that members, as volunteer workers, can productively assist in caring for the poor and needy. Church-service missionaries and large numbers of volunteers prepare food for distribution. The use of member volunteers and Church-service missionaries internationally to distribute food allows the Church to respond quickly and ensure that the food gets to the intended user

---

5. J. Reuben Clark Jr., special meeting of stake presidencies, October 2, 1936, as cited by Marion G. Romney, in Conference Report, October 1981, 130.

in good condition. Recently, members in England packaged wheat grown on a Church farm in England and shipped it to Ethiopia.

Priesthood organization. A fourth element of the infrastructure that allows us to respond effectively internationally is the organization and growing maturity of the priesthood leadership. The establishment of regional welfare committees and the establishment of agent stake presidents and operating committees provide the leadership and oversight necessary for the ongoing successful operation of bishops' storehouses and home storage centers. These local organizations are in the best position to teach welfare principles, coordinate volunteer labor, call Church service managers, review the services offered by the bishops' storehouses and family storage centers, and recommend needed improvements.

International Activities

Family gardens. Member families, in many parts of the Church, could become more self-reliant if they had access to land or water for growing food in family gardens. Excess Church property, or suitable property that can be leased, will be made available for needy members to produce food for themselves and others. In some cases, there is excess Church property or property already owned by members, but it is in need of water. In these cases, simple, effective irrigation systems will be installed using member resources and labor to make this land productive family gardens.

The model for these family gardens is the Kapaka project in Laie, Hawaii. The Kapaka project consists of 270 acres owned by the Church. The tillable ground has been divided into family garden plots that average about 40 feet by 110 feet. Four hundred eighty families are currently growing gardens on this project. An agent stake president and an operating committee are assigned to oversee the operation. Each family needing assistance is assigned a plot by its bishop according to the needs of the family. They grow basic foods indigenous to their culture such as taro, bananas, bread fruit, yams, beans, and corn.

Family gardens, following the Kapaka model, are being established in Tonga, Kenya, and the Democratic Republic of Congo.

Bishops' storehouses. Bishops' storehouses have been in operation in Mexico since 1997. Currently there are seven storehouses providing food in common use, such as corn flour, wheat flour, rice, dry beans, powdered milk, sugar, salt, and cooking oil. The commodities are purchased locally in bulk at wholesale prices and then repackaged by volunteers into smaller packages for distribution. As in the United States and Canada, all distribution from the bishops' storehouse is under the direction of local bishops and is based on the needs of each family. The average value of the bishops' orders indicates that needs are being met modestly. Bishops are taught to provide welfare assistance to members to help them develop spirituality, become self-reliant, and learn to provide for others.

Storehouses have been approved and are in the process of being established in Chile, Ecuador, and the Dominican Republic. Like the Mexico bishops' storehouses, they will distribute a limited stock list of life-sustaining foods as directed by local bishops. Each storehouse is assigned an agent stake president and an operating committee to provide oversight, coordinate volunteer labor, call Church-service managers, and review the services offered.

Home storage centers. Home storage centers will give members the opportunity to be more self-reliant through dry-pack storage of basic life-sustaining foods. Food such as wheat, flour, rice, and sugar is purchased in bulk to take advantage of lower prices and is then resold to members for packing in foil pouches. The items to be packaged in each country will be determined by what is generally eaten in that country as well as what will store for extended periods considering local climatic factors. The opportunity is very similar to the dry-pack canneries offered for the use of members in the United States.

The first home storage centers were opened in Mexico in 1996. There are now seven centers co-located with the Mexico storehouses.

There are six locations operating in England, and one in South Africa, Hong Kong, and Taiwan. Home storage centers have been approved and are in process of being set up in Chile, Ecuador, the Dominican Republic, Tonga, and American Samoa.

Home storage centers increase member self-reliance. The members are able to purchase basic commodities at a lower price than they otherwise would because the items are purchased in bulk at favorable prices by the home storage centers. Since these products are part of the daily diet of the member, they are able to reduce their food costs. Also, as members are financially in a position to do so, they have the opportunity to increase their self-reliance and personal sense of security by following the prophet's counsel to store food against a day of need.

Family food boxes. One of the best examples of how the capabilities and infrastructure of the Production and Distribution division has been brought together in a unique way is the preparation of family food boxes for international distribution. A family food box is a ten-by-fourteen-inch box, weighing about thirty pounds, which contains various basic foods that will sustain a family of four for about a week. The contents of the box are determined by matching the kinds of food normally eaten in the recipient country with the food that is in inventory in the bishops' storehouse. Because the Church has farms, canneries, processing plants, strategic reserves of food, and the organization and tradition of volunteerism, the Church has been able to respond quickly to the need for food boxes with a variety of food that matches the needs of very diverse countries. Depending on the destination, food boxes may contain rice, soup mix, powdered milk, beans, canned meat, cooking oil, flour, sugar, and other products.

When family food boxes have been approved for distribution, a local stake is called and asked to provide up to three hundred volunteers to pack the commodities in the boxes. The response from the stakes has been almost overwhelming. Usually, more people show up than we have asked for, and everyone has a great experience. They feel productive and grateful to be able to help those in need. Generally, two oceangoing containers can be filled with 1,350 family food boxes in about an hour and a half.

In the past, food boxes have been sent to Mexico, Kosovo, Venezuela, West Africa, Sierra Leone, Korea, and Mongolia. They have been very well received with high praise from governments and relief agencies because of the quality and variety of food they contain and the ease with which they can be distributed to and used by those in need.

All of this is possible because of Church welfare facilities and production capabilities, Church food reserves, member volunteers, and priesthood leadership.

Harold C. Brown is the Welfare Services managing director; A. Terry Oakes is the LDS Employment Resource Services director; and E. Kent Hinckley is the Bishops' Storehouse Production Distribution director. These essays were presented at "Development Assistance and Humanitarian Aid: The LDS Perspective," the International Society's eleventh annual conference, August 2000, Brigham Young University, Provo, Utah.

Chapter 11

Building Bridges of Understanding through Church Humanitarian Assistance

Garry R. Flake

MANY OF YOU have had such extensive experience in many countries throughout the world. We are here because of our interest to see the influence of the gospel expand to these people we love. The humanitarian effort of The Church of Jesus Christ of Latter-day Saints is part of the whole effort of expansion. It is a way of helping the needy of the world and, at the same time, increasing awareness of the Church. We are interested—through humanitarian services of the Church—in helping to build bridges of understanding wherever we can. I would like to respond to the most common questions we receive about Church humanitarian work.

Why is the Church involved in providing worldwide humanitarian assistance?

Foremost, the Church provides assistance simply for the good it does. Our Christian giving demonstrates that the gospel is a gospel of love. Spiritual and temporal well-being results for both the giver and the receiver. An important benefit for the Church, where feasible, is to help open doors of nations that have been closed to the Church and its message.

How extensive is Church humanitarian aid?

Church humanitarian aid has tripled in the last five years. This, of course, is due to the generosity of members and friends of the Church who sustain this effort with cash and in-kind donations. Assistance was provided in over one hundred countries last year in about fifteen hundred different projects. Literally millions have been blessed.

What is the focus of Church humanitarian aid?

The focus continues to be on providing life-sustaining goods as emergency response to an increasing number of disasters. Humanitarian Services is part of the inspired Welfare Services program of the Church. The focus of Welfare Services has always been to help people become more self-reliant and to provide effective temporary assistance as needed.

Humanitarian emergency response has the unique ability to draw quickly on the resources of the Bishops' Storehouse Services and Deseret Industries. With the immediate availability of organized labor, needed goods can be packaged for shipment in a matter of hours. These two organizations, coupled with a worldwide Church organization ready to receive goods and quickly distribute them, enhances Church response to any disaster. The Church is recognized worldwide as a premier emergency relief agency.

In 2002 the Church delivered in-kind assistance directly to needy flood victims in Chile, to those affected by mammoth forest fires in Arizona, to those severely affected by a devastating typhoon on the remote Chuuk Island in the Pacific, and to members and others on the brink of starvation due to drought in Southern Africa. It has actively participated with many local and national governments in Central Europe to provide aid in response to extensive flooding.

In addition to emergency response, what else does the Church do to assist the needy not of our faith?

Since the Church emphasizes helping people help themselves, there are humanitarian missionary couples currently serving in approximately thirty countries. Development projects are focused on the skills of missionary couples who share their expertise. This has included laboratory technologists improving the blood bank services in Mongolia and dentists who trained instructors in a dental school in Peru. The Church has established food-processing training programs at universities in Cambodia and Syria. There is English and vocational teacher training in many countries.

Hundreds of tons of used clothing and donated medical and educational supplies are distributed each year. Humanitarian missionary couples, among other assignments, ensure these donations reach the needy. Their field presence reduces theft and misuse.

What is the relationship of Church Humanitarian Services and Latter-day Saint Charities?

All Church humanitarian effort is given without regard to race or religion. Latter-day Saint Charities is the registered nongovernmental agency of the Church. It is a delivery agency. The primary focus is on the Church as the donor agency, whenever possible. However, there are countries where the Church is not officially recognized, but Latter-day Saint Charities has been registered. Latter-day Saint Charities also allows often improved access to other international agencies.

Does the Church work with partnership organizations?

Yes. Over the last decade, the Church has collaborated with over five hundred local and international organizations and agencies, drawing on their strengths to deliver goods and services. The Church has always had a good relationship with the Red Cross. It works closely with Catholic Relief Services and other faith-based organizations. There has been a unique partnership with the Wheel-chair Foundation, providing nearly ten thousand wheelchairs to those who cannot afford them in fourteen countries. These have been provided through the First Lady's charitable organization in most locations. There has been favorable public recognition, but the most important result is providing mobility to individuals who otherwise would be homebound.

Church humanitarian aid desires full participation with partnering agencies. It does not want to only be a funding source.

How are Church humanitarian efforts financed?

Church members have been generous in their support of Church humanitarian aid. Many friends of the Church participate as well. Contrary to the practice of so many other organizations, there is no pressure and no funding campaigns. Every donation is an individual, voluntary initiative. In addition, as President Gordon B. Hinckley explained in a general conference session, LDS Philanthropies also supports the Church humanitarian cause.

What is the overhead cost, and who pays it?

The Church, from its general budgeted funds, covers the minimal overhead costs that occur. This allows every donated humanitarian dollar to go to those being assisted. Since there is such an extensive volunteer effort, the overhead is very low—far below that of most other humanitarian organizations.

How else do members of the Church support humanitarian efforts?

Literally thousands of hygiene, school, and newborn kits are prepared and brought to the Church humanitarian center. Many are made by individuals and families. Since the Kosovo refugee crisis in the spring of 1999, over two hundred thousand quilts have been donated. Thousands of tons of clothing come through regular Deseret Industries donations.

Recently the leadership of the Gresham Oregon South Stake thought if the Lord could feed five thousand, stake members could make five thousand hygiene, school, and newborn kits. They applied for an eight-thousand-dollar grant from Church humanitarian funds to purchase materials, then multiplied the value many times over. One Relief Society sister sewed 117 infant blankets. Another sister in a retirement home with arthritic hands slowly crocheted 100 pairs of baby booties. Two Laurel girls who had never sewn before made 250 blankets. The stake president reported, "As with the loaves and fishes, the true miracle was manifested in the lives of our stake members that were changed forever. We want the approximately ten thousand children who receive these kits to know of our love for them, whoever and wherever they are."

Does the Church assist Muslims?

Yes. Church humanitarian aid is provided throughout the world to those in need, regardless of race or religion. The Church is balanced in its assistance, helping Muslim, Christian, and Jew alike.

The Church provided substantial support following the earthquakes in Turkey. Nearly one hundred thousand hygiene kits were prepared in Indonesia in partnership with an Islamic humanitarian organization for Timorese refugees. Church members and Muslims worked jointly in assembling these kits. With the focus on those in need, the result was more tolerance and understanding, touching the lives of both givers and receivers.

The Church has worked with several partnering organizations in Jordan and in Egypt. The expertise of humanitarian missionary couples has been well received in Pakistan, Syria, and other Islamic countries in Africa, Asia, and the Middle East. Humanitarian initiatives are just part of the whole as the Church continues to extend a hand of friendship to the Islamic world.

Church humanitarian aid continues to demonstrate a gospel of love and a caring attitude for those in need throughout the world. It is part of building bridges of understanding.

Garry R. Flake is the director of Humanitarian Emergency Response for The Church of Jesus Christ of Latter-day Saints. This essay was presented at "Muslims and Latter-day Saints: Building Bridges," the International Society's thirteenth annual conference, August 2002, Brigham Young University, Provo, Utah.

Part IV

Church Education Initiatives in an Era of Globalization

Chapter 12

The Globalization of the Church Educational System

Elder Joe J. Christensen

From the very beginning of this dispensation, the Prophet Joseph Smith and his successors have spoken in global terms in a remarkable and amazing way. For example, beginning with the first verse of the first section of the Doctrine and Covenants, we read: "Hearken ye people from afar; and ye that are upon the islands of the sea, listen together. For verily the voice of the Lord is unto *all* men, and there is *none* to escape; and there is *no* eye that shall not see, *neither* ear that shall not hear, *neither* heart that shall not be penetrated. . . . Wherefore the voice of the Lord is unto the ends of the earth, that *all* that will hear may hear" (D&C 1:1–2, 11; emphasis added).

In this dispensation, the Prophet Joseph Smith received a charge similar to that which the Savior gave to His Apostles following His Resurrection and just before ascending to heaven: "Go ye into *all* the world, preach the gospel to *every* creature, acting in the authority which I have given you, baptizing in the name of the Father, and of the Son, and of the Holy Ghost" (D&C 68:8; emphasis added; see also Matthew 28:19).

Wilford Woodruff, shortly after his conversion, received a glimpse of what the destiny of The Church of Jesus Christ of Latter-day Saints was to be when he attended a remarkable testimony meeting in which all of the priesthood brethren, then in Kirtland, met in a little log schoolhouse room that was fourteen square feet. He heard testimonies for the first time from Oliver Cowdery, Brigham Young, Heber C. Kimball, the Pratt brothers, Orson Hyde, and others. President Woodruff later recalled what the Prophet Joseph said after hearing those testimonies: "When they got through the Prophet said, 'Brethren I have been very much edified and instructed in your testimonies here tonight, but I want to say to you before the Lord, that you know no more concerning the destinies of this Church and kingdom than a babe upon its mother's lap. You don't comprehend it.' I was rather surprised. He said 'it is only a little handful of Priesthood you see here tonight, but this Church will fill North and South America it will fill the world.'"[1]

In 1842 the Prophet Joseph reiterated the intention for the work of the Restoration to become globalized when, at the request of Mr. John Wentworth, editor of the *Chicago Democrat*, he wrote a "sketch of the rise, progress, persecution, and faith of the Latter-day Saints."[2] Toward the end of his letter, he declared: "The Standard of Truth has been erected; no unhallowed hand can stop the work from progressing; persecutions may rage, mobs may combine, armies may assemble, calumny may defame, but the truth of God will go forth boldly, nobly, and independent, till it has penetrated *every* continent, visited *every* clime, swept *every* country, and sounded in *every* ear, till the purposes of God shall be accomplished, and the Great Jehovah shall say the work is done."[3]

Globalization Facilitated by Technology

Considering the circumstances in Kirtland, Ohio, the following prophecy, received in 1833, is truly remarkable: "And then cometh

1.   Wilford Woodruff, in Conference Report, April 1898, 57.
2.   Joseph Smith, *History of the Church of Jesus Christ of Latter-day Saints*, ed. B. H. Roberts, 2nd ed. rev. (Salt Lake City: Deseret Book, 1957), 4:535.
3.   Smith, *History of the Church*, 4:540; emphasis added.

the day when the arm of the Lord shall be revealed in power in convincing the nations, the heathen nations, the house of Joseph, of the gospel of their salvation. For it shall come to pass in that day, that every man shall hear the fulness of the gospel in his own tongue, and in his own language, through those who are ordained unto this power, by the administration of the Comforter, shed forth upon them for the revelation of Jesus Christ" (D&C 90:10–11).

One of the factors that makes this such an impressive prophecy is that when the revelation was received, the Prophet Joseph Smith could not travel or communicate from one place to another any faster than the pharaohs in Egypt thousands of years before. To that point in time, and for the preceding thousands of years, the fastest means of travel and communication at a distance was a good rider on a fast horse.

The possibility for the globalization of the Church was facilitated following the Restoration of the gospel, as the spirit of innovation and invention was indeed poured out on so many, and man's circumstances began to rapidly change. Like an avalanche, developments came such as photography, telegraph, transatlantic cable, telephone, radio, television, jet-propelled aircraft, advances in medicine, satellite communication, computers, the Internet, fiber optics, and on and on.

I am confident that so many of the technological developments came in direct fulfillment of Joel's prophecy, which some biblical scholars estimate was recorded approximately eight hundred years before the birth of the Savior, when he spoke for the Lord and predicted: "And it shall come to pass afterward, that I will pour out my spirit upon all flesh; and your sons and your daughters shall prophesy, your old men shall dream dreams, your young men shall see visions: And also upon the servants and upon the handmaids in those days will I pour out my spirit. And I will shew wonders in the heavens and in the earth" (Joel 2:28–30).

Remember when the angel Moroni appeared to the Prophet Joseph in 1823, he quoted Joel's prophecy and let him know "that this [prophecy] was not yet fulfilled, but was soon to be" (Joseph Smith—History 1:41). And thus the flood of technological developments occurred after so many centuries in which there was little or no change.

Along this line, I remember hearing President Spencer W. Kimball mention that in his opinion, the scientists who developed jet aircraft were inspired by the Spirit in order to enable the leaders of the Church to travel rapidly from one place to another around the world to supervise the Church and its progress. He added that "of course, we let other people ride them."

The seriousness with which the Brethren have taken that responsibility to carry the gospel to all the world is evidenced by so many of the early mission calls to elders to leave their families and go into the far reaches of the earth. Among my own family's ancestors, Robert Owens, a great-great-grandfather, marched with the Mormon Battalion, and, when released from his military obligation in San Diego, California, made his way to the Salt Lake Valley, where he was reunited with his wife and surviving children—his wife, Catherine, had buried three of their children at Winter Quarters. Within just a few years, he experienced one of those calls over the pulpit in the morning session of a general conference in 1852. He was called again to leave his family—to go on a mission to India and Australia, with the assurance that the announced missions were "generally, not to be very long ones; probably from three to seven years will be as long as any man will be absent from his family."[4] To respond to such calls required great faith because you can't get much farther away from home than that!

After much challenge and travail, the territory was colonized, and the roots of the Church sunk deep into the soil of America's western inland empire. Speaking of education, efforts were made from the beginning to establish schools to educate the children of the Church.

---

4.   Heber C. Kimball, *Deseret News*, September 18, 1852, 1.

Education Important from the Beginning

As Latter-day Saints we are recipients of a remarkable heritage because that same intense and diligent concern for education of the Church membership has existed from the very beginning, whether the Church was struggling against the elements, sickness, persecution, disappointments, or apostasy. Classrooms were set up in the frontier of Missouri; the poverty of Ohio; the swamps of Illinois; the cold of Winter Quarters; in covered wagons crossing the plains; in log cabins and dugouts; from the center of the Salt Lake Valley to the peripheral colonies throughout Utah; in significant portions of Arizona, Nevada, Idaho, and Wyoming; and even in Mexico and Canada.

In far-flung, less-developed areas of the Church, where basic education was not available, Church-sponsored schools were established and operated until public-sponsored educational opportunities became available. In a few locations, they still exist.

Yes, this is a church that believes in education, and though our tactics, communications media, and economic circumstances vary greatly from those of the young Church of so many years ago, our strategy and goals are precisely the same. Religion, true religion, lies at the heart of our efforts and quest.

It was in 1832 and 1833 that the Prophet Joseph Smith received revelations that are now contained in section 88 of the Doctrine and Covenants. In this section, you will note this same emphasis on education with religious roots. In my opinion, no treatment of the Latter-day Saint viewpoint of education would be complete without reference to this significant latter-day scriptural injunction, which applies to all members wherever they are in the world. Remember, we were counseled to "teach one another the doctrine of the kingdom" and also to teach "of things both in heaven and in the earth, and under the earth; things which have been, things which are, things which must shortly come to pass; things which are at home, things which are abroad; . . . wars [and] perplexities . . . [and] judgments; . . .

and a knowledge also of countries and of kingdoms. . . . Teach one another words of wisdom; yea, seek ye out of the best books. . . . Seek learning, even by study and also by faith" (D&C 88:77, 79, 118).

The Charge to Internationalize the Seminaries and Institutes of Religion

Geographically, in the 1950s and early 1960s, the bulk of the seminary and institute of religion programs and faculty were located in a rather compact area. Almost any faculty member, serving even in the outer limits, could be reached personally by a supervisor getting into his car and traveling no more than one full day. That situation was to change greatly in the months and years ahead, because the challenge had been much expanded.

After all those early developments that had been made to establish the Church essentially in the intermountain area, California, and, to some degree, throughout the United States, the time came particularly for the international expansion of the religious educational efforts of the Church. As it turned out, that was where I had the personal opportunity to make some contribution to the efforts. I will tell you a little about how that happened.

In 1970, after serving for eight years as director of the Institute of Religion adjacent to the University of Utah, my wife and I received a call to preside over the Mexico City Mission. We leased our home for the anticipated three years, bundled up our six children, and moved to Mexico City. We were deeply immersed in all that goes on in a mission. We had enrolled our children in school, and one afternoon we had been out purchasing school supplies. Upon return to the mission home, I was told that President Harold B. Lee had called and wanted me to return his call. It was our wedding anniversary, September 2. I did not know that the First Presidency made a practice of calling mission presidents to wish them well on their anniversary! I discovered that they do not.

President Lee's first words were, "Joe, are you sitting down?" I assured him I was. He then shared the purpose of his call with this message: "Today, in the Board of Education meeting, it was determined that we would like you to serve as associate commissioner of education to serve with Brother Neal A. Maxwell, the commissioner. Your assignment will be to administer the seminaries and institutes of religion and, in effect, to succeed Brother William E. Berrett, who is retiring. We would like you to return home as soon as we can find a replacement for you. You may call Brother Maxwell for more details."

I do not remember ever being more surprised—even shocked. We had settled into the mission. The children had adjusted, we were enjoying the challenge of the work, and things seemed to be going well. I had anticipated returning to the Church Education System (CES) for employment in some capacity after finishing the mission. I remember facetiously having said to some of my colleagues in CES that if Brother Berrett were to retire while we were gone, "I hope that a new 'pharoah' doesn't arise who 'knows not Joseph'" (see Exodus 1:8).

Within three weeks, President Eran Call and family had been called, and we were home by the end of September 1970 to begin serving in the new assignment. What an experience lay ahead!

The Board of Education, at that time, consisted of the entire First Presidency, all of the Quorum of the Twelve, the Presiding Bishop, and Sister Belle Spafford, who was serving as the Relief Society general president. Commissioner Maxwell and the rest of us as his associates were asked to study the direction of Church education in all of its facets and make recommendations to the Board of Education and the Board of Trustees for any developments or adjustments.

It seems significant to note that in the November 1970 meeting of the Board of Education, it was determined that the seminaries and institutes of religion, in one form or another, should follow the membership of the Church throughout the world—as soon as was practical. Through the efforts of assistant administrators Frank D. Day, Dan J. Workman, Frank M. Bradshaw, and, a little later, Bruce M. Lake, and other competent and dedicated staff, we tackled the assignment.

At that time, as many of you would know, the weekday religious educational program at the secondary and college levels was located only in English-speaking areas of the world, such as England, Australia, and New Zealand. The high school seminary program was primarily taught in the released-time format in Church-owned buildings adjacent to high schools throughout the Intermountain West and in some early morning settings—particularly in California. In a few less-populated areas, early experimentation had begun with a home-study seminary format that seemed to be well received by those who would not have any other form of weekday religious educational opportunity.

It was the home-study seminary format that was developed in the late 1960s that made the international movement feasible. The home-study program consisted of a class meeting once a week in a ward or branch, and the students were expected to study their course materials daily in their homes. Efforts were made through content and layout to make the course interesting and student friendly.

Once a month students would be brought together for a meeting on a district or stake basis. For a time this meeting came to be known as Super Saturday. This gathering was usually conducted by the individual CES employee assigned to the area. This system proved to be successful from a cognitive learning standpoint. Many of the students became remarkably proficient in learning and rapidly finding key scriptures, and their skills were tested in what then came to be known as "scripture chase" activities that generated a lot of enthusiasm.

One of the significant side benefits of bringing the young people together on this monthly basis was that many came from widely scattered areas where there were very few youth who were members. This social contact gave them reinforcement, and many long-standing friendships were established that undoubtedly led to more marriages within the Church than would otherwise have occurred.

At the time the charge was given to have the program follow the membership of the Church throughout the world, there was not one seminary or institute course that existed in any language other than English. The translation, publication, and distribution of home-study course materials presented challenges. There was no international non-English faculty or staff in place or anyone trained in the non-English international areas who was acquainted with the program.

The next nine years proved to be very interesting, challenging, and stimulating. Our early decisions had to deal with where to start first—which languages and in which countries. After studying the international membership populations, we decided that we should begin with the Spanish, Portuguese, and German languages. Brother Robert Arnold was sent to Guatemala, Brother David A. Christensen to Brazil, and Brother Richard Smith to Argentina and Uruguay, with Brother James Christiansen soon to follow in Germany. They were the first CES personnel to be sent to non-English speaking countries.

From the standpoint of moving these educational programs throughout the world within a three-year period, three very important guidelines or objectives were given to these first brethren assigned as CES pioneers in non-English-speaking areas: (1) Develop a positive working relationship with priesthood leaders. (2) Start the home-study seminary program, enrolling interested secondary *and* college-age students. (3) Find and train a person who could provide local native leadership, thus removing the necessity of exporting others from the United States. We took seriously Alma's message from the Book of Mormon: "For behold, the Lord doth grant unto *all* nations, of their *own* nation and tongue, to teach his word, yea, in wisdom, all that he seeth fit that they should have; therefore we see that the Lord doth counsel in wisdom, according to that which is just and true" (Alma 29:8; emphasis added).

Work in Japan, Korea, Taiwan, the Philippines, and several other locations was soon to follow. In short, the goal was to start the program and have it nationalized within three years. Some remarkable local brethren were found and trained. I know of no other Church program that moved toward globalization and nationalization so quickly.

Student Response to Seminaries and Institutes

The response of the students to seminary and institute was overwhelmingly positive and went far beyond what we expected. We had thought that the efforts would be successful if even one or two hundred students were registered in the first year. What a surprise it was during on-site visits in July of 1971 to find that more than seven hundred students were enrolled in Guatemala, a comparable number in Argentina and Uruguay, and more than nine hundred in Brazil.

At that same time, we made a feasibility study for starting the seminary and institute program in Chile. We held meetings with priesthood and mission leaders and determined that we would recommend to the Board of Education to begin the program at the start of the next school year. Upon return, the report and recommendation were made to President Harold B. Lee. In this case, the proposal to initiate the program was approved, but, surprisingly, his instruction to us was not to wait but to "start the program now." That counsel proved to be inspired because many political changes were to come in Chile before the beginning of the next school year. President Salvador Allende became the first communist leader to come to power in a democratic election. Starting the program the next school year would have been more difficult.

The students who enrolled around the world seemed especially hungry and thirsty to learn more about the scriptures and the gospel. Among so many, there was a genuine feeling of excitement. Brother Frank D. Day reported that on one of his supervisory visits to Asia, he observed a Book of Mormon class being taught in a rented classroom in a commercial building in downtown Seoul, Korea. He wondered if any students would come to that location, but at the appointed hour the students poured into the classroom. The teacher mentioned that he had a one-page handout describing the various groups of plates from which the Book of Mormon was translated and that he would distribute it at the end of the class period. A young girl picked up one of the sheets and asked, "Is this for me?" "Yes, it is for you to keep." She literally started to dance for joy at the thought of having something she could keep and study on her own. The teacher, Brother Seo Hee Chul, said, "You can be sure that when she comes to class next week, she will have memorized the detail on the whole page."

We felt confident that if we could get the students into the scriptures, there was a good chance of getting the scriptures and what they teach into the students. Using the students' later willingness to respond to missionary calls as a measuring tool, in many cases that proved to be true.

A Prophetic Clarion Call for Missionaries from International Areas

Within the next few years, what was once a monolingual seminary and institute program, operating mainly in the western United States, was established in sixty-six countries and in seventeen languages around the world. Obviously, those numbers have continued to expand during the last several years. The teenage and college-age students were studying the scriptures and doctrines of the Restoration just in time to receive the prophetic missionary clarion call which President Kimball made with his characteristic candor and clarity in 1974, in which he called on all of us to lengthen our stride and raise our sights. He emphasized that each country should break with prior tradition and be providing its own missionaries. Here are a few selected quotations from that monumental address:

> When I read Church history, I am amazed at the boldness of the early brethren as they went out into the world. . . . As nearly

as 1837 the Twelve were in England fighting Satan, in Tahiti in 1844, Australia in 1851, Iceland 1853, Italy 1850, and also in Switzerland, Germany, Tonga, Turkey, Mexico, Japan, Czechoslovakia, China, Samoa, New Zealand, South America, France, and Hawaii in 1850. . . . Much of this early proselyting was done while the leaders were climbing the Rockies and planting the sod and starting their homes. It is faith and super faith. . . . Today we have 18,600 missionaries. We can send more. Many more! . . . When I ask for more missionaries, I am not asking for more testimony-barren or unworthy missionaries. . . . I am asking for missionaries who have been carefully indoctrinated and trained through the family and the organizations of the Church. . . . I am asking . . . that we train prospective missionaries much better, much earlier, much longer. . . .

The question is frequently asked: Should every young man fill a mission? And the answer has been given by the Lord. It is "Yes." Every young man should fill a mission. . . . There is ample argument that Mexico, with its nine stakes and five missions, should furnish its own missionaries, or the equivalent.

Suppose that South Korea with its 37,000,000 people and its 7,500 members were to take care of its own proselyting needs and thus release to go into North Korea and possibly to Russia the hundreds who now go from the states to Korea.

If Japan could furnish its own 1,000 missionaries and then eventually 10,000 more for Mongolia and China, if Taiwan could furnish its own needed missionaries plus 500 for China and Vietnam and Cambodia, then we would begin to fulfill the vision. Suppose that Hong Kong could furnish its needed missionaries and another 1,000 to go to both of the Chinas; suppose the Philippines could fill its own needs and then provide an additional 1,000 for the limitless islands of southeast Asia; suppose the South Seas and the islands therein and the New Zealanders and the Australians could furnish their own and another several thousand for the numerous islands of south Asia and for Vietnam, Cambodia, Thailand, Burma, Bangladesh, and India. . . . Suppose that Mexico and Central America provided far more missionaries than they needed themselves and the people of South America had reached the point where they could export numerous fine missionaries and then suppose that the United States and Canada awakened to their real responsibility, sending thousands of missionaries to join them.

President Kimball later quoted President Brigham Young: "This kingdom will continue to increase and to grow, to spread and to prosper more and more. Every time its enemies undertake to overthrow it, it will become more extensive and powerful; instead of decreasing it will continue to increase; it will spread the more, become more wonderful and conspicuous to the nations, until it fills the whole earth."

And finally, President Kimball said that he envisioned "great numbers qualifying themselves for missionary service within their own country and then finally in other lands until the army of the Lord's missionaries would cover the earth as the waters cover the mighty deep."[5]

That powerful prophetic message came in such a timely way because it was just a few years after the young people in these non-English-speaking areas of the Church had begun to study scriptures and doctrines of the gospel in the weekday seminary and institute classes. Their knowledge and increased testimonies helped prepare them to respond positively to the mission calls that would come.

One concrete example of the response of young people to this clarion call came forcibly to my mind in the country of Brazil. When Brother Frank Bradshaw and I made that first on-site visit to Brazil in 1971 to see how the seminaries and institutes were progressing, we were informed that the number of full-time native Brazilians serving missions could be counted on one hand, or at the most, on two. When I returned to Brazil as a Seventy to serve in an Area Presidency in 1989, more than one thousand Brazilians were serving full-time missions. According to information received from the Missionary Department in August 2001, that number increased to over twenty-six

---

5. Spencer W. Kimball, "When the World Will Be Converted," *Ensign*, October 1974, 6–8, 12–14; see also *Deseret News*, January 5, 1854, 2.

hundred, of whom 180 have been exported to other countries. Interestingly, thirty native Brazilian missionaries are serving in Japan. Not only will they accomplish much good there among Portuguese-speaking members, but when they return to Brazil, they will have a much greater entrée into the Japanese population there. Some of you may know that there are more Japanese living in São Paulo than in any other city of the world outside of Japan itself—over one million.

Almost without exception, the young missionaries called in these countries have had prior seminary or institute of religion experience, and the personal growth and development during the mission provides a powerful contribution to leadership in this Church in which the leadership comes from among the members—people like you and me. To illustrate, any elder who follows the prescribed missionary schedule for his two years of service receives more than seven thousand hours of specialized instruction in the following areas: scriptures; basic doctrines of the Church contained in the discussions; how to teach those doctrines; how to relate with leaders, members, and nonmembers; and how to get along with companions. If a person were to attend the three-hour block of meetings every Sunday without fail, it would take him more than forty-six years to accumulate that much specialized instruction.

The whole procedure of having more returned missionaries who are native to their countries makes for a relatively young corps of competent priesthood and sister leaders, who are more committed and better prepared than ever before.

In a personal conversation I had with Elder Bruce R. McConkie, he shared an interesting experience he had after being in Mexico and calling a twenty-five-year-old returned missionary to be a stake president. He wondered how he was going to explain this action to the other General Authorities when he returned to Salt Lake City. Finally, he decided that the best approach would be to mention that he thought it best to call a stake president who was older than the bishops.

Growth Exceeds Expectations

The globalization of the Church's weekday religious educational programs has not only been amazing to those of us who were directly involved in their implementation in their early years, but apparently, it is also of even greater surprise to Church members generally. In the Sydney B. Sperry Symposium in 2000, Dr. Victor Ludlow presented a paper entitled "The Internationalization of the Church," in which he reported members' estimates in several indicators as to whether they thought that more was occurring outside the United States and Canada than inside. The perception of the members was reasonably accurate with regard to general Church membership, Book of Mormon sales, and number of missions. But there was a wide divergence with regard to seminaries and institutes of religion. Generally, members estimated that perhaps 25 percent of the students would be enrolled outside of the United States and Canada.

Brother Ludlow noted that the international growth of seminaries and institutes "is the biggest surprise to most Latter-day Saints. They assume that the seminary and institute program is primarily a USA-Canada phenomenon. They are aware of the elementary school programs for LDS children in the South Pacific and some other underdeveloped areas, but they have no idea how rapidly the CES seminary and institute enrollment has exploded throughout the world."[6]

To place the growth more fully into perspective, when I was first appointed as a seminary teacher adjacent to Granite High School in 1955, the international enrollment in seminaries and institutes was listed at zero. In the report given in 2001, the total outside the United States and Canada is listed at 340,026—almost 50 percent of the total worldwide enrollment. The seminary and institute program now functions in eighty-two countries, and course materials have been translated into fifty-eight languages! All of this has occurred thanks

---

6.   Victor L. Ludlow, "The Internationalization of the Church," in *Out of Obscurity: The Church in the Twentieth Century* (Salt Lake City: Deseret Book, 2000), 213.

to the efforts of hundreds of dedicated full-time staff and thousands of faithful and effective volunteers.

Although the numbers of young people enrolled are impressive, I do not wish to convey an impression that there is not much more that needs to be done. Activity ratios need to be increased in every country, and the percentage of eligible young men serving full-time missions should be greatly enlarged.

Gospel Truths Taught to Meet Challenges of Our Time

Why do we do all of this? Why do we go to all this effort as a Church? Let's face it, as a society, we are immersed in some serious problems. There is a decided weakening of the capacity of institutionalized churches to influence their members at the level of personal conduct. We see ample evidence that so many in public and private circles do not conduct themselves consistently with Judeo-Christian moral and ethical values. Scan any newspaper and you will see what I mean.

There are many in secular education today who believe that truth is relative to time, culture, and circumstance. We hear of "situational ethics," of individuals saying that peculiar circumstances determine the "rightness" or "wrongness" of actions; or that it may be right for you, but it is not right for me; or that it may have been right for me in the past, but it is not right for me today. We see emphasized in so much of our educational efforts today "what is," to the neglect or exclusion of "what ought to be," to such an extent that in many ways our continued existence as a civilized people is threatened. It is true, as someone said, that one of our weaknesses in America and so many parts of the world today is that we "aim at nothing, and hit it with accuracy." So much of what we do educationally in our society generally lacks direction and commitment.

This is not true with The Church of Jesus Christ of Latter-day Saints, for we hold that there are absolute truths. In other words, true principles are eternal; they never change. They are the same yesterday, today, and forever, in all cultures, in all times, and in all places.

The commandments, the standards, the word of God stand firm and unalterable. Someone has said that the Church is never more than a generation away from extinction, and so it is if truths are not taught effectively. Each generation has the responsibility of teaching these truths effectively to each succeeding generation. In other words, an effective religious educational program must exist. I remember that someone said, "Religion is always the search for the meaning of life. ... The religious problem is therefore the ultimate issue in education."

I believe that one of the major reasons why many in the world have been so weakened in their moral fiber is because they have not had operating in society an effective religious educational program based on true principles. In the Church, we have that; and furthermore, we are committed. Our leaders are committed. We make no apology to anyone that we plan, organize, and invest resources of time and money. We drive countless miles to haul children to and from early morning seminaries and Church sponsored activities of all kinds. We print manuals by the hundreds of thousands for teachers and parents to use in teaching. We establish seminaries, institutes of religion, schools, colleges, and universities. Why? So that these truths can be taught and learned; so that circumstances can be created in which the Spirit can testify to all our spirits of the eternal truths of the gospel. Without this Spirit, we cannot succeed, and when teachers and students have it, we cannot fail. Our course is charted, and our goals are set.

The entire religious educational effort of the Church centers in Christ today, as it did in Book of Mormon times centuries ago: "For we labor diligently to write, to persuade our children, and also our brethren, to believe in Christ, and to be reconciled to God; for we know that it is by grace that we are saved, after all we can do. . . . And we talk of Christ, we rejoice in Christ, we preach of Christ, we prophesy of Christ, and we write according to our prophecies, that our children may know to what source they may look for a remission of their sins" (2 Nephi 25:23, 26).

The Church, an Educational Institution

This Church is an educational institution. It is made up of teachers—all of us, wherever we are in the world. As President David O. McKay has said: "We are a Church of teachers. In the Latter-day Saint home the father and mother are required to be teachers of the word—expressly required so by the revelation of the Lord. Every auxiliary organization, every quorum, is made up of a body of men and women or of men who are in the ultimate sense of the word, teachers."[7]

A basic question is, "For what purpose do we teach?" I am reminded of an impressive experience we had while we served at the Missionary Training Center. On one occasion during a mission presidents' seminar, a member of the Quorum of the Twelve was addressing the group of newly called mission presidents and their wives. He asked them, "What is your most important responsibility as a mission president?" Hands went up all over the room. He called on one of them, who responded with enthusiasm, "Baptize converts!" The brother agreed that baptizing converts was a very important responsibility, but he went on to say, "But that is not your most important responsibility as a mission president. Your most important responsibility is to facilitate the sealing of families."

One of the major goals of this Church is to strengthen families and, through effective religious education, to raise up a membership throughout the world worthy of current temple recommends—a people fully qualified to enter into the sacred covenants that are performed in the houses of the Lord that bind on earth that which will be bound in heaven. These temples, through the efforts of President Gordon B. Hinckley and all who serve with him, are becoming available in ever-increasing numbers and in closer proximity to the membership of the Church. If all of us, as members of the Church, could genuinely come to the point in our lives "that we have no more disposition to do evil, but to do good continually" (Mosiah 5:2) and

---

7.   David O. McKay, "That You May Instruct More Perfectly," *Improvement Era*, August 1956, 557.

honestly qualify for a temple recommend throughout our entire lives, we wouldn't have much to worry about in this life or the life to come.

As mentioned, there is so much more yet to be done, but what an impressive array of developments has occurred within the last several decades to fulfill, at least partially, the prophetic pronouncements that The Church of Jesus Christ of Latter-day Saints will eventually become globalized.

The Brethren who lead this Church are committed to the idea that families must be strengthened, and to assist in this process, teenagers and young adults all over the world should have the opportunity afforded to them to enroll in weekday religious education, prepare to fulfill full-time missions, and qualify for temple marriage. Much progress has been made to make this possible, and there is much more that needs to be done.

I testify that our Heavenly Father lives, that Jesus is the Christ, that this is His Church led by living prophets, and that, as we have heard, "The Standard of Truth has been erected; no unhallowed hand can stop the work from progressing; persecutions may rage, mobs may combine, armies may assemble, calumny may defame, but the truth of God will go forth boldly, nobly, and independent, till it has penetrated every continent, visited every clime, swept every country, and sounded in every ear, till the purposes of God shall be accomplished, and the Great Jehovah shall say the work is done."[8]

This Church will go forward with or without you and me. I am confident that it can go forth a lot better with us than without us. May we all work with diligence and in harmony.

© by Intellectual Reserve, Inc.

Elder Joe J. Christensen is an emeritis member of the First Quorum of the Seventy. This essay was presented at "Education, the Church, and Globalization," the International Society's twelfth annual conference, August 2001, Brigham Young University, Provo, Utah.

8.   Smith, *History of the Church*, 4:540.

Chapter 13

Education, the Church, and Globalization

Elder John K. Carmack

THE LORD HAS made it clear that our salvation is tied in with our attitudes and actions toward the poor. Apparently God loves the poor since He has made so many of them. Now President Gordon B. Hinckley and his associates in the First Presidency and the Quorum of the Twelve Apostles have given a tremendous new emphasis on sharing with the poor in announcing the formation of the Perpetual Education Fund and department. The sole purpose of this fund is to help our young men and women in poor communities of the world gain opportunities beyond what their resources allow.

As far as I can tell, every prophet of God has loved and served the poor. While President Hinckley is proud of our institutions of higher learning, he recognizes that most of the opportunities in these universities are for people of means, and these opportunities are not generally available for those coming from poor backgrounds. He has been asking for a long time, "What are we doing for the poor of the Church, especially the young people who are trying to get a start in life?" That may be more important to him than establishing the best research and teaching university possible. He wants action. He insists that we act to assist those less fortunate than others of us who are so greatly blessed materially.

This has been one of his themes in sermons for a long time. For example, in 1978, at Brigham Young University, he said, "I heard a man of prominence say the other day, 'I have amended the language of my prayers. Instead of saying, "Bless the poor and the sick and the needy," I now say, "Father, show me how to help the poor and the sick and the needy, and give me the resolution to do so."'"[1]

A Parable

A keen matter of equity and justice is involved in the effort of opening opportunities for the poor. We find a parable in section 38 of the Doctrine and Covenants that has become something of a spiritual theme for the Perpetual Education Fund: "For what man among you having twelve sons, and is no respecter of them, and they serve him obediently, and he saith unto the one: Be thou clothed in robes and sit thou here; and to the other: Be thou clothed in rags and sit thou there—and looketh upon his sons and saith I am just? Behold, this I have given unto you as a parable, and it is even as I am. I say unto you, be one; and if ye are not one ye are not mine" (D&C 38:26–27).

With this parable in mind, consider President Hinckley's introductory comments about the Perpetual Education Fund. He said:

> We have many missionaries, both young men and young women, who are called locally and who serve with honor in Mexico, Central America, South America, the Philippines, and other places. They have very little money, but they make a contribution with what they have. They are largely supported from the General Missionary Fund to which many of you contribute. . . .
>
> They become excellent missionaries working side by side with elders and sisters sent from the United States and Canada. . . . They return to their homes. Their hopes are high. But many of them have great difficulty finding employment because they

---

1.   Gordon B. Hinckley, "'And the Greatest of These Is Love,'" *BYU Devotional Speeches of the Year*, February 14, 1978, 24.

have no skills. They sink right back into the pit of poverty from which they came.[2]

These returned missionaries fit the parable's description of twelve sons who served their father obediently. Some come home to rich educational and job opportunities. They are the ones in the parable clothed in robes and occupying the place of honor. The ones who are clothed in rags are those who go home to nothing but grinding poverty and hopelessness. It is for that second group of sons that the program has been announced and is being readied. We are positioning the Church to reach out to our young men and women in less-advantaged parts of the world.

There is no quick fix for this global concern, but we are starting and moving forward. Help is on the way. Experience has shown that sprinkling money in a show of benevolent giving is not the answer and, in fact, will usually weaken and harm rather than help. Almost all of our members want to assist, including both those with modest means and those with substantial means. Many approaches have been tried, with some good results and some not so good.

Training and Education

Opening opportunities for education and training—leading to jobs—seems the best way to help those facing a bleak future. Although the Prophet Joseph Smith had little formal education, he and the Church have, from the beginning, emphasized education. Everyone knows, for example, that "the glory of God is intelligence" (D&C 93:36). We all know the scripture that says, "It is impossible for a man to be saved in ignorance" (D&C 131:6). The doctrine and literature of the Church abound in admonitions to improve ourselves; to gain knowledge, wisdom, and understanding; and to progress, not only in this life but also in the eternal realms.

---

2. Gordon B. Hinckley, "The Perpetual Education Fund," *Ensign*, May 2001, 51.

The education promoted by the Church in this new program lays a heavy emphasis on studying the scriptures and treasuring up words of life, but the curriculum does not stop there. The scriptures advocate diligence in teaching and learning "in theory, in principle, in doctrine, in the law of the gospel, in all things that pertain unto the kingdom of God, that are expedient for you to understand; of things both in heaven and in the earth, and under the earth; things which have been, things which are, things which must shortly come to pass; things which are at home, things which are abroad; the wars and the perplexities of the nations, and the judgments which are on the land; and a knowledge also of countries and of kingdoms" (D&C 88:78–79).

The scope of such a curriculum is breathtaking, requiring a lifetime of study—continuing beyond this life. In his books and sermons, President Hinckley often counsels the Saints to get all the education, knowledge, and training they can. And where the economies of the countries allow it, the Saints are making great strides in education, knowledge, and training. Church researchers, moreover, have found that the greater the attainment of formal education, the more likely it is that the person will be found attending Church meetings regularly and giving service to others.

President Hinckley, however, put his finger on a serious concern the Brethren have for members that live in parts of the world where education, training, and good jobs are generally unavailable or are very difficult to obtain. With the increasing globalization of the Church, how do we help members attain the dignity, financial stability, training, and education they need? From what source will our leaders come in those parts of the world?

Success in making new converts is often enjoyed among the poorer and more humble brothers and sisters. How can we help them without destroying their dignity, self-reliance, and initiative? It is a great concern. We are searching for the answers. Just adding to the enrollment of our few great institutions of higher learning, though very important, is not the answer to this larger question we have raised. We know the doctrine. It admonishes us to help the poor, be one, be just in the treatment of our sons and daughters. As James points out, we can't just say, "Be ye warmed and filled" to a brother or sister who is naked and destitute of daily food. Rather, "faith, if it hath not works, is dead, being alone" (James 2:17).

Just as the Church grappled mightily with the plight of the Saints during the Great Depression, the First Presidency and Quorum of the Twelve have agonized, pondered, and planned to find ways of meeting the plight faced by many of our members in less-advantaged countries. How can we help without bringing greater harm and misery to our people? Like the medical profession, the Church has the obligation, above all, not to harm its members by placing them on what we used to call a dole. That kind of assistance can paralyze and stultify the initiative and self-reliance of our people and rob them of their self-respect.

Many wonderful initiatives and procedures are already in place to assist the poor and disadvantaged Saints. We have a way of helping the poor that has stood the test of time in our fast-offering program. We have also developed many employment centers. We have given loans and grants to some for education. On their own initiative, many of our members with means and skills have done their best to lift and touch members and others less advantaged throughout the world. These continue to be important and wonderful, but something more needed to be done.

In announcing the Perpetual Education Fund and new Church department, President Hinckley addressed the major concern head-on. After describing and raising the concern, as outlined above, he announced a bold new program, international in scope, to meet the challenge, at least for our younger returned missionaries and other young adults. We will talk more about that later, but let us see what we can learn from some other initiatives, in and out of the Church.

Similar Initiatives

Those of us who are older remember the tremendous debt of gratitude we felt for what Tom Brokaw called "the Greatest Generation."[3] Millions of our youth had been in the service of the country for four or five years, forgoing the years they would otherwise have been working, gaining an education, and starting a career. They had performed, on the whole, a magnificent service for their countries and for the free world in the fight against tyranny. To help them, bold action was required. The nation created what became known as the GI Bill of Rights. Literally millions received education and training under this powerful program. Other millions received loans for starting businesses, buying farms, and acquiring homes. The program was a tremendous boost to them and to the nation. This bold program laid a new foundation of prosperity and opportunity.

Brokaw said, in the introduction to his best seller, that these soldiers "became part of the greatest investment in higher education that any society ever made, a generous tribute from a grateful nation. ... They were a new kind of army now, moving onto the landscapes of industry, science, art, public policy, all the fields of American life. ... They helped convert a wartime economy into the most powerful peacetime economy in history."[4] On a global and international scale, is that not what the First Presidency and Quorum of the Twelve have in mind with the Perpetual Education Fund?

Another bold initiative followed World War II, named the Marshall Plan after President Harry S. Truman's secretary of state, George Marshall. This program of assistance saved the economies and independence of many nations that faced ruin without resources to meet the horror and chaos of World War II. The Church, though small, acted quickly and magnificently during that same era to help

---

3. See Tom Brokaw, *The Greatest Generation* (New York: Random House, 1998).
4. Brokaw, *The Greatest Generation*, xx.

its own and others under the noble administration of Elder Ezra Taft Benson.

Earlier, in 1903, the Church found itself faced with a shortage of well-educated teachers for its young people. To meet that problem, the Board of Education of the Church established the Education Fund of 1903. This fund granted loans to worthy and ambitious young people to gain greater competence, particularly in the profession of teaching. The fund was revolving in nature in that as the recipients completed their education, they repaid their loans. This replenished the fund for others to use.

Now, back to our present dilemma, we find that the kind of assistance needed in less-advantaged countries is training for our young men and women who want to find good jobs, marry, have families, and serve in the Church. The priority is for training that leads to occupations and jobs, not college or university training, although that too is needed. First and foremost, however, they need training that will lead to jobs.

We are reminded that, while serving as an envoy in Europe for his new country, John Adams, in a letter to his wife, Abigail, once said: "I must study politics and war that my sons may have liberty to study mathematics and philosophy. My sons ought to study mathematics and philosophy, geography, natural history, naval architecture, navigation, commerce, and agriculture in order to give their children a right to study paintings, poetry, music, architecture, statuary, tapestry, and porcelain."[5]

Perhaps President Hinckley is saying that our young adults need to study computer technology, bricklaying, electrical installation, design and drafting, teaching skills, automobile repair, and nursing in order to allow them to marry, serve in the Church, pay tithing and fast offerings, and become contributing members of their communities. Later some of their children may have the means and

---

5.   David McCullough, *John Adams* (New York: Simon and Schuster, 2001), 236–37.

background to study a profession and gain all that universities have to offer. In the meantime, the work available and the skills needed should be our curriculum and the place to use our resources to help. Much of Thomas Jefferson's effort was to lead "a crusade against ignorance, establish and improve the law for educating the common people."[6] Is that not the essence of the bold new initiative of the Church? Is it not a crusade against the lack of opportunity for the common people of the Church? Shouldn't that be a major emphasis of Church members today?

Looking Back for Answers

History often gives us context and answers to present concerns. For example, after the death of Joseph Smith and his brother Hyrum in Carthage Jail, Brigham Young and the Quorum of the Twelve moved into the place of leadership. They did not forget the poor. In a meeting held in the Nauvoo Temple to discuss and plan the migration to the West, Elder George A. Smith of the Twelve recalled the covenant they had made in Missouri—not to leave behind any of the poor—and suggested it was time for another such covenant. President Brigham Young moved "that we take all the saints with us to the extent of our ability."[7] They did that to their great credit and to the credit of the Church members who shared with each other.

Having succeeded in establishing a foothold in these valleys, they faced another great need—to emigrate the thousands of converts in Europe who wanted to join them. But how were they to do it? Knowing that a huge and complex organizational task faced them, they incorporated a new organization under the laws of the

6. Thomas Jefferson, *The Jeffersonian Cyclopedia: A Comprehensive Collection of the Views of Thomas Jefferson* (New York: Funk and Wagnalls, 1900), 274.

7. "Circular Regarding When Saints Were Leaving, October 11, 1845," *Messages of the First Presidency,* comp. James R. Clark (Salt Lake City: Bookcraft, 1965), 1:284.

provisional state of Deseret. They called it the Perpetual Emigrating Fund Company. President Young, at the organizational meeting, reminded the Saints of the covenant to "never cease our exertions, by all the means and influence within our reach, till all the Saints who were obliged to leave Nauvoo should be located at some gathering place of the Saints."[8] He was elected president of the company and others were elected to various offices. A fund separate from tithing was established. He then called the people of Europe to gather here. They built into the program the requirement of repaying their loans to maintain self-reliance and dignity in the people. Many could and did pay their own way. Others needed partial loans to make it. Some needed assistance for all of their expenses. Never mind, they did it.

The Perpetual Emigrating Fund Company required agents to organize and commence the journey across the sea from Great Britain and Scandinavia. The Perpetual Emigrating Fund Company appointed agents to meet them when the ships arrived in America. Other agents had the duty to find the wagons, provisions, oxen, cattle, and all the things needed to cross a wide wilderness.

They boarded in Liverpool. The noted author Charles Dickens boarded one of the emigrant ships carrying the Saints to the New World and published this report:

> Two or three Mormon agents stood ready to hand them on to the Inspector, and to hand them forward when they had passed. By what successful means, a special aptitude for organisation had been infused into these people, I am, of course, unable to report. But I know that, even now, there was no disorder, hurry, or difficulty. . . . I went on board their ship to bear testimony against them if they deserved it, as I fully believed they would; to my great astonishment they did not deserve it; and my predispositions and tendencies must not affect me as an honest witness. I went over the Amazon's side, feeling it impossible to deny that, so far, some remarkable influence had produced

8.   "Second General Epistle, October 12, 1849," *Messages of the First Presidency*, 2:34.

a remarkable result, which better known influences have often missed.[9]

What these approximately 100,000 Saints added to the Church in these valleys is impossible to estimate. They became the Church in large measure. And a great many owed their ability to come to the West to the loans from the Perpetual Emigrating Fund. Repayment was hard and was often made in labor and in kind. Leaders extended tremendous efforts to keep the fund equal to its task. The Moroni Fund, the Provo Fund, the Ephraim Fund, and the Scandinavian Concerts helped. Sarah Ann Peterson's plan to have sisters donate eggs laid on Sundays spread from her community in Ephraim to surrounding communities. The plans and thoughts of the Church revolved around and were dominated by this program of emigration. There was nothing like it anywhere.

After Brigham Young died, President John Taylor took the oar as President of the Church and forgave half of the remaining debts of the emigrants as an act of celebrating the year of jubilee. When the United States disincorporated the Perpetual Emigrating Fund Company and the Church, the fund and company had fulfilled its essential purposes. The Church and its growing communities were well supplied with boot- and shoemakers, accountants, boilermakers, cabinetmakers, engineers, miners, masons, printers, spinners, weavers, and many others representing specialized skills and occupations.

Back to the Present and Future

We no longer need all these people and their skills in these valleys—they are bursting with growing population. We need to do the same thing in less-advantaged countries that we once had to do here. And President Hinckley, on behalf of the Brethren, announced the plan and way to do it. Before making that announcement, he began

9. Charles Dickens, *The Uncommercial Traveller and Reprinted Pieces* (London: Oxford University Press, 1958), 228, 232.

developing a plan to organize a new department and establish a plan to accomplish the purposes of the new Perpetual Education Fund. He invited contributions. All contributions would go to assist the needy young adults in less-advantaged areas of the Church. The local administration of the program was delegated to institute directors in those countries.

The Perpetual Education Fund Board of Directors has approved the program designed by the new Church department. The plan of action has been created. The expenses of the department will be minimal because the only paid employee is its secretary. The budget for travel and other expenses will be paid not out of the fund but by the Church budget. The department is establishing the program on a small basis, as President Hinckley counseled, and, by the end of the year [2001], loans for worthy and needy recipients will be available in all the less-advantaged countries of the world where we have institutes of religion and a number of returned missionaries. The scope of the plan is enormous, limited only by the size and income of the fund. The fund is rapidly growing due to the generosity of the Saints. This program greatly enhances the future of disadvantaged returned missionaries and other young adults.

The President and the entire Church are behind this bold new program. The policies designed by the Perpetual Education Fund Department have built self-reliance into the program by requiring commitment to repay the loans with modest interest once the training has been received. We are all committed to it—like the covenant the Saints entered into in the Perpetual Emigrating Fund Company to bring the Saints here. This fund does not replace other programs to help the poor. Fast offering continues to be a grand and fundamental program and principle.

Conclusion

The meaning and value of the Perpetual Education Fund will probably not be known and appreciated for a decade or two. Surely the Perpetual Education Fund will help the Church fulfill its destiny to roll forward until it fills the whole earth. It is patterned after the old Perpetual Emigrating Fund Company and, in fact, is based on heavenly and spiritual patterns. The course of God is one eternal round. Principles of equity and justice underpin it. We are remembering all twelve of our sons and not forgetting less-advantaged returned missionaries who have served so well. It is magnificent. One reason it will work is that "the earth is full, and there is enough and to spare" (D&C 104:17). We need no new organization, except for the focus on a new fund with its special mission, but we will use volunteers and our magnificent institutes of religion. Under the direction of prophets of God, like we did with the old Perpetual Emigrating Fund, we will do things that will amaze the world around us! May God grant us the intelligence, energy, and faith to make our principles a reality.

© by Intellectual Reserve, Inc.

Elder John K. Carmack is managing director of the Perpetual Education Fund and an emeritus member of the First Quorum of the Seventy. This essay was presented at "Education, the Church, and Globalization," the International Society's twelfth annual conference, August 2001, Brigham Young University, Provo, Utah.

Chapter 14

Education and Provident Living in an Expanding Church

A. Bryan Weston

WHAT A WONDERFUL occasion to talk about The Church of Jesus Christ of Latter-day Saints as it moves out into the world! In the early days of the Church, the effort was to gather the members of the Church to Zion and to help establish in their hearts and in their lives a society in which they could grow up and make their contributions in their communities and, subsequently, the world. The efforts of our day have changed a little bit from that early effort. Whereas we first brought Zion to these valleys of the mountains and to these concentrations, where we could be unfettered in some ways in living our religion, now there is a major effort to take Zion to the world and to establish Zion in the world—wherever there are stakes and wards of the Church established. Years ago, we were in a meeting with President Spencer W. Kimball with Church Educational System (CES) administrators, and his early comments were, "Brethren, we follow the priesthood, don't we?" And literally that has been the effort in Church education: to follow the priesthood; to support, assist, and sustain their efforts; and to strengthen the members of the Church, whom we are charged to serve. My desire is to describe briefly some things that are happening in Church education—meaning religious education, especially as it expands out into the world.

I have titled this chapter "Education and Provident Living in an Expanding Church." Provident living, as the Church has used it over the years, really speaks about preparing wisely for the future—living providently while doing our best to both prepare for the future and also enjoy those blessings that are presently available to us.

I represent CES on the religious education side, and we have special appreciation in this day for the things that are happening in a concentrated effort from many departments of the Church. This includes priesthood leaders, Area Presidencies, CES leaders, the Church Board of Education, and some thirty-eight to forty thousand volunteers who help throughout the world in teaching and administering CES programs. The new Perpetual Education Fund, in many ways, has brought together and allowed some things to happen between CES, welfare, and a number of other Church departments in serving these young people of the Church. I think this is providential and part of the destiny of this Church, as we consider this statement from the Prophet Joseph Smith, "The greatest temporal and spiritual blessings . . . never attended individual exertion or enterprise."[1] There are some unique blessings coming to the Church because of the working together and teamwork of the agencies of the Church. There is an urgency in this day in which we live in assisting priesthood leaders working with young adults internationally. Some quick statistics: In Brazil alone there are 230,000 young adult members of the Church. About forty-five thousand of them are considered active or attend Church at some point during a given month. About 5 percent of those serve missions. After their missions, many of them become less active in the Church because of the lack of education, jobs, and Church association. As President Gordon B. Hinckley has said, they go back to their poverty and to the difficult circumstances from which they have come.

---

1. Joseph Smith, *Teachings of the Prophet Joseph Smith*, comp. Joseph Fielding Smith (Salt Lake City: Deseret Book, 1976), 183.

Let me share with you a few statistics in terms of six countries which are all heavily populated in terms of young adult members of the Church. These six countries—Mexico, Brazil, Chile, Ecuador, Peru, and the Philippines—are all Latin American, except the Philippines. There are great numbers in those various countries, totaling 1.7 million young adult members of the Church. The activity rate of those members that we can anticipate would be in church on a given Sunday is about 300,000 of the 1.7 million overall. Institute enrollment in the various institutes in all these countries is less than 10 percent of the total members and about just over half of the active members. We have some work cut out for us in terms of working with potential institute students. The percent of active members enrolled ranges from a high of 77 percent in Peru down to 26 percent in Mexico; overall, 54 percent of the active members of the Church are involved in the institute program. Of that total pool of young adult members of the Church, there are a number who are serving missions or who have recently served missions.

A couple years ago, we had a preliminary effort in a pilot program that President Hinckley and the Board of Education authorized to be extended in Mexico and Brazil to try and reach some of these young adult members. In this expanded program, we offered, in addition to our normal institute classes, some English classes and computer literacy classes to try and help these young returned missionaries learn English, for which there were jobs available in most cases. It has been about three or four years since that effort was initiated. It has now blended into the Perpetual Education Fund as a joint effort.

To demonstrate this effort, I will illustrate using the Lima North Institute. There was an explosion of enrollment when these new classes were offered. In ten months, we went from an enrollment of 195 to 1,136 students. We did not know where to put them. We had two small homes rented—and we still do. We have not been able to get our building built yet. The other Lima institute showed an equal explosion of growth. The use of the institute building was dramatic. They started in most cases at 6 a.m. and would finish at 11 p.m. or later. The desire of these young people to get on a computer was tremendous. They would sign up not only to take the computer classes, which were taught by volunteers, but they would also sign up to do their practicing on the computer, starting at six in the morning and going until midnight or thereabouts—as late as we would let them stay in the building.

We found that starting the English and computer class in the institute program spawned a number of other programs with the young people—twenty-seven other "classes." We put classes in quotes because none of them were for credit at the institute but came about because of interest and the abilities of these young people to stimulate interest in special programs. These classes enhance the sociality of the institute program in many ways, with offerings in dance, piano, organ, aerobics, French, Portuguese, Italian, and Russian. They had music classes where they learned to sing, and then they would sing for one another at the start of their classes. In Peru there was a finance class in Quechua, and there were some preuniversity classes so that some of the students could be admitted to universities. They had a wonderful experience with some eight hundred students involved. The institute became a hive of activity, and it was and still is a wonderful place to be. Those young people are hard to turn off once they get started and have such a good experience.

There are scriptures that support what is happening in Church education: "Wherefore, the things of which I have read are things pertaining to things both temporal and spiritual." The Lord speaks about both sides of our nature. Nephi records, "It appears that the house of Israel, sooner or later, will be scattered upon all the face of the earth, and also among all nations. . . . Nevertheless, after they shall be nursed by the Gentiles, and the Lord has lifted up his hand upon the Gentiles and set them up for a standard, and their children have been carried in their arms, and their daughters have been carried upon their shoulders, behold these things of which are spoken are temporal; for thus are the covenants of the Lord with our fathers" (1 Nephi 22:3, 6).

Nephi goes on to say:

> And after our seed is scattered the Lord God will proceed to do a marvelous work among the Gentiles, which shall be of great worth unto our seed; wherefore, it is likened unto their being nourished by the Gentiles and being carried in their arms and upon their shoulders. . . .
>
> Wherefore, he will bring them again out of captivity, and they shall be gathered together to the lands of their inheritance; and they shall be brought out of obscurity and out of darkness; and they shall know that the Lord is their Savior and their Redeemer, the Mighty One of Israel. (1 Nephi 22:8, 12)

I have been in Lima, helping with some of this initial effort in implementing some of the Perpetual Education Fund as it works with institutes and in the institute program. I trained some of our local institute directors for the role they will play. We asked some of the students who came and who were applying for some of these first loans from the Church what their reaction was when they heard President Hinckley's announcement. It was interesting to hear their response. Most of them said that they wept. They knew that the Lord was conscious of their needs and their desperation when they did not know what to do or where to turn. They were so grateful. This response is interesting in light of the scripture that says they will "be brought out of obscurity and out of darkness; and they shall know that the Lord is their Savior and their Redeemer, the Mighty One of Israel" (1 Nephi 22:12). In discussing linkage of institutes with education, job placement, and a broader role, President J. Kent Jolley of the Brazil South Area said, "This is the most important thing that could be done for the Church in Brazil. We have to act now, or we will lose this whole generation of members."

We have asked ourselves a few questions. First, can the institute program become a catalyst to provident living—both to have the sociality and the enjoyment of membership now but also to prepare for the future among Latter-day Saint young adults? Second, as the institute is such a great gathering place for young adults, how can we assist the students to seek educational training, obtain job placements, and prepare to arise out of obscurity in context of an institute? How do we stay true, in our CES role, to our trust and also implement these important and good developments in international institutes?

Our objective given to us by the Church Board of Education is to assist in accomplishing the mission of the Church—to teach students the gospel, to provide a spiritual and social climate, and to prepare young adults for Church service. It seemed that the board had already put in place the basic parameters in which we could operate. Then we made recommendations, within the context of the Perpetual Education Fund, to work with priesthood leaders to get newly returned missionaries and all young adults to become actively involved in the institute, because of the association and the spirituality that occurs there and the strengthening of young people and their testimonies. Another objective is to work with Employment Resource Services to get career planning and training for students. A third objective is to bring family history courses into institute during this time of temple building, including computer usage. That seemed to be a natural solution because it would give students the opportunity to become a little more confident on computers, within context of what the Church has asked institute programs to do.

The institute must enhance the idea of a gathering place of young single adults; the activities should facilitate the gathering. We would add, as we proposed, a wraparound class in institute, one which could be started at any time. When young men and young women come off of their missions or when they are activated in the Church and enrolled in this class, they could start the class at any point and then continue through the next semester with the first few classes they had missed as they enrolled. This class is now in a draft form, we have it out, and it is going the same places the Perpetual Education Fund is; it is called Provident Living. We have given it a tentative number, and there are some marvelous things in it. When

Elder John K. Carmack read the draft, he said, "I think those principles were never taught before in the Church, but there is surely a need now." We look forward to what this might add to the institute in terms of provident living, to help students prepare for the future and answer the questions: How am I going to support a family? What can I do so I can eventually give service to the Church? And what can I do to then prepare to be in a situation as a mother and father to raise my children in the Church in faithfulness?

We have thought we could set up computer training—where appropriate—to enhance the students' use of the family history course and their general literacy with computers. We could encourage other enhancements to the institute classes and activities as budgets, talents, and interests may allow. This means that if a group of students had certain talents and abilities, they could be involved in serving one another and preparing themselves for effective Church service.

We are currently working to provide buildings and full-time employees to support the enrollments and programs. In our institutes internationally we are sharing office space for employment resources and family history. We are jointly serving these young people. Another factor we are actively involved in is using Brigham Young University interns and faculty, as available, to support career planning, family history, and so forth, in institutes, with accountabilities, job descriptions, and budgets set up to allow those things to happen.

The context of our efforts would be first to teach the gospel of Jesus Christ. We use scriptures to teach English, enhanced by the use of computers, whether using the TALL or Elis or other programs that would be appropriate. And as a peripheral step, we would provide computer training to enhance family history and the use of computers among the students. Again, President Jolley said, "This is the most important thing that could be done for the Church in Brazil. We have to act now, or we will lose this whole generation of members."

In conclusion, the Doctrine and Covenants says: "Ye cannot behold with your natural eyes, for the present time, the design of your God concerning those things which shall come hereafter. . . . Behold, verily I say unto you, for this cause I have sent you, . . . that you might be honored in laying the foundation, . . . that a feast of fat things might be prepared for the poor . . . unto which all nations shall be invited. . . . And after that cometh the day of my power; then shall the poor, the lame, and the blind, and the deaf, come in unto the marriage of the Lamb, and partake of the supper of the Lord, prepared for the great day to come" (D&C 58:3, 6–9, 11).

We are taking Zion to the nations of the world where the stakes and the young people already are and where the gospel is established, and we are trying to help them build themselves strong in a way that will allow the Lord to do His marvelous work among them in preparation for those days to come.

I express gratitude to so many, those who are here, and a number of others who are not, all of whom have been part of this ongoing effort. I think we are just on the threshold. The tip of the iceberg seems to be in sight. We have no idea of all the dimensions of this wonderful iceberg that we are starting to float on in this world of building Zion throughout the world. I pray that the Lord's blessings be with us in this effort.

A. Bryan Weston is a retired Church Educational System administrator. This essay was presented at "Education, the Church, and Globalization," the International Society's twelfth annual conference, August 2001, Brigham Young University, Provo, Utah.

Chapter 15

Private Education Initiatives by Latter-day Saints

E. Vance Randall and Chris Wilson

EDUCATION HOLDS A prominent place in Latter-day Saint theology. Well-known verses from revealed scriptures in the Doctrine and Covenants quickly come to mind: "The glory of God is intelligence" (93:36). "Whatever principle of intelligence we attain unto in this life, it will rise with us in the resurrection. And if a person gains more knowledge and intelligence in this life through his diligence and obedience than another, he will have so much the advantage in the world to come" (130:18–19). "Seek ye out of the best books words of wisdom; seek learning, even by study and also by faith" (88:118). "Teach ye diligently and my grace shall attend you, that you may be instructed more perfectly in theory, in principle, in doctrine, in the law of the gospel, in all things that pertain unto the kingdom of God, ... of things both in heaven and in the earth" (88:78–79).

For Latter-day Saints, acquiring a good education is a religious duty. Education provides us with the mental tools and knowledge to read, understand, and apply gospel principles; to better provide for the temporal necessities of life; and to make us more serviceable in building the kingdom of God. Thus, The Church of Jesus Christ of Latter-day Saints has been very involved in K–16 education since the early days of the Restoration, though the nature of the involvement has changed over the years due to changing circumstances.

The purpose of this chapter is twofold: (1) to provide a very brief historical sketch of the Church's involvement in formal K–16 education; and (2) to present major highlights of some of the current efforts of individual Latter-day Saints in providing K–16 education, especially K–12, with a special interest in developing countries. We deliberately do not give much attention to the important topic of religious education, which is beyond the scope of this chapter. An excellent source of the history of religious education can be found in William E. Berrett's *A Miracle in Weekday Religious Education.*[1]

Historical Sketch of K–16 Education in the Church

The historical development of the Church's provision of K–16 education can be divided into four eras: 1830–47, beginnings; 1847–90, early Utah period; 1890–1935, time of transition and retrenchment; and 1935–2001, expansion, internationalization, and contraction.

1830–47, beginnings. It was not long after the Saints had relocated to Kirtland, Ohio, from New York that the call for the provision of a common school or elementary education went out. In a revelation to W. W. Phelps, the Lord instructed him to assist Oliver Cowdery "to do the work of printing, and of selecting and writing books for schools in this church, that little children also may receive instruction before me as is pleasing unto me" (D&C 55:4). In June 1832, a column titled "Common Schools" appeared in the *Evening and Morning Star.* Members of the Church were admonished to "lose no time in preparing schools for their children, that they may be taught as is pleasing unto the Lord, and brought up on the way of holiness." The preparation and selection of schoolbooks for the children were to wait until more urgent matters were completed, but "parents and

---

1.   See William E. Berrett, *A Miracle in Weekday Religious Education: A History of the Church Educational System* (Salt Lake City: Salt Lake Printing Center, 1988).

guardians in the Church of Christ need not wait—it is all-important that children to become good should be taught."[2]

The appearance of these Church organized and supported K–12 schools had to wait for another two years. In December 1834, the Kirtland [Elementary] School started with around 130 students under the tutelage of William E. McLellin, a schoolteacher by profession, who had taught school in five different states. Classes were held in the printing office. In the "Report of the Kirtland School," dated February 27, 1835, Joseph Smith Jr., Frederick G. Williams, Sidney Rigdon, and Oliver Cowdery were listed as trustees. Some thirty students were dismissed from the school because they were too young. A final enrollment of 100 students pursued their studies in "penmanship, arithmetic, English grammar, and geography."[3] The following year a high school was established in November 1836. The Kirtland High School was held in the attic of the Kirtland Temple, and the 140 students were taught by H. M. Hawes, Esq., a professor of Greek and Latin languages. He was assisted by two other instructors. The curriculum was divided into three departments: classical languages; English (comprising mathematics, common arithmetic, geography, English grammar, writing, and reading); and the juvenile department.[4]

The other major educational development in Kirtland was the School of the Prophets, a combination of secondary education and religious instruction. This adult education movement, or School of the Elders, was for adult males to prepare them for their missions and other callings related to building the kingdom (see D&C 88:77–80, 127; 90:7, 15). The School of the Prophets was held during the winter months of 1833, 1834–35, 1835–36, and 1836–37. Instructors included

---

2. Joseph Smith, *History of the Church of Jesus Christ of Latter-day Saints*, ed. B. H. Roberts, 2nd ed. rev. (Salt Lake City: Deseret Book, 1957), 1:276.

3. Smith, *History of the Church*, 2:200.

4. See Smith, *History of the Church*, 2:474.

Joseph Smith, Orson Hyde, Sidney Rigdon, William E. McLellin, and Joshua Seixas. Topics of instruction included theology, English grammar, penmanship, arithmetic, geography, reading, writing, and Hebrew.[5]

With a Church center in Missouri as well as Ohio, schools continued to be organized by Latter-day Saints. In 1831, Church members in Kaw Township laid the foundations for the first school in Missouri. Members also established the first school in Jackson County in 1833. As the Saints were driven out of Jackson County and surrounding areas to the northern part of Missouri, they built more schools. A large schoolhouse was built at Far West, where it also served as a church and a courthouse. In the *History of Caldwell County*, reference is made to the keen interest the Mormon settlers had in education: "There were also many persons of education and accomplishments. School teachers were plenty and schools were numerous. . . . The Mormons very early gave attention to educational matters. There were many teachers among them and schoolhouses were among their first buildings."[6] As in Kirtland, a School of the Elders, or School of the Prophets, was organized for adult males and was under the direction of Elder Parley P. Pratt (see D&C 97:3–6).

The determination of the Saints to secure good education did not diminish with the loss of their homes in Missouri and subsequent move to Nauvoo. On December 16, 1840, the city of Nauvoo was granted a charter for the University of Nauvoo by the state of Illinois. In addition to providing postsecondary education, the University of Nauvoo had the role as "parent school," which provided support and supervision for all other K–16 schools organized in

---

5. See Lyndon W. Cook, *The Revelations of the Prophet Joseph Smith: A Historical and Biographical Commentary of the Doctrine and Covenants* (Provo, UT: Seventy's Bookstore, 1981); see also Smith, *History of the Church*, 1:342.

6. *History of Caldwell County*, 121, as quoted in B. H. Roberts, *A Comprehensive History of the Church of Jesus Christ of Latter-day Saints* (Salt Lake City: Deseret News, 1957), 1:425n18.

Nauvoo.[7] Concern for good textbooks and education was repeated as part of the Church conference in 1845. Elder Heber C. Kimball reminded the Saints of the need for "school books printed for the education of our children, which will not be according to the Gentile order." W. W. Phelps was commissioned to write some of these schoolbooks.[8] However, gathering storm clouds of persecution would soon drive the Saints from Nauvoo to Utah.

1847–90, early Utah period. Like their Pilgrim forefathers, Mormon pioneers arriving in the Salt Lake Valley faced the incredible task of recreating a society with its social and religious institutions out of the barren wilderness. True to their beliefs in the Restoration, two of their initial tasks were to select a site for a temple and to organize a school. The first school in Utah opened its door (or tent flap) in October 1847. The teacher, seventeen-year-old Mary Jane Dilworth, began the school day with nine pupils. As more pioneers arrived and moved to settle other areas, schools increased in number and in location. Eventually, five types of K–12 schools dotted the Utah landscape: private free schools, private tuition schools, ward schools, territorial or common schools, and specialty schools.

In 1851 the first public school law was passed, which sought to establish a system of schools and allowed towns and cities to provide support for these schools through taxation. The University of Deseret, later to become the University of Utah, was also established by the territorial legislature. For the first twenty years, these publicly supported schools were Latter-day Saint schools. They were often organized at the ward level, and classes were held in the ward meetinghouse and were frequently taught by someone called or hired by the bishop. Many opposed the concept of using taxes to support schools,

---

7. See Ernest L. Wilkinson and W. Cleon Skousen, *Brigham Young University: A School of Destiny* (Provo, UT: Brigham Young University Press, 1976).
8. Smith, *History of the Church*, 7:474.

"because institutions supported by general taxes cannot be conducted on a religious basis."[9]

In the late 1860s, Gentiles began to move into Utah. Some were seeking silver, others establishing businesses, and others hoping to redeem Latter-day Saint children from their benighted religious beliefs. The introduction of religious and social diversity into Utah society had an important impact on Utah education. It became increasingly difficult to explicitly imbue public schools with Latter-day Saint theology. Protestant denominations, with some help from the federal government, sent missionaries to Utah to set up private Protestant schools. The objective of these schools was to enroll Latter-day Saint children and wean them away from their religious beliefs. These Protestant schools sought the redemption of the children from false religious beliefs and the eventual eradication of the "Mormon problem" in one generation. Although many Latter-day Saint children enrolled in these Protestant schools, very few were converted to Protestantism.

The increased secularization of Utah society, with its impact on public schools, the rise of private Protestant schools, and even the hiring of Gentile teachers in some ward schools were of great concern to Church leaders. Control of education and schools was gradually eroding and falling into the hands of those outside the faith. The response by Church leaders was to admonish the Saints to hire members as schoolteachers and to get more involved in the educational decision-making process, both at the territory and town levels. The final blow, however, came with the Edmunds-Tucker Act of 1887, when control of public schools was placed under the direction of an appointed commissioner, and the sale of Church assets was to be used to support the public schools of the territory.

The response of Church leaders to the loss of control over public schools was to establish their own school system "independent of

---

9. *Deseret Evening News*, November 26, 1884.

the District School system . . . in all places where it is possible."[10] In June 1888 a letter from the First Presidency stated: "We feel that the time has arrived when the proper education of our children should be taken in hand by us as a people. Religious training is practically excluded from the District Schools. The perusal of books that we value as divine records is forbidden. Our children, if left to the training they receive in these schools, will grow up entirely ignorant of those principles of salvation for which the Latter-day Saints have made so many sacrifices. To permit this condition of things to exist among us would be criminal."[11] The First Presidency asked that each stake form a stake board of education to oversee educational matters in the stake and to establish an academy in every stake. Some academies had been established prior to this letter from the First Presidency. Union Academy was the first academy and was established in Salt Lake in 1860. Brigham Young Academy, later to be known as Brigham Young University (BYU), was established in 1875. Between 1860 and 1909, thirty-five Church academies were established from Canada through the western United States and into Mexico. These academies gave Church leaders control over the curriculum and who would be hired to teach.

1890–1935, transition and retrenchment. 1890 was a watershed year for the Church and the beginning of a major transition from a Mormon theocracy and society into the mainstream of American life.[12] Through revelation, plural marriage was discontinued. In education, the territorial legislature established a system of free public elementary schools. These schools were to be supported by taxes

---

10. "Epistle to Saints in Semi-Annual Conference, October 6, 1886," *Messages of the First Presidency*, comp. James R. Clark (Salt Lake City: Bookcraft, 1965), 3:86–87.

11. "Establishment of Stake Boards of Education, June 8, 1888," *Messages of the First Presidency*, 3:168.

12. See Thomas G. Alexander, *Mormonism in Transition: A History of the Latter-day Saints, 1890–1930* (Urbana and Chicago: University of Illinois Press, 1986).

collected by the territorial government. The territorial government soon began to provide financial support of public high schools in nearly every county. Church members now found themselves in a financial dilemma. They had been asked to support stake academies by Church leaders, and now they also had to pay taxes to support the public schools. The financial burden was too great.

The response of the Church was twofold. First, seminaries were established adjacent to public schools, where children could receive religious instruction. The first seminary was established in 1912 next to Granite High School. The second major change in Church educational policy was the closure of the stake academies. In 1919, Apostle David O. McKay was appointed commissioner of education with Adam S. Bennion as superintendent of Church schools. President Heber J. Grant assigned them to examine the Church's education policy with regard to stake academies. They decided that to ask members to financially support both stake academies and public schools was too heavy a burden. Furthermore, the Church did not have sufficient resources to fund the academies. The proposed solution was to close the academies. By 1935 all the academies had been closed, transferred to the state as high schools, or transformed into two-year public colleges (for example, Weber College, Snow College, and Dixie College) and then given later to the state.

There were several exceptions. The stake academy at Colonia Juárez remained open as a stake academy, Ricks was converted into a two-year private college and retained by the Church as Ricks College (renamed BYU–Idaho), and Brigham Young Academy became Brigham Young University. Also, an elementary school in Laie, Hawaii, continued and was elevated to junior college status in 1954 by President David O. McKay. This college was initially named the Church College of Hawaii. It is now a four-year institution and is known as BYU–Hawaii. The Church also kept the LDS Business College, which was organized by Karl G. Maeser and William B. Dougall in 1886.

BYU's major role was to prepare teachers of faith who would then teach in the public schools. This would help ensure that public schools would not become godless schools, but the school culture would be indirectly influenced and shaped by Latter-day Saint values and beliefs. The seminary and institute programs, providing religious instruction for high school students and college students, continued to expand, as did provision of higher education at Brigham Young University and Ricks College. In contrast, the Church's direct involvement in K–12 education decreased to the stake academy in Colonia Juárez.

1935–2001, expansion, internationalization, and contraction. In 1953 all Church education programs were consolidated under one organization, the Unified Church School System. The organizational change allowed for better coordination and correlation of educational programs and initiatives. Two major things happened. First, enrollments in seminary and institute programs exploded during the following twenty years. Seminary enrollment increased from 34,467 in 1953 to 141,514 in 1970. Institute enrollment shot up more than tenfold, from 4,555 in 1953 to 49,168 in 1970. The second major event, which foreshadowed the major focus of the 1970s and 1980s, was the internationalization of the seminary and institute program. In 1953 the only place outside the United States where seminary and institute programs were held was Canada. By 1970 programs were established in twenty-five countries and territories.[13]

In 1970 the Unified Church School System was reorganized into the Church Educational System (CES) with Neal A. Maxwell as commissioner of education. CES was given the mandate that seminaries and institutes should follow the Church throughout the world. In addition to religious education, CES also "operated seventy-five elementary and middle schools and seven secondary schools in Bolivia, Chile, Fiji, Mexico, New Zealand, Peru, Western Samoa, American

---

13. Berrett, *A Miracle in Weekday Religious Education*, 240.

Samoa, Tahiti, and Tonga in 1970."[14] As Elder Neal A. Maxwell, then Commissioner of Education, reported to the Church General Board of Education, "Without literacy individuals are handicapped—spiritually, intellectually, physically, socially and economically. Education is often not only the key to the individual member's economic future, but also to his opportunities for self-realization, for full Church service and for contributing to the world around him—spiritually, politically, culturally and socially."[15] By 1976 the Church operated fifty-one elementary and twenty secondary schools in fourteen countries. However, in harmony with a change in Church policy that the Church should not sponsor K–12 education in areas where the government is able to do so, many of these schools were closed. By 1986, CES operated only thirty schools: eight elementary schools, thirteen middle schools, eight secondary schools, and college preparatory schools in Mexico and the South Pacific.

The period of 1935 to the present time has witnessed extraordinary growth, both in enrollment in seminary and institute programs and the number of countries where these programs are found. The involvement of Church education in K–12 education programs saw a brief increase in the 1970s but a retraction in the late 1970s and early 1980s. The recent inauguration of the Perpetual Education Fund to provide financial assistance in the form of loans to assist young adults with postsecondary education is not so much an expansion of Church education programs as it is a modest effort to assist young adults, especially in developing countries, to continue their education.

It appears that current Church policy does not foresee expansion of K–16 schools sponsored by the Church. This does not, however, preclude efforts by individual Church members from providing K–16 educational opportunities. The second part of this chapter

---

14. Berrett, *A Miracle in Weekday Religious Education*, 185.
15. Quoted in Berrett, *A Miracle in Weekday Religious Education*, 185.

describes the efforts of these individuals to furnish formal education at the K–12, as well as the college, levels.

Private K–16 Education Initiatives by Church Members

As the period of expansion, internationalization, and refocusing of education progressed to its present state, a number of private international education initiatives (PIEI) have begun to emerge. These PIEIs vary considerably in both their composition and focus. The descriptive research that follows is a preliminary step to a more systematic inquiry that will yield a greater understanding of these initiatives. This type of descriptive data gathering is an ongoing process, never a finished step. Therefore, expansion and clarification of these initial efforts is welcomed and encouraged.

A PIEI is defined as a formal or nonformal international education activity not officially sponsored by the Church but originating and continuously sustained by the private efforts of Church members. Education, as used in this definition, can be divided into two distinct types. The first is formal education or instruction leading to a formal certification or degree. The second type is nonformal education or instruction that focuses on self-help and skills improvement and does not directly lead to a certificate or a degree. With these working definitions, it is possible to describe the current status of PIEIs and ask specific questions regarding education, globalization, and the Church.

To this point, nineteen specific PIEIs have been identified; seventeen of these could be contacted. Information regarding the seventeen accessible PIEIs was gathered from individual PIEI Web sites and through individual telephone interviews. Inquiries were made in three general areas: history and perceptions for their future, the scope and focus of their operations (geographical as well educational), and, finally, their perceptions of the nature and role of formal Church departments and programs in their unique operations. To facilitate the discussion of these three areas of inquiry, we will begin with PIEIs engaged in primarily formal education.

Formal education initiatives. Four of the nineteen PIEIs have been involved in the process of providing formal education. These include the Rose Education Foundation (REF), Future Hope International (FHI), Southern Virginia University (SVU), and the now-defunct Alma Success Academy (ASA). The first of these formal education initiatives began in 1996 (SVU), and the most recent commenced operations in the year 2000 (FHI). Like many young organizations, the major perception for their future activities is growth. Expansion of both existing schools and programs and the introduction of new schools in new places is a major goal of formal PIEIs. The existence of the necessary government connections and skilled people fluent in the cultural context are vital in selecting sites for expansion. Private formal international education initiatives are truly in their infancy. The impact and challenges faced by these pioneering groups deserves greater study.

The geographical distribution of formal education initiatives by Church members is limited to two continents, South America and Asia, and three countries within those continents, Guatemala (REF), Haiti (FHI), and Cambodia (FHI). Within each country, the size of operations is diminutive, with operations being limited to one or two schools. There are significant questions to consider: Why did formal PIEIs begin in the locations they have and not elsewhere? What role, if any, has the Church played in influencing the location of these formal PIEIs? Why does a returned missionary from Cambodia, for example, establish Future Hope International, while returned missionaries from numerous other countries do not? What attributes, skills, and opportunities existed to make operating formal PIEIs possible? While the descriptive data conducted thus far are helpful in raising questions, they are not suitable for answering these questions. Further research is required to form a clearer picture of the explanations to such questions. While geographic focus is important to consider, population and curriculum focus within countries is also significant and varies considerably.

The focuses of formal PIEIs vary, both in the population they wish to serve and the curriculum they work to provide. FHI, for example, focuses on Vietnamese minority children not served by the Cambodian government. It attempts to accomplish this by embracing a nondenominational approach. Others, like REF, attempt to focus first on the indigenous population and then the broader population in Guatemala. Currently, formal PIEIs choose to focus on one level of education rather than provide a comprehensive system that spans primary, secondary, and higher education.

Curriculum within these organizations also varies according to the historical and social context of the different countries, the specific standards for certification in the respective countries, the financial and personnel conditions of the organizations, and also according to the broader developmental vision of the individual PIEI. The implications of choosing differing arrangements and populations have yet to be examined. In concluding this section, the perceptions of nonformal PIEIs concerning the role of the Church will be introduced.

In researching PIEI perceptions of the role of the Church departments and organizations, we focused on the following: CES, Church welfare, Latter-day Saint Charities, BYU, the Missionary Department, and local stakes, wards, and branches. Responses from both formal and nonformal PIEIs were similar at the general level. For example, both groups see CES as a prime location for conducting recruitment of both students and local field personnel. Latter-day Saint Charities is recognized as a financial resource capable of contributing to certain projects. Both formal and nonformal groups see BYU as fulfilling a research and training role. Local missionaries and wards are seen as sources of volunteer support. The only major difference discovered at this level is that formal PIEIs did not perceive Church welfare as being related to their activities, while nonformal PIEIs do. When we move from the general level of perception to the more specific level, we begin to notice differences that carry implications for the relationship between PIEIs, Church departments, and affiliated organizations.

Perhaps these specific differences and their implications are best illustrated by using BYU as an example. Formal PIEIs perceive BYU as providing research and training relevant to formal education in various international contexts. Formal PIEIs see themselves as future partners in developing a body of knowledge that would be useful in establishing and maintaining operations and training of both foreign and domestic teachers and administrators, who would then take positions in formal education in various country contexts. The nonformal PIEIs, in contrast, are much less interested in building capacity in terms of the existing formal education structures within a country. Their level of analysis focuses on the individual and economic development through the less-structured approaches of nonformal education. The research and training for nonformal initiatives would be positions in development NGOs, rather than formal education positions. The implications of these differing PIEI perceptions for BYU are research and training programs heading in two directions based on differing strategies of educational development. This seems to be a pattern that relates to the perceptions of other Church departments as well. The difference in strategies leads to differing needs, which leads to different perceptions of the role Church departments and affiliated organizations might play. We will now turn our attention to the discussion of nonformal PIEIs.

Nonformal education initiatives. Nonformal PIEIs[16] are more common than formal PIEIs. One reason for this may be the flexibility of nonformal initiatives in terms of length of projects, financial requirements, and so forth. Nonformal private international

---

16. The following is the list of identified, nonformal, private Latter-day Saint international education initiatives: Choice Humanitarian, UNITUS, JUCONI, Chasqui Humanitarian, Enterprise Mentors International, Called 2 Serve Foundation/Academy for Creating Enterprise, Reach the Children, Norma I. Love Foundation, Rose Foundation, Help-International, American Indian Services, Huntsman Armenian Projects, Ouelessebougou-Utah Alliance, Norman Gardner/Braille Resource and Literacy Center. (The status of Engage Now and Mesa International is uncertain.)

initiatives began earlier than their formal PIEI counterparts. Three were founded during the period from 1980 to 1985, four from 1986 to 1990, one from 1991 to 1995, and five from 1995 to 2001. Many of these nonformal PIEIs are spin-offs from earlier projects and organizations. They continue to define and redefine themselves at a rapid pace. As with formal PIEIs, their perceptions for the future are the expansion of both the geographical scope and the content of their projects. Therefore, the questions regarding where and why a PIEI forms in a given location apply to nonformal initiatives as well. The majority of nonformal PIEIs are involved in some configuration of microenterprise.

Geographically, nonformal PIEIs are represented on four continents, although they are most heavily concentrated in Latin American countries. In Latin America, three organizations operate in Mexico, three in Bolivia, one in Guatemala, three in Honduras, two in Peru, one in El Salvador, one in Venezuela, and one in Ecuador. Africa has two organizations with active operations, both in Kenya. Armenia, in Eastern Europe, has one organization actively working, while Asia has three different countries represented. One group has operations in Vietnam; Nepal is served by one group, as is the Philippines. Currently, the scope of operations is somewhat larger than the formal PIEIs, serving a greater number of people, with a wider range of programs.

In terms of curriculum focus and population there is a broad mix. As stated previously, microenterprise is part of the majority of nonformal PIEIs. An initiative like JUCONI, which focuses on street children, uses a comprehensive human development approach that addresses biological, cognitive, affective, and communicative development and social integration. In contrast, the Academy for Creating Enterprise's curriculum focuses specifically on providing entrepreneurial skills training in microenterprise to returned Filipino missionaries. While some initiatives have a broad focus in terms of the populations they serve, the majority focus on women, children, and minorities within the broader population. Like their formal educational counterparts, some focus specifically on Latter-day Saint populations and work outward, while others prefer to work in a nondenominational fashion.

Nonformal PIEIs' perceptions regarding the role of the Church, its departments, and its affiliated organizations has been introduced previously. While at the general level the perceived role of the Church is very similar, at a more specific level the difference in perception begins to become apparent. While difficult to determine with the young organizations involved, it seems that the greater flexibility of nonformal PIEIs enables them to find more ways to link their activities with the Church, and they are therefore more common than formal PIEIs. Nonformal PIEI projects require smaller, shorter, and more flexible commitments by Church departments and organizations and therefore find support more frequently. While nonformal PIEIs are currently more prevalent, there is insufficient research to demonstrate which approach might be more successful in building local capacity through education.

In summary, private international Latter-day Saint initiatives are a recent and growing attempt to meet the individual educational needs of people internationally. Currently, two approaches are represented, one that provides formal educational opportunities and a second that concentrates on nonformal education. The geographical trend of these initiatives is diverse, but it is concentrated in Latin American countries. Within countries being served by PIEIs, there are a wide variety of configurations. Some initiatives signify Latter-day Saint populations as their focus, while others have a broad non-denominational approach. Nonformal PIEIs often employ some arrangement of microenterprise as a means of developing local capacity. At the general level, both formal and nonformal PIEIs have similar perceptions of the role they would like the Church departments and affiliated organizations to play. However, at the more fundamental level, formal and nonformal PIEIs have differing developmental agendas. These similarities at the general level and divergent paths at the fundamental level create implications for the present and future relations of PIEIs and Church departments and organizations. The history of the Church and K–16 education, from its beginnings in 1830 to the current period of expansion, internationalization, and refocus, affirms that the Church has always been, and continues to be, dedicated to education. Where governments and private sources can offer education, the Church encourages their efforts to do so. Internationally, the Church does not provide formal education (schooling) in areas where government-sponsored schools are adequate to provide appropriate education for Latter-day Saint members. Globalization creates a space for both formal and nonformal Latter-day Saint private education initiatives to operate. The descriptive information provided herein raises questions that should be considered. For example:

- What should be done with regions without any private Latter-day Saint formal or nonformal education opportunities? Should expansion of these opportunities be encouraged in some way? How?
- How successful have formal and nonformal PIEIs been in building local capacity?
- Finally, what role should private Latter-day Saint formal and nonformal education initiatives and the Church play in support of each other's efforts to provide quality education in areas where members do not have access to adequate educational opportunities?

Doubtless, additional questions can and should be raised regarding PIEIs, globalization, and the Church. The descriptive research presented here is only a starting point for future consideration. The help and collaboration of all interested parties in clarifying and expanding these research efforts is welcomed and appreciated.

E. Vance Randall is a professor of educational leadership and foundations at Brigham Young University. Chris Wilson is a PhD candidate at Loyola University. This essay was presented at "Education, the Church, and Globalization," the International Society's twelfth annual conference, August 2001, Brigham Young University, Provo, Utah.

Part V

International Challenges Facing the Church

Chapter 16

The Tumultuous Twenty-first Century:

Turbulence and Uncertainty

Elder Alexander B. Morrison

IT IS OBVIOUS to even the most casual observer that we are in the midst of transformations so broad and comprehensive that they are revolutionizing the world in which we live, think, work, play, and pray—as never before in human history. The physical, intellectual, and social world we inhabit has changed more—faster and more often—in the past century than in the previous twenty thousand years. The ground is still shifting under us as relentless technological progress in the postindustrial world, coupled with social changes, as diverse as redefinition of the value and nature of work; the changing roles of men and women and changes in the nature of the family; the distribution of wealth; and the attitude toward others not of our racial group, all combine to radically alter the way we think and act. In so-called advanced societies, such as that of the United States, stress levels are becoming increasingly difficult to sustain as we separate the rhythms of our life from those of nature. Perhaps it is only to be expected that in the face of such persistent change and the lack of firm and unchangeable anchors that provide needed stability and constancy we see such alarming levels of depression, anxiety, violence, and hedonism. One example will illustrate my point: changes in the family, which, in this and many other lands, is under continuous and determined attack.

The family in America and elsewhere is not only changing under the pressures, but it is also becoming weaker. Two notable trends of the past generation—the rapid increase in divorce rates and out-of-wedlock childbearing—are particularly indicative of the weakened state of the family. Other danger signs include a decrease in the two-parent family as the traditional setting in which most children are raised; a decrease of the influence of the extended family; the documented impact of fatherlessness on a multitude of social problems—ranging from crime to domestic violence against women; increased numbers of latchkey children, both of whose parents work outside the home; competitive demands from a variety of community and school activities, which weaken family cohesiveness; and aggressive, well-financed attempts to legitimize same-sex unions, according them all of the rights, powers, and privileges that have since time immemorial been restricted to marriage between a man and a woman.

Another transformation, unlike any other in our history, is changing our world. A new international system, that of globalization, is replacing the Cold War system. Unlike the Cold War system, which froze the world into static competing blocks for nearly half a century, globalization is a dynamic, ongoing process. Globalization involves the inexorable integration of markets, nation-states, and technologies to a degree never witnessed before, in a way that is enabling individuals, corporations, and countries to reach around the world farther, faster, deeper, and cheaper than ever before and in a way that is producing a powerful backlash against those who are being left behind or victimized by this new system. Recent violent demonstrations at the G-8 meetings in Genoa (July 2001) were fueled by the anger and fear felt by millions around the world who sense, increasingly, that they are held captive by changes they neither understand nor embrace.

Globalization is not all smiles and sunshine. It has a number of potentially disastrous downsides as well. When the infection of financial panic spreads in a globalized world—and it can do so literally overnight, as the Asian flu of the late 1990s showed—it causes ripples, even tidal waves, across the whole global system.

I think it is not improbable that globalization, by raising both fears and expectations, may contribute to the development of what Robert D. Kaplan terms "the coming anarchy." In a bleakly realistic and frankly frightening collection of essays, which provides "a refreshing corrective to the dogma of globalization," Kaplan points out that the glaring global reality "is not that we [in the U.S.] are becoming like the Third World, but rather that they have so little chance of becoming like us."[1]

Kaplan uses West Africa to illustrate the worldwide demographic, environmental, and social stresses occurring in our "brave new world"—a world in which criminal anarchy emerges as the paramount danger for the future. Disease, overpopulation, crime and violence, scarcity of resources, environmental degradation, migration of refugees fleeing ethnic cleansing, tribalism with its concomitant erosion and instability of nation-states, the empowerment of private armies, and inept and corrupt governments—all portend the dangers that will soon confront our civilization in the West. Sad to say, West Africa is reverting to the Africa of the nineteenth century—a series of coastal trading posts (Accra, Kinshasa, Lagos, Monrovia, and others) and an interior that again is becoming unexplored and off-limits to foreigners. As national boundaries in Africa continue to erode, a more impenetrable boundary is being formed—the barrier of disease, which threatens to separate Africa and other parts of the Third World from more developed regions of the globe. Each year, there are three hundred to five hundred million clinical cases of malaria worldwide, 90 percent of which occur

1. Robert D. Kaplan, *The Coming Anarchy: Shattering the Dreams of the Post Cold War* (New York: Random House, 2000).

in Africa, and each year an estimated one million African children die from that ancient scourge. A dramatic example of the ravages of disease is provided by the AIDS epidemic—a scourge of medieval proportions, which is leaving a whole generation of African children without parents. Some twelve million African children already have been left as orphans, innocent victims of the AIDS epidemic. Some six thousand African children are dying from AIDS daily. Millions of people are being infected each year with the HIV virus; nearly all will die from AIDS.

Through 1999, 450,000 people in North America had died from AIDS, but in sub-Saharan Africa the figure was 13,700,000. The percentage of adults ages fifteen to forty-nine already infected with the AIDS virus is as high as 30 percent in several African countries— more than one hundred times the rate in the United States. Half of South African boys age fifteen will not live to age thirty. Uganda has the dubious honor of having the highest number of AIDS orphans in the world: 1.1 million in all; in some districts in Uganda one-third of all children are orphans. Destitute African orphans, most of whom end up on the streets, turn to prostitution or violence. None among us can be oblivious to or unconcerned about this terrible tragedy as AIDS tightens its death grip on a whole continent. Despite naively optimistic assertions to the contrary, there seems little reason to believe that meaningful remedies to the current AIDS epidemic will or even can be found and applied on a broad scale in Africa over the next decade or more. And if AIDS establishes a firm lodgment in the villages of Southeast Asia, as seems likely, today's epidemic could become a veritable maelstrom of death worldwide.

Kaplan asserts, and I fear he may be right, that "Africa may be as relevant to the future character of world politics as the Balkans were a hundred years ago, prior to the two Balkan wars and the First World War."[2] A century ago, Kaplan notes, the threat was the collapse of empires and the birth of nations based solely on tribe. Now,

---

2. Kaplan, *The Coming Anarchy*, 18.

the threat is nature run amok, with all that implies in terms of environmental scarcity, disease, cultural and racial clashes, and war.

Indeed, Kaplan is of the view that the environment—broadly described—will be *the* national security interest of the early twenty-first century worldwide. Surging populations, deforestation, soil erosion, scarcity of fresh water, climatic change, and the probability of rising sea levels in critically overcrowded regions such as the Nile Delta and Bangladesh will trigger potentially cataclysmic events which initiate and sustain group conflict. In the twenty-first century, freshwater will be in dangerously short supply in such diverse locales as Saudi Arabia, Australia, Central Asia, and the western U.S., including California. The Ogalalla aquifer, which for more than a century has provided groundwater for the Great Plains of the U.S., is drying up. As this proceeds, it will only accentuate major demographic shifts already occurring in that part of the continent. Further north, the Canadian prairie province of Saskatchewan already has fewer people than in 1905. Wars over water, whether in the Nile or in the Tigris and Euphrates rivers, seem a likely possibility. In July 2001 the Canadian prime minister, Jean Chretien, proclaimed that Canada's abundant freshwater supplies are not for sale to the United States at any price. How sustainable that assertion will be in the long run is problematic at best.

Another great environmental issue, the availability of energy supplies, also will pose immense difficulties over the next century. Unless some other cost-effective source can be found in the form of fusion reactors, solar energy conversion, fuel cells, wind energy, or something else, humanity will continue to drive its technology, lifestyle, and growth with fossil fuels. The willingness of technologically advanced countries to go to war over oil supplies has been demonstrated within the last decade, and the potential for future conflicts remains very high indeed.

Increasing deficits in resources will not only engender violent conflicts but also will be instrumental in redefining who people are in terms that do not coincide with the borders of existing states. Religion and tribal ethnicity, not national governments or international organizations, will define political realities. Islam, which from its beginnings has been characterized by militancy, can be expected to become increasingly attractive to the downtrodden of the world, in an era driven by environmental stress, increased cultural sensitivity, heightened ethnocentricity, and erosion of national boundaries. Indeed, Islam is already the world's fastest growing religion. Conflicts between Hindus and Muslims in the Indian subcontinent and between Turkic Muslims and Slavic Orthodox Christians in the Caucasus and the Caspian littoral will be increasingly likely in the next few decades. Professor Thomas Homer-Dixon of the University of Toronto has summarized the new world that is upon us, with all its disparities and dangers: "Think of a stretch limo in the pot-holed streets of New York City, where homeless beggars live. Inside the limo are the air-conditioned post-industrial regions of North America, Europe, the Pacific Rim, parts of Latin America, and a few other spots with their trade summitry and computer-information highways. Outside is the rest of mankind, going in a completely different direction."[3]

The ineluctable truth is that we are entering a bifurcated world, with comparatively few healthy, well-fed techno-elites, and a much larger number of people condemned to a life that, in the words of Thomas Hobbes, is "solitary, poor, nasty, brutish and short."[4] The techno-elites, with a struggle, to be sure, will master or at least contain their most critical environmental stresses of the next century, but the vast majority of mankind, crippled by poverty, a lack of technology, and their rich neighbor's indifference will be unable to do so.

3. As quoted in Nuruddin Farah, "Highway to Hell: The Travel-Writing of the Disaster," *Transition* 70 (1996): 62.

4. Thomas Hobbes, *Leviathan*, ed. Marshall Missner (New York: Pearson-Longman, 2008), 83.

Even in the U.S., where the gap between rich and poor is steadily widening, we are witnessing an increasing polarization between the techno-elites and the techno-illiterates. The fact that many of the latter are African-Americans and Hispanics only exacerbates problems in an already racially divided country.

Make no mistake about it, the brave new world of globalization is filled with uncertainties and replete with dangers, even here in the land of techno-elites. Technology so dazzling and relentless that it may well exceed the capacity of the human species to understand its implications and adapt to its consequences will have immense impact on our perceptions of humanity's uniqueness. None of us can fully comprehend the moral and ethical implications of such advances as mapping of the human genome; transplanting organs from bio-engineered animal species; chemical therapies custom-designed to correct deficiencies in the genomes of patients; artificially enhanced domestic animals; cloning of animal species, perhaps even humans; interspecies hybrids; genetically altered plant species; or computing devices which equal or exceed some attributes of the human mind. No wonder thoughtful observers ask, will the human species adapt or be overwhelmed?

If we are to make our way safely through the uncharted waters of the next century, we must, in my view, look increasingly beyond the lure of technology to the deeper roots of human community, rebuilding positive aspects of the social cohesiveness of earlier times, and learning to put aside the ancient tribal hatreds that have divided and destroyed civilizations from time immemorial. We must consider all of the inhabitants of this globe as fellow travelers on a spaceship, endowed with glorious yet finite resources, and we must learn to replace the selfishness of "the natural man" with a genuine concern for the good of all mankind. Continuance of the current disparity between rich and poor—for every sixty-five dollars earned in rich countries, one dollar is earned in poor ones, and the gap is widening—is simply a recipe for disaster on a scale never before seen in human history.

We begin to understand the interconnectedness of all peoples everywhere as we internalize the Apostle Paul's famous statement to the Athenians: "[God] hath made of one blood all nations of men for to dwell on all the face of the earth" (Acts 17:26). The implications of Paul's prescient observation are clear: all men and women everywhere literally are brothers and sisters, members of the same spiritual family, with all the obligations and responsibilities of sibling relationships that implies. If we value the future, then prejudice, bigotry, and racism—all of which have caused so much suffering and harm since time began—must be replaced with the brotherhood of which Jesus and every other great religious leader in history taught.

We reaffirm our familial relationships with others as we join in loving, serving, and suffering together. As we do so, we find that the superficial differences that have kept us apart fall away, and we see others not as stereotypes or caricatures, but as real people, not much different than we are ourselves.

I finish where I began: it seems apparent that the century we are now entering will be tumultuous and turbulent. That should hardly surprise us. We are, after all, living in the great winding-up scenes of human history. Amidst all the turmoil that will surround us in coming years, we have the divine assurance that "the righteous need not fear" (1 Nephi 22:17). Secure in our knowledge that we are engaged in God's work, anchored in our testimonies of the strength of this great latter-day work, firm in our faith in God and His prophets, we can face the future with equanimity and optimism, doing our duty as God has revealed it to us, and entrusting the future to Him whose servants we all are.

© by Intellectual Reserve, Inc.

Elder Alexander B. Morrison is an emeritus member of the First Quorum of the Seventy. This essay was presented at "Education, the Church, and Globalization," the International Society's twelfth annual conference, August 2001, Brigham Young University, Provo, Utah.

Chapter 17

Family and the Global Church:

Cultural and Political Challenges

Elder Bruce D. Porter

I will begin by making some general points about the worldwide Church of Jesus Christ of Latter-day Saints and the growth of the Church internationally and then turn to what I know is your specific interest in this conference, the proclamation on the family and how our family values may assist us as the Church expands internationally. I will make five points, and I will elaborate on each of them regarding the growth of the Church across the world.

First, God is in charge. This is His kingdom, His plan, and He has a way and a means prepared for it to succeed.

I had an interesting experience several years ago. I was living in Frankfurt, Germany, as a member of the Europe East Area Presidency. Other members of the presidency and I were driving to the office in Frankfurt. Now, at this particular time we were having political troubles all across our area. We were having tremendous difficulty with the government in Bulgaria; we were even fearful that our missionaries might be expelled. There was unrest in Albania. There had been several Russian cities that our missionaries had had to leave or were faced with the threat of having to leave. We had problems in Ukraine and so forth. As we drove into the office, we began talking about all these various challenges. The picture looked rather bleak, and it was not clear what we could even do about most of these things.

As we drove farther and talked a little more, one of the members of the presidency suddenly began to laugh. There was not anything obviously funny about the situation, but he started to laugh. We said, "What are you laughing about?" He said, "Isn't it wonderful to discuss problems that we all know will be resolved? To know that everything will work out, because the work cannot fail." We thought about it, and we started laughing too.

It is a great advantage to be part of a work in a kingdom where you know that victory is certain in the long run and that any problems that may exist are but temporary setbacks along the road to that ultimate success.

I learned a lot from Elder Charles A. Didier, under whom I served in the Europe East Area Presidency. Whenever problems came up, of whatever nature it was, political or otherwise, Elder Didier would never panic. He would never say the situation is grim. He would never send off a letter to the First Presidency and tell them we needed help. Elder Didier simply would smile and say, "The Lord will take care of it," and He did again and again and again. I mentioned that long list of challenges that we faced. Every one of those challenges was resolved or at least tempered within a week or two of that conversation, and we had nothing to do with it. The miracles took place; the Lord took care of the vineyard.

Now nearly ten years have passed since communism collapsed in Eastern Europe. I am not sure even today that we fully appreciate what a remarkable and miraculous event that was. I was, at the time, heavily involved. I was with the federal government, and I was involved with international broadcasting, specifically Radio Free Europe and Radio Liberty. We were broadcasting to those countries on the front lines of the Cold War, so to speak. We had the best information available anywhere in the world on what was happening. Yet we had no inkling of what was about to hit. I can tell you that across the spectrum of specialists on Russia, on communism, on Soviet economics, sociology, whatever it is, no one expected it to happen. No one predicted that it would happen. It came as a complete and total surprise. To this day scholars are arguing about what caused the collapse of communism. They cannot agree, they cannot explain it, and it does not fit any of their theories. But there is an explanation, and it is a very simple one: a decree went forth from God Almighty that the time had come for His gospel to be preached in Poland, in Hungary, in Bulgaria, in Russia, in Ukraine, and so forth. When that decree went forth, the governments of men and the power of man wilted and became as naught before the power of God.

A revolution took place—a peaceful, largely nonviolent, velvet revolution across Eastern Europe. Within months we had missionaries going into those countries. For twenty years prior to that, I had spent my life studying Russia, studying Russian politics, and international relations. Like many members of the Church who did that, one of the reasons I studied it is that I wanted to see the gospel go forth to those countries. I would occasionally meet with other Latter-day Saints who were Russian specialists, and I would say, "How is this going to happen? What will bring this to pass?" And we would speculate about how the gospel could ever be preached in Russia. I remember many times thinking we would send clandestine missionaries or we would begin radio broadcasting and all kinds of things. But the conversation would almost always end by our agreeing that whatever else happened, we would not see young elders from the United States with name tags going into Russia. So you can imagine my feelings in 1991 when I walked into the branch in Moscow and was greeted by a missionary from the United States with a name tag right in the middle of what we previously had thought of as enemy territory, or at least communist-controlled territory.

I do not want to focus just on Eastern Europe, but I emphasize this point that when the time came that our Father in Heaven knew it was right for His gospel to be preached in those countries, it happened. It happened overnight. It was so quick and so sudden that the Church had to scramble to find mission presidents and literally hundreds of missionaries, all who went within a short period.

In the preface to the Doctrine and Covenants, the Lord said: "And the voice of warning shall be unto all people, by the mouths of my disciples, whom I have chosen in these last days. And they shall go forth and none shall stay them, for I the Lord have commanded them" (D&C 1:4–5). We have certainly seen that happen not only in Eastern Europe but in country after country across the world. In that same section, a few verses later the Lord explains how it will happen: "The weak things of the world shall come forth and break down the mighty and strong ones. . . . That the fulness of my gospel might be proclaimed by the weak and the simple unto the ends of the world, and before kings and rulers" (D&C 1:19, 23). Now, I think that the "weak and simple" and "the weak things of the world" refer to our young men and women who serve missions. For that matter, it refers to all of us. We are weak and simple before the powers of the world, and yet the Lord has made us and those missionaries His instruments to take forth His gospel.

In September 1996, I traveled to Siberia and toured the Yekaterinburg mission of the Church. This was the first mission in Russia to be headed up by a native Russian mission president. One of the cities we went to was an industrial city called Cheliabinsk. We had a little branch there of about fifty members. Incidentally, they had all been baptized within the last six months, all fifty members. We had six full-time missionaries serving there. We held a zone conference with those missionaries, just the six of them, myself, and the mission president. One of those missionaries was from Mexico. He was a humble, sweet, pure-hearted young man. Like so many people from his country, he grew up humble. You could read it in his face. As the zone conference proceeded and I spoke, the young man was touched and tears began to roll down his cheeks. As I looked at him, I thought of this scripture, "That the fulness of my gospel might be proclaimed by the weak and the simple unto the ends of the world" (D&C 1:23).

There we were, literally at the end of the world, and here were the weak and simple proclaiming the Lord's gospel.

You may recall that in 1995, a new law was passed in Russia governing religion, denominations, and the preaching of the gospel. I was back in the United States at that time, no longer in the East Europe Area Presidency. That law was getting tremendous headlines in Utah: an interview with a missionary or mission president that had just come home,[1] statements from U.S. senators on how they would deal with the new law,[2] and legislation being passed in the U.S. Congress cutting off aid to Russia if this religious oppression continued.[3] It was a big event.

I called Elder Didier, who was then the East Europe Area President. We had a nice conversation, but he never mentioned anything about the law. So finally I said, "Elder Didier, how is this law going to affect the Church?" And he said, in effect, "What law?" I explained that I was thinking of the Russian law on religion. He said, "Oh, that thing. We're not concerned about that. The Lord has always taken care of us in the past, and He will take care of us again." And that is exactly what happened. That law did not slow the growth of the Church at all. It had no effect on our bringing missionaries into the country. It had no effect on the growth of the Church. If there was any effect at all, it was to give us a little free publicity, which we can always use, and that was all.

What appeared to be a huge threat to the future of the Church proved to have little effect. Now, I am not saying there will never be setbacks, because there will be, or that we will not occasionally have

---

1. See Michael Nakoryakov, "Mission Impossible Spread the Word: Russian Law May Rein in Mormons," *Salt Lake Tribune*, January 21, 1995, A1.

2. See Christopher Rosche, "Bennett Talks Religion with Top Russians," *Salt Lake Tribune*, September 10, 1997, A8; Don Baker, "Hatch Turns Up Heat on Russia Religion Law," *Deseret News*, July 15, 1997, A1.

3. See Lee Davidson, "U.S. Seeks Religious Freedom Worldwide," *Deseret News*, July 3, 1997.

to leave a country for a time, but what I am saying is that the Lord has all these things in His hands. We need not fear. We need not panic. This is His work.

Now, a second point. The Church, wherever it has gone, has been built on the foundation of the most humble, simple people in those countries. In an organization such as yours, the International Society, you have many talented people with contacts around the world. There may be a tendency to think that the Church goes forward the same way other organizations go forward—through networking and contacts and gaining influence with the powerful of the world. Occasionally it is true that someone who is powerful has proven to be a friend of the Church, but that is not generally how the Church is built up.

The Church is built up by the most ordinary and humble people who hear the message of the gospel and enter the waters of baptism. As the Apostle Paul said, "Not many wise men after the flesh, not many mighty, not many noble, are called: but God hath chosen the foolish things of the world to confound the wise; and God hath chosen the weak things of the world to confound the things which are mighty" (1 Corinthians 1:26–27). When I read that scripture, I think of the experience of Elders Heber C. Kimball and Brigham Young and the first Apostles who went to England.

Kimball and Young had tremendous success out in the English countryside. But when they tried to open London to missionary work, they had little success for several weeks. London was a very worldly city. They were trying to find leaders, as we often do; therefore, they were going to the more prosperous parts of the city. They were trying to meet local leaders in government, industry, and so forth, and they were getting absolutely nowhere, not a single baptism. Finally the Spirit moved upon Elder Wilford Woodruff and others, and they went down to the industrial quarters of the city where the common laborers, just off the farms, were working. We know from Charles Dickens and other sources that the working conditions were terrible. These people were in abject poverty, almost slavery. They were truly the most humble of the earth. They were baptized by the hundreds, and the Church began to be built up in London. They were the weak and simple things of the earth, but their descendants became apostles and prophets, great leaders in the world and in the Church. And so it has been in every country that we have ever gone into. We almost always start out with the most simple and ordinary of people, but they become great through the power of the message. Now there are occasional exceptions, and I will give you one.

Elder F. Enzio Busche of the Seventy, now in the Area Presidency in Eastern Europe, was a very prominent man in Germany at the time of his baptism. He was heir to a large fortune and a printing company that was one of the largest in the world. He was highly educated and affluent, yet after lengthy study he received the gospel and joined the Church. His joining the Church and his influence proved to be a great blessing for the Saints in Germany. So there are exceptions to the rule that only the poor and simple of the earth join the Church, although if you know Elder Busche his case is not really an exception, for Elder Busche is one of the most humble men I have ever known in my life. There are few humble men among the mighty and great of the world. Elder Busche happened to be one of them, and he was able to receive the gospel—taught by simple ordinary American missionaries with their thick accents—and perceive its truth, then join the Church.

I have a friend who, a number of years ago, was reading about the handcart companies in the book *Handcarts to Zion* by LeRoy and Ann Hafen.[4] As he was reading this book, he came across a passage that talked about a particular company of handcart pioneers in which there were two blind people, a man who could not walk, a man with one arm, and a single sister with several children and no husband to help her. As he read that passage, he was struck that in

---

4. See LeRoy R. and Ann Hafen, *Handcarts to Zion: The Story of a Unique Western Migration, 1856–1860; with Contemporary Journals, Accounts, Reports, and Rosters of Members of the Ten Handcart Companies* (Glendale, CA: Arthur H. Clark, 1960).

his ward, just in the past year, there had been baptized two blind persons, a man who could not walk, a man with one arm, and a single sister with several children. He observed that they had a hard time finding callings for these people. It was a ward with an abundance of talent, and these converts were handicapped to some degree. The ward leaders were not sure what they could do. For a long time these newly baptized members went without a calling. How interesting, he thought, that 150 years ago we took people like that, assembled them into companies of pioneers, and demanded greatness of them. We sent them across the plains and said, "You can do it. You can do anything." That is the spirit we need to have as we go forth and build up the Lord's Church.

Now a third point. I have heard a certain phrase used many times by members of the Twelve and of the First Presidency. When we go to new countries and open them up to missionary work, we always go through the front door. Now what does that mean, the front door? We do not hide who we are. We do not do anything clandestinely. We obey the laws of the land and knock on the door and say, "May we come in?" to the powers that be. That is how we always do it. That is how it will happen in China, Cuba, Bangladesh, or any of the nearly one hundred countries where we still do not have missionaries. We will go right in the front door. That may seem virtually impossible, but it will happen. Some of those doors are still closed, tightly closed. But if it is not possible to go through the front door, we will wait patiently, and the time will come when God will open those doors and we will go through them.

I do not know how many of you have been in the chapel of the Joseph Smith Memorial Building. I think it is one of the most beautiful rooms in the world. There is a powerful spirit there. The General Authorities of the Church meet there during every general conference for training. In that chapel, as you look up to the stand and above the organ, there is a beehive carved in wood, the symbol of the state of Utah. But it is more than that. I believe that the beehive is a symbol of the Church and kingdom of God in the last days, but not in the way we usually think about it. We usually think of a beehive as highly organized, and the bees are all very diligent. We as Latter-day Saints do tend to be very organized and, for the most part, fairly diligent. But that is not the analogy I would use. Every early spring or late winter when the earth is dead and the flowers and plants have retreated into their hibernation for the year, the bees begin to go forth. By their diligent labors, they pollinate those dormant flowers, trees, other plants, and grasses, making possible the renewal of the earth each spring. As I think of the Church and kingdom of God, I think of us here in the tops of the mountains as a beehive that sends forth tens of thousands of missionaries and other leaders to renew the earth and prepare the way for the spring and the summer of His coming.

Now another point about the growth of the Church worldwide. We must not fear opposition or persecution. If there is one thing that spreads as fast the gospel, it is anti-Mormon literature. I was astonished to see in Russia how fast anti-Mormons would catch up with us. We were always one step ahead, but not by far. We would open up a city, and within a few weeks some minister would pass through, handing out anti-Mormon literature beautifully translated into Russian. When we dedicated our first chapel in Russia in the city of Vyborg, which is just north of St. Petersburg, a center devoted to the distribution of anti-Mormon literature opened up, complete with full-time employees, a building, and everything else right in that same city. I used to worry about that. I used to worry that our Saints would get hold of this stuff and be poisoned by it or disillusioned. I do not worry about that anymore. I have come to understand what President Brigham Young meant one time when he said that the more it is attacked, the stronger it will become. On one occasion he put that in a more colorful way when he said, "Every time you kick 'Mormonism,' you kick it up stairs: you never kick it down stairs. The Lord Almighty so orders it."[5]

---

5.   Brigham Young, in *Journal of Discourses* (London: Latter-day Saints' Book Depot, 1854–86), 7:145.

You may recall another so-called crisis that took place in Russia when a very prominent military officer made some very unkind statements about the Church. He said that Mormons were, in effect, idiots, that the Church was a cult, that it was evil, and that it had to be eradicated from Russia. Now we know that someone was putting words in his mouth because he did not know a thing about the Church, which he later admitted. But someone with influence on him had gotten him to put that into the speech. We were very concerned. This got quite a bit of publicity in Russia and abroad. Members of the Church were frightened. They thought the officer might become president of Russia, and he still might. They did not know what this meant for their future. But again, you can kick Mormonism, but you will only kick it upstairs.

In the months immediately following his statement, our missionaries had a notable increase in success. Why? Because, number one, there had been so much publicity about it that people were curious. They wanted to know, what in the world is this? And, number two, as several people said to the missionaries, Russians have learned from a lifetime of experience that when a prominent leader says something is bad, it has got to be good. We had a sudden flood of discussions and baptisms. In the end, the military officer in question apologized for his remarks and admitted that he did not know what he was talking about. We got another burst of publicity. I can honestly say that the whole incident turned to the good of the kingdom. Again, it appeared to be a crisis, but it turned to our good.

A fifth point about preaching the gospel. More people are born into the world every few months than the entire population of the Church. Our task from this perspective may seem hopeless, but in the long run the gospel will indeed be preached to every creature and will resound in every ear. The long run may include the Millennium, and it certainly includes the vast work taking place in the spirit world. It is prophesied in the scriptures that the gospel will be preached to every nation, kindred, tongue, and people before the end shall come (see D&C 42:58). I believe that literally means that every nation and every people will have an opportunity to hear the gospel in some form or another. But it does not necessarily mean that every individual on the face of the earth will hear the gospel message before the Savior comes. Every people, to some degree, or in some degree of representation, will hear the gospel message, but not necessarily every person. Why do I say this?

It is clear from prophecies about the last days and the Millennium that when Christ comes, there will be at least three categories of people on the earth. There will be the righteous remnant waiting to meet Him. There will be the wicked who will be destroyed. The wicked, I take to mean, are those who have willfully rejected the gospel, willfully rejected every call to repentance and gone on in pursuit of evil things. But it is also clear that there is a third group sometimes referred to in the scriptures as the "heathen nations" (D&C 45:54) who will remain but will not yet be members of the Church.

The prophet Zechariah prophesied that after the Lord comes the rain would not fall on those nations until they submit to the Lord's law (see Zechariah 14:17–18). I do not know who those nations are, but I suspect that they may include some of the larger nations of the earth where we will preach the gospel but be unable to reach every last person. I share this thought with you—and it is my personal thought—but I share it because we need to understand that God has a timetable, that no one will be left out. No one will fail to receive their salvation, either because we did not do our part or because there was not enough time. God will allow all to hear His word before the Judgment Day.

I want to turn now to the proclamation on the family and talk specifically about families and what I would call the Church's competitive advantage as we go forth into the world. About twenty years ago, I was a graduate student in Cambridge, Massachusetts, and an unusual opportunity came for me to attend a conference in Italy. This was a conference of the International Society of Strategic Studies, and it brought together prominent political, industrial, and academic leaders from around the world—cabinet members, CEOs from the defense industry, and some of the world's most prominent specialists on national security.

I hasten to add that I was not there because of my own prominence. I was only a graduate student, but I had been able to go represent an organization that had a permanent membership. So there I was in Stresa, Italy, this beautiful resort town, staying at a five-star hotel, rubbing shoulders with very prominent people before whom I felt very intimidated. As the conference went on—it was about a three- or four-day conference—I became more and more overwhelmed by the people I was meeting just casually at dinner and before dinner—names I had heard about, titles that sounded very important, and so forth.

On about the third day of the conference, I took a break and walked up to the train station in Stresa to buy a ticket for my departure following the conference. The conference meetings had been in a large hotel by a lake, and as I walked up the hillside into the town, I left the resort area of five-star hotels. I found myself in a very ordinary, quiet, little Italian town. I think I had been feeling a little bit tense at this conference, always wanting to be on my best behavior. As I walked into the little town of Stresa, I relaxed. I felt very peaceful and calm. I no longer felt that I had to be on guard to say the most intelligent thing at every moment. I could just be myself. As I walked, I saw a little Italian family, a mother and her little children playing in the street. The children were running back and forth playing some kind of a game, and the mother was watching over them. I felt a great love for this family. Looking at them, I also felt an impression that it is of such people that the kingdom will be built. It will not be built by our networking with the most famous people in the world, making contacts with them, and using their leverage and power to somehow open those doors. It will be built by the plain and simple of the earth. They will hear our message because they are plain and simple and because what we have for them will bless their lives and the lives of their families.

BYU's Kennedy Center studies culture extensively. It even publishes *Culturgrams* that try to help people understand different cultures, how they think, how they operate, and their manners and traditions. It is a very important and worthwhile endeavor, and I think that it has been recognized not only within the Church but more broadly by industry and others who use *Culturgrams*. It is important that we study culture. It is important that we understand the languages, history, literature, and sociology of other nations and ethnic groups. But the human family has more commonalities than differences among us. Among the things that unite us is the great human universal—the family.

There may be various cultures with different wedding traditions, different courtship traditions, different degrees of patriarchy versus matriarchy, and so forth, but the fact remains that the concept of a family, of a biological father and mother who raise their children, teach them what is right and wrong, socialize them into the values of their culture, is virtually universal. The exceptions, if there are any, are very minor and might generally occur in some very primitive, throwback-type cultures. But where you find civilization in any degree, you find family. We understand as Latter-day Saints the importance of families. The Turkish people understand that, the Mexican people understand that, the Lebanese people understand that, the African people understand that, the Chinese people understand that, and the Japanese people understand that. The only people who seem to not understand anymore are our fellow Americans.

It is here, and to some degree in Europe, that intellectual movements have arisen in the last forty years that deliberately and openly seek to undermine the family as the fundamental unit of society. As a result we are heading toward disaster in our own country. In the proclamation on the family, the Brethren say, "Further, we warn that the disintegration of the family will bring upon individuals, communities, and nations the calamities foretold by ancient and modern prophets."[6]

In the last ten years, believe it or not, the crime rate in the United States has been dropping. There are a lot of reasons for that, but among one group it has been rising, and rising dramatically. Do you know what group that is? Children. Crimes committed by children and juveniles are going up at a stunning rate. Crimes committed by other age-groups are going down. What is happening and what will continue to happen with increasing frequency is that as the family breaks apart, as children are raised without fathers by single mothers or sometimes simply by institutions, including day care, they are often not socialized, not taught what they need to know about right and wrong, not taught love and affection, and not taught how to compromise or how to get along with others.

A generation is being raised without conscience. The amazing thing about the terrible crimes that have been committed by children and juveniles has been the complete lack of remorse on the part of the perpetrators. In many cases, they do not feel any sense of guilt nor any sense of sorrow. They did what they wanted to do. They had never been taught differently. It is literally an impending disaster for our nation.

I am going to recommend a book, and while I do not usually do this, this book did not get the attention it deserved. Published by Oxford University Press in 1991 (and I am still amazed to this day that they published it), it was written by cultural historian James Lincoln Collier and is called *The Rise of Selfishness in America.*[7] It shows how at the turn of the century there was a culture of vice that existed in ghettos of our inner cities, where prostitution, drug use, crime, and the like was contained. The values held to by those little

6. "The Family: A Proclamation to the World," *Ensign*, November 1995, 102.

7. See James Lincoln Collier, *The Rise of Selfishness in America* (New York: Oxford University Press, 1991).

pockets were values of selfishness. "I can do whatever I please. I do what satisfies me alone." The author, in exquisite detail, shows how that culture of selfishness has spread and been adopted more widely until it has become the culture of U.S. society. He also makes this interesting observation about families. He talks about the fact that we are abandoning our children to an enormous degree. Between a soaring divorce rate and the number of children born to unwed mothers, a majority of our children will spend at least a portion of their childhoods in single-parent homes, in effect being raised without fathers.

This is an extremely unusual circumstance, perhaps unique in human experience. In no known human society, past or present, have so many children been raised outside of an intact nuclear family. The author goes on to talk about the consequences of that. His solution (and this is why I say it is astonishing to think this was published in the 1990s by Oxford University Press) is for sexual morality to be reinstituted in our society, including premarital chastity, for women to stop working and come back home to raise children, and for the family and family values to be made the crowning values of our whole society.

If we do not do this, he predicts, we will have a disaster on our hands, just as the Brethren suggested in the proclamation. Another article that recently appeared in the *Wall Street Journal* talked about the consequences of day care for children.[8] It pointed out that dozens of studies by social scientists, many of whom do not share our values, show that with few exceptions, children who are raised in day-care centers, particularly young children—one-, two-, and three-year-olds—become much more aggressive in their dealings with other people. They prove to be unable to compromise. They prove to be

8. See Sue Shellenberger, "Child Care Is Worse than Believed, with Safety Jeopardized, Study Suggests," *Wall Street Journal*, February 6, 1995; Sue Shellenberger, "Impact of Child Care Is Mixed, Study Says," *Wall Street Journal*, April 4, 1997.

unable to show affection. They prove to be more abusive in all their relationships. These are not ideologically biased studies; they are simply scientific studies on the impact of day care on children.

If I were to say this at almost any other university across our country, it would be very controversial, cause a big uproar in the audience, and I would not be invited back again because these are not popular views. They are not politically correct views. But if I were to go to almost any country in the so-called Third World—Africa, Asia, the Middle East, and Latin America—these views would be accepted as common sense and normal. Perhaps these views would not be accepted in every university by every professor, but in general those societies still defend and still understand the importance of traditional family values.

I hope you are familiar with the work that Brother Richard Wilkins is doing, a professor at the BYU law school, and the organization he has established, NGO Family Voice. His organization is going to United Nations–sponsored conferences on the family and other world conferences to defend the traditional family against the wave of antifamily values that are being spread, mostly by U.S. social scientists and by some European social scientists. What he is finding is that while he and his colleagues are pariahs among those from the United States, they are winning friends and influence across these other countries and cultures who are appalled by what they see happening in the United States.

These countries for decades have looked up to the United States as a model of what a country can be because of our prosperity, technology, freedoms, and human rights. Many of those people still see the United States as a model. But when they send their children to U.S. universities and those children come home, they are shocked by the experiences their children have had and the strange ideas they have in their heads. They do not want to send their children back to the United States.

We have had an interesting experience here at Brigham Young University bringing students from Jordan and other Arab countries, but especially Jordan. These are the children, sons and daughters, of the elite of Jordan, who in increasing numbers are anxious to have their children come to BYU—not Harvard, not Yale, not Princeton, not Berkeley, but BYU. Why? Because here their children can find some refuge from the vices and aberrant social philosophies that are so prominent at other universities. Here they find support for the traditional family, for high moral standards, for good health practices, for wholesome living.

In other words, what we believe in and what we stand for may not be highly popular in elite circles in our own country today, but it makes eminent sense to most of the people of the world. In increasing numbers, they will flock to our banner. Our love and support for the family thus gives us a great comparative advantage as we strive to build the kingdom of God around the world. It is one of the strongest and straightest arrows in our quiver. It will soften hearts and prepare people everywhere to accept the fulness of the restored gospel.

I have spoken today of five ways in which the kingdom of God will go forth across the earth. In conclusion, I would bear witness of him who is the author of this work, whose power and glory makes it all possible. When all is said and done, The Church of Jesus Christ of Latter-day Saints will prevail not because of the efforts of man but because of the power of God working miracles across the face of the earth, preparing the hearts of God's children to receive their Lord and Redeemer. I bear witness that He lives. I bear witness that this is His Church and kingdom. I bear witness that He will come again and the day shall come when the knowledge of God will cover the earth as the waters cover the sea.

© by Intellectual Reserve, Inc.

Elder Bruce D. Porter is a member of the First Quorum of the Seventy. This essay was presented at "Family and the Church: Cultural and Political Challenges," the International Society's ninth annual conference, August 1998, Brigham Young University, Provo, Utah.

Chapter 18

An Ethical Dilemma:
The Imposition of Values on Other Cultures

David A. Shuler

THIS CHAPTER IS based on the assumption that an examination of ethics, particularly the ethics of change as it relates to international development, is not only interesting but needed in the current development discourse. Particularly, I would argue, it is a subject that has special implications and importance to Latter-day Saints.

Below is a reproduction of an interesting correspondence that I came across from Mahatma Gandhi to Adolf Hitler in the earlier years of World War II:

> As at Wardha,
> C. P.
> India,
> 23.7.39
> Dear friend,
>
> Friends have been urging me to write to you for the sake of humanity. But I have resisted their request, because of the feeling that any letter from me would be an impertinence. Something tells me that I must not calculate and that I must make my appeal for whatever it may be worth.
>
> It is quite clear that you are today the one person in the world who can prevent a war which may reduce humanity to a savage state. Must you pay that price for an object however

worthy it may appear to you to be? Will you listen to the appeal of one who has deliberately shunned the method of war not without considerable success? Any way I anticipate your forgiveness, if I have erred in writing to you.

I remain,
Your sincere friend,
(Signed M. K. Gandhi and addressed to Herr Hitler in Berlin)[1]

The process of change and its internal and external conditions are commonly examined and discussed in academic circles, but the ethics of change seem less frequently questioned. In this chapter, I question the colloquial use and definition of *idealism* and suggest that inherent to our vernacular use of the term *idealism* is the notion of change. All idealists seek for change. I also propose that there exist *change orthodoxies*, certain assumptions—akin to types of ethnocentrisms—that dictate our views on what needs to change and what does not, which direction to change and the speed of that change. Too seldom individuals, institutions, and even academic disciplines question these orthodoxies; they are often given free passage. I will finally suggest that change involves ethics, in that ethics is the study of good and bad, right and wrong, and just and unjust, and that change can, and often does, fall into the categories of what we would call good and bad, right and wrong, or just and unjust. A discussion of international development is a discussion of change, and a discussion on change requires a consideration of ethics.

An idealist. There seems to be a lot of unanswered questions around the notion of idealism. What are people implying when they say this person or that person is an idealist? Is it true that most of us as children and youth were more idealistic? If so, why? What would be the cause of this phenomenon—this pattern of beginning life with idealism, then losing it? As adults, most of us have not ended up as idealists. Is this trend of youthful idealism a onetime and unique fallout of the sixties generation? Or is it the historical norm since

---

1.   From Peter Rühe, *Gandhi: A Photo Biography* (New York: Phaidon Press, 2001).

the beginning of the human race, repeated each generation as the consequence of loving parents wishing to shelter us as children, thus giving us the illusion of impossible things—*idealistic* things? Or is this phenomenon simply due to young, innocent minds that are unwilling to accept what we adults might term the ugly things of life (e.g., brutality and greed)? Why is it that some individuals persist in their idealism well into adulthood, while rare individuals persist to deathbed in pure idealism? I think we often label these people with titles of hero, martyr, great leader, or even prophet.

Though I have some confusion about the nature and usage of idealism, I would wager that many people would describe the participants at this conference on international development as idealists. Are you an idealist? The sloppy definitions of idealism, as well as the ambiguity of whether it is a good or bad quality to possess, may be disconcerting to an audience wanting to change the world for good. The ambiguity may also reflect a need to analyze the definition more carefully.

For a start, does idealism have more to do with naïveté or with hope? This association makes a considerable difference. Is idealism gullible and irrational, or is it looking for the bright side and accentuating the good? Is it connected to hope? To faith? To tolerance? Tolerant people are often labeled as idealists. I personally cannot support a Pollyanna idealist, but on the other hand those who aspire to sophistication by finding the worst in everything—and everyone—seem to me to be equally useless and much less enjoyable to be around. Tolerance seems not only *politically* correct but also *morally* correct.

I believe it is axiomatic to say that every idealist seeks and supports some type of change. If a person was completely satisfied with the status quo, then I do not believe anyone would call them an idealist. An idealist, regardless of our definition, is, ultimately, a person with elevated ideas, or *ideals*, of how the world, or some part of it, *should* be and not how it *is*. If this assumption is true, then both Hitler and Gandhi were idealists. But if this were the case, what, then, is the difference between the two? Just saying, "One guy is good, and one guy is bad," seems to deny us of the opportunity to discover more completely what we mean by good and bad as well as a more thoughtful understanding of the concept of idealism. I keep coming across the question, "What is the difference between historical colonialism and present-day international development efforts?" This question, I believe, challenges some assumptions of what idealistic change is. Will future generations read textbooks less forgiving of our present-day efforts "to bring prosperity" than even the efforts of colonialists "to bring civilization"? Will we be held accountable for setting in motion certain cause and effect sequences that led to bad, wrong, and unjust events, just as we hold the colonial powers responsible for their initiation of changes that led to undesirable consequences? Who decides what change is good and needed and what change is bad? Which criteria are used in these determinations? In light of the predicament in the Middle East and in other parts of the world, when are people freedom fighters and when are they terrorists? When are development workers humanitarians and philanthropists, and when are they cultural and even political imperialists?

Many of us work in development at a much smaller scale and on less grandiose projects than the above questions seem to be addressing. But undesirable, even destructive, consequences can be initiated at the community level. In fact, our potential to have impact—lasting impact—is much greater at the community level than at regional or even national levels of even the smallest countries. In some ways we perhaps need to be most cautious in instigating change.

Culture and Cultural Values

I will not bore readers with a lengthy discussion of the definition of culture. Those working both within and without the social sciences who are very experienced in international environments will verify the complex and profound nature of the notion of culture. Many bookshelves are full of books dedicated to this one subject. Culture is real, and its effects and manifestations are real and often profound. Anyone, whether or not from academia, who has lived for any extended period of time in a foreign community will verify the significance of culture. Still, I would agree with those who claim that few individuals, regardless of their education and intellect and regardless of how extensive their intercultural living, truly comprehend the scope and magnitude of what the notion attempts to convey in the simplicity of one word—*culture.* Noted anthropologist Clifford Geertz defined culture as simply a set, or system, of symbols and meanings.[2] But when we consider that virtually *anything* and *everything* in life can be a symbol—a wink, a sound, the volume of sound (such as a whisper), a color, clothing, food, architecture, how we stand or sit, a tone of voice, an adornment, body parts and sizes, stories, proverbs, metaphors, writing itself (that is, the letters and words on this page), flora, fauna, social positions and titles, religious rites, myths, and so forth—then we realize that his definition may be simple, but its implications are not.

Another point regarding culture: human beings place meaning, and sometimes what we call *value*, on everything they see, hear, taste, touch, smell, or think of in their life, and the meaning, or value, they place is greatly affected by their upbringing within their social and physical environments. From the perspective of religion, particularly a Latter-day Saint perspective, most of us would not argue with this viewpoint, since there seems to be little or no contrasting points with our theology. Most religions would add the factors of spirituality, divine or supernatural interventions, and characteristics brought from a premortal or another mortal life as affecting mean-

---

2. Clifford Geertz is sometimes referred to as "the father of interpretive anthropology" and is perhaps the most influential anthropologist of our time. Some of his most popular works include *The Interpretation of Cultures: Selected Essays* (New York: BasicBooks, 1973); *Local Knowledge: Further Essays in Interpretive Anthropology* (New York: BasicBooks, 1983); and *Available Light: Anthropological Reflections on Philosophical Topics* (Princeton, NJ: Princeton University Press, 2000).

ing and values. As Latter-day Saints we certainly would not hesitate to include these factors as contributing to our identities, that is, who we say we are and what we say we value.

Cultural values are commonly discussed and defined as the most central paradigms within a culture. In the overly simple, and perhaps overly used, model of an iceberg to represent culture, the cultural values are analogous to the deep heavy mass far below the surface of the water. Unlike those evident parts of culture near or above the surface, such as clothing, body language, eating habits, and religious rites, values are not easily discernible, though they are the hidden bulk of the iceberg that gives rise to the surface characteristics.

In 1961 two scholars, Florence Kluckhohn and Fred Strodtbeck, published a somewhat classic work, which since has been frequently quoted in anthropological publications, as well as publications in intercultural communications and various other social sciences.[3] In their publication, the authors discuss the significance of what they call *cultural value orientations*. They define cultural value orientations as "complex but definitely patterned principles . . . which give order and direction to the ever-flowing stream of human acts and thoughts."[4] Stella Ting-Toomey, commenting on their work, describes cultural value orientations as "the basic lenses through which we view our own actions and the actions of others. . . . They also set the emotional tone for how we interpret and evaluate cultural strangers' behavior . . . and influence our overall self-conception, and our self-conception, in turn, influences our behavior."[5]

In their work, Kluckhohn and Strodtbeck focus on five areas that they felt were universal or common to the human experience: (1) people's relationship to nature (do they submit to it, live in har-

3. See Florence Rockwood Kluckhohn and Fred L. Strodtbeck, *Variations in Value Orientations* (Evanston, IL: Row, Peterson, 1961).

4. Kluckhohn and Strodtbeck, *Variations in Value Orientations*, 4.

5. Stella Ting-Toomey, *Communicating across Cultures* (New York: Guilford Press, 1999), 58.

mony with it, or control it?); (2) people's time sense (are they past-oriented, present-oriented, or future-oriented?); (3) people's belief in human nature (is it basically evil, neutral, or good?); (4) people's concept of activity (being, becoming, or doing); and (5) people's concept of social relations (lineality/authoritarian, collaterality/group decisions, or individualism/autonomy). There are many and varied cultural values and value orientations—perhaps hundreds, even thousands could be identified—and many social and cultural experts have spent years identifying and discussing similarities and differences in human societies.

When speaking of values, people often assume that values have moral or ethical underpinnings that are considered inherent to the word. This assumption is perfectly logical and understandable. We often use the term *value* when explaining or exploring highly ethical and moral topics. However, I will risk suggesting that the use of the term in the social science realm is not necessarily implying a moral or ethical dimension. Often values—in the social science sense of the word—are complex and difficult to isolate and therefore difficult to determine if linked to ethics or morality. Also clouding the issue is the ambiguity that cross-cultural comparisons can yield, simply due to our own ethnocentrisms and interpretations from our own cultural context or even our personal point of view. For example, in the study of Kluckhohn and Strodtbeck and with regard to the cultural value orientation concerning human nature—being basically evil or basically good—one might possibly argue a moral superiority of one or the other depending on circumstance or context. As a Latter-day Saint, I might argue for "basically evil" when referring to "the natural man" (see Mosiah 3:19; 16:3–5) and then conversely, at a different time or place, argue that our nature is basically good—we are the offspring of God (see Acts 17:28). Both these divergent views are valid Latter-day Saint perspectives in certain conditions and contexts.

Some values and principles lie at the heart of the gospel and would not be subjective or relative to context or conditions. These principles are well established and should guide us in everyday life.

But even these more absolute principles, I would propose, have a relative dimension. For example, Christ, being a Jewish male in His community and culture, would most likely have showed reverence and respect to the Father by covering His head with the *tallit*, or prayer shawl, as He taught or prayed in the synagogue, the temple, or even in the Garden of Gethsemane. In the community and culture where I live, I demonstrate that same principle of respect and reverence by uncovering my head when in church or when I pray. The significance of Geertz's definition of culture as "systems of symbols and meanings" thus becomes apparent. The meaning, or principle, of respect and reverence is maintained and manifested by two very different symbols of two cultures. The importance and focus on the principle is well established, but how it is demonstrated is left to the history of humankind and the relative development of cultural traditions throughout the ages. Meanings may be absolute or well established, but symbols can still vary and be relative to context and environment.

Development as Imposition

In light of the nature and importance of culture, its relevance becomes quite obvious to the field of international development. Trying to implement change in a cross-cultural relationship is challenging and can even be dangerous. As participators in development, we naturally are attempting to bring about change with the assumption that we can gauge and guess what the rippling effect of our actions will bring. The complication comes when the environment and context within which we initiate change (speaking of all the aspects of environment, for example, social, religious, political, economic) is different from our own and is unfamiliar, or worse, unknown. Colonialism is one historical example in regard to this discussion of change and culture. Most students of history need little convincing that colonialism, regardless of intention or motive, brought change—change that was to a large extent imposed. These changes led to longer lasting effects—some good, some bad. In reference to the negative, sometimes colonial activities were immediately nefarious in nature, while at other times activities took years, even decades, to lead to undesirable outcomes. The same attitudes, assumptions, and processes of cultural imperialism continue to occur today. Whether it is worse in our day, with regard to the intensity of the imperialism or breadth of its influence, I am not qualified to say. I only can attest to its presence in many development activities and in the attitudes of many development workers. Sometimes it exists in concepts like *modernization, westernization,* and *globalization.*

Modernization theory is one theory accused of ignoring differing environments or contexts—in short, ignoring culture and cultural values. This theory would be described by those opposing its views as purporting that "poor" individuals or communities have been made poor or are being kept poor by the fact that they are not modern, that either they refuse or have not had the opportunity to modernize. The theory can be, and often is, used by those who speak of economic systems, technology, medical methods, health-care systems, agricultural practices, or political systems and ideologies, just to give a partial listing. At the center of all this theorizing is the belief of a type of unilinear evolution—that all societies evolve in the same way and along the same line of progressive stages, with our Western culture being the most evolved and advanced. Change toward modernization seems to be orthodox—that is, generally accepted with little questioning and with the assumption that it is a change toward the better.

In a very cheeky essay, written several years ago, I played the role of a cynic and attacked several theories in development. Modernization theory was one of the orthodoxies I heavily criticized. This was very "tongue-in-cheek" and was meant for the eyes and ears of students in a course I was then teaching, an introduction to development studies. It was meant to elicit discussion. Although I exaggerated my disdain, in reality I do find modernization theory to be not just arrogant and condescending but also dangerous and perhaps leading to unethical decisions and behavior. If you will forgive me, I will share with you some parts of this essay which I shared with my class:

> The concept of *modernity* cannot be very modern—I just cannot believe it. Surely all of history, from the beginning, is filled with example after example of societies, communities, and individuals holding themselves up as specimens of modernity—the "latest and greatest"! So, why does each rising *modern* society, community, or individual think and act like they are so unique, so special, so enviable? And why do they convince themselves, and everyone else, that no one can be happy, content, or "developed" unless they become *modern* like themselves? (But then, this same society just one or two generations later will be seen as old-fashioned, out of date, ineffective, and even foolish!)

I then go on to tell the students of a lecture I heard from a very capable professor:

> I once heard a speaker being very critical of our general approaches in development. I remember him raising his voice and saying, "Development has always been about one group of people *doing* development *to* another group of people," then he really raised his voice and said, "Development should not be about *doing*." At the time I was not sure what he meant or whether I agreed with him. I have had a number of years to wonder what he meant by his statement "doing development." I think what he meant has everything to do with this obsession of being modern. Modernization theory dominated most of the decades of the last century. Many spoke against it, but it persisted and still persists. I do not think much has changed except our language of how we talk about it. Even the use of the word "participatory," a word describing a very popular approach of development organizations today, does not guarantee freedom from modernization theory, since it can also mean "Come, all you poor backward people, and participate in our modern way of making you modern." What is our goal? To make *them* like *us*—modern—and to allow them to have modern things like us? This belief and approach must be questioned, and fortunately, has been questioned by many, such as

authors Katy Gardner and David Lewis: "Modernisation, as both a theory and a set of strategies, is open to criticism on virtually every front. Its assumption that all change inevitably follows the Western model is both breathtakingly ethnocentric and empirically incorrect. . . . While theories of modernisation assume that local cultures and 'peasant' traditionalism are obstacles to development, . . . 'actor-oriented research' has consistently found that, far from being 'irrational,' people in poor countries are open to change if they perceive it to be in their interest. They often know far better than development planners how to strategise and get the best from difficult circumstances, yet modernisation strategies rarely, if ever, pay heed to local knowledge. Indeed, local culture is generally either ignored by planners or treated as a 'constraint.'"[6]

Westernization is a more ambiguous term. It could be defined as the trend of non-Western societies to embrace the symbols of those referred to as Western nations. Some people tend to use the term as being synonymous with modernization, which may be appropriate in some cases. However, westernization seems to imply a process of cultural domination, and, I should add, a process that seems not so much imposed as it is invited and desired by those being westernized. Westernization is not so much considered a theory or set of assumptions as modernization theory is, but it is rather a description of a process taking place. It enters our discussion not so much as a factor in development or underdevelopment but as an outcome, which can be encouraged and supported by some change agents. I will not attempt the same criticism with those promoting westernization as I did with those believing in modernization theory mainly because I think there are few who feel it is necessary to westernize in order to "develop." Still, it is a concept that development organizations should be aware of, as well as its potential consequences on individuals, families, and communities, particularly with regard to their concept and value of self.

---

6.   Katy Gardner and David Lewis, *Anthropology, Development, and the Post-modern Challenge* (London: Pluto Press, 1996), 14–15.

Globalization consists of very real processes with very real consequences, but nobody really seems to know what they are or how
they actually function. Those who speak against globalization and
seek to stop it are perhaps as naive as those who promote it. As with
all social and cultural changes, there will be those who benefit from
change and those who will get hurt, and it is probably true that no one
person, government, or group of governments can stop globalization
from advancing, even if there were a consensus and desire to do so. But
any change agent, whether a large multilateral agency or a tiny nongovernmental organization (NGO), should be aware of the existence
of globalization and seek to protect local individuals and communities, especially those who are most vulnerable, from harmful and
unjust consequences. Some cultural environments, including sociopolitical systems, have few built-in protections against certain
nefarious influences of globalization. Family life, kinship relations,
reciprocity, religious beliefs and behaviors, ecosystems, and local
economies and vocations can all be debilitated and in some cases
devastated by the process of globalization.

Safeguards against Imposition

This is the section about which I would very much like to receive
suggestions. This is where we need our collective wisdom in meeting
some very large challenges, doing so ethically while preserving the
agency of those we seek to help. Very briefly I would like to speak
of two safeguards against imposition: *cultural congruence* and *true
participation*.

When speaking of cultural congruence, an element or activity
of a development effort would not only be appropriate and effective
to the cultural environment, but the attitudes and perceptions of
everyone involved, including the change agents, would be respectful and reinforcing of cultural values. Obtaining cultural congruency requires considerable effort and longitudinal study. It requires
genuine concern and respect. The characteristics required to achieve
cultural congruence are best obtained through working among the

people and living as they live. Many hours of conversation, interviewing, observing, and participating in local life will be needed, and the level of success will directly correspond to the level of involvement and the total amount of time spent in meaningful activity and living. Methods of rapid appraisal and assessment most likely will not be adequate to assure congruency.

The method of participation was an idea too long in coming to the field of development. We would think that such a basic and commonsense idea would have been instinctive to development workers and organizations, but it was not. Perhaps it was not the overwhelming influences of certain orthodoxies such as modernization or even the good old-fashioned ethnocentrism that contributed to the assumption that we knew all the solutions and answers, so why bother involving the locals? Whatever the reason now, participatory approaches are virtually accepted and extolled by every camp. Robert Chambers, at Sussex University, has promoted participatory approaches with much success through the last decade or more. His book, *Whose Reality Counts? Putting the First Last,*[7] has influenced literally every level in development from the World Bank down to the smallest of NGOs. However, it seems that there is some debate as to what participation means. Several scholars and practitioners recently have started to question the extent and sincerity of certain efforts in participatory approaches. Bill Cooke (University of Manchester), David Mosse (University of London), R. L. Stirrat (Sussex University), and others make some salient points in the edited publication *Participation: The New Tyranny?*[8] These authors have concerns that modern-day versions of the old modernization strategies and even colonial mindsets are being disguised and labeled as participatory strategies in some current development projects.

---

7. See Robert Chambers, *Whose Reality Counts? Putting the First Last* (London: Intermediate Technology Publications, 1997).
8. See Bill Cooke and Uma Kothari, eds., *Participation: The New Tyranny?* (London: Zed Books, 2001).

In conclusion to these comments on the importance of participation, I should say that true participation requires an environment of trust, openness, respect, and friendship, where locals' input is highly valued and guides all decision making. When this type of participation exists, then the last becomes first, as Chambers recommends; that is, the local input and insider perspective takes precedence over foreign or outsider opinion. And when this occurs, true participation is fostered and imposition becomes less of a threat.

The Gospel, Agency, and Development

When speaking of idealism, we, as Latter-day Saints, will sometimes speak of the "ideal world" as a world without violence, hunger, sickness, exploitation, and abuse; but in our theology, is this really the ideal world? I would suggest that the restored gospel principles teach us that the world of agency is the ideal world, or at least the beginning of it. Herein lies the problem, or paradox: a world of agency inherently allows for violence, hunger, sickness, exploitation, and abuse. This paradox suggests that free and uncoerced agents will, and do, make mistakes and misjudgments, which result in the creation or promotion of the unhappiness we witness in every society. Then what is the ideal world? I fear that this would be a hot debate, even among Latter-day Saints. I will suggest one answer that presents itself: the ideal world is a world where free agents choose to educate themselves concerning, then actually live by, the principles of happiness; subsequently these same agents then, in nonselfish and nonmanipulative ways, help others to see the mistakes and misjudgments that lead to their unhappiness (for example, violence, hunger, sickness, exploitation, and abuse).

When I first started thinking about the ethics of those striving for change, I looked for counterexamples—extremists, if you will—and rather quickly came up with the almost diametric opposites of Gandhi and Hitler. Of course they were contemporaries, but I did not think of this, since it is difficult and unlikely to think of the pair sharing anything—one just does not put the two in any common category or simultaneous thought. Then, just several weeks later a friend gave me a beautiful book on Gandhi—a coffee-table book—and as I flipped through the pages, my eye caught the photocopied letter (the one placed at the beginning of this paper), and I saw the two men's names there on the same page. It then occurred to me that they did have things in common, and many of these are the same things that we idealists share and desire. Idealism can be a very good thing that motivates great women and men to do great things. But since what motivates us quite regularly deals with right or wrong, good or bad, and just or unjust, we must be aware, or beware, of its potential to do harm.

Like most people, I aspire to be a Gandhi, not a Hitler. I aspire to liberate and help and to facilitate change in favor of the greater good. But the specifics of *how* it is done and *for whom* that greater good is accomplished remain debatable. They, Gandhi and Hitler, were alike in many ways: men focused and dedicated to a cause, confessing deep concerns about the welfare of their people, being fully convinced of the greatness of the motherland (India) and the fatherland (Germany), and being committed to a destiny that they envisioned. I see both of them striving to bring change, a change that would bring to pass their vision, their version of the ideal. Still, even considering these similarities, they were very different men, and they lived by different principles. Gandhi led by example, not by imposition. He loved his people, but he did not allow that love to diminish their agency. He loved democracy, and he consistently strove to give the poor a voice and to empower them. His idealism drove him to a lifetime of service and unselfishness, and in the Ammon fashion of the Book of Mormon, he won himself into the heart of almost every man, woman, and child of the subcontinent, as well as the favor of common folk in many Western nations. He traveled the length and breadth of the subcontinent in the common-class train. He wore his people's clothes, common clothes, ate common village food, and slept in common traditional housing. He practiced subsistence horticulture and even spun his own clothing. His development project was culturally congruent and truly participatory!

I apologize for using the dramatic distinction of Hitler and Gandhi to make my less dramatic points concerning ethics and development. It was a dramatic distinction indeed. But somewhere between Gandhi and Hitler are the rest of us. And surely somewhere between the extremes of these two idealists is a large middle ground where most of life happens and where things blend, bend, and become less clear. Finding an idealist or leader near the middle of this middle ground may leave us to wonder as to which side we fall. In the middle, with all the visions and all the efforts to change, we can wonder whose idealism is more right than wrong. Are there absolutes and universals in idealism, or are there only preferred particulars and relativity? And what of change? When does the end justify the means when moving toward the ideal? Does a quest for the most just ideal ever condone the most unjust of actions to achieve it? As Gandhi queried Hitler, "Must you pay that price for an object however worthy it may appear to you to be?" Do *injustices* ever support and promote *just* causes? Can imposition, manipulation, or force ever be condoned or considered ethical when they support a worthy end? Are *unjust* actions ever *justified*? I wish the answer were as simple as a resounding "No, never," but something tells me that this response would be naive. I think it would also be naive to think that Gandhi was always *Gandhian* and never *Hitlerian*. These are all further questions for a study in the ethics of change.

Let us be idealists that recognize and respect agency and are aware of our motives, predispositions, and areas of ignorance. It is safer for us to submit to the will of others when it is their decisions and their stewardships; ethics, if not gospel principles, require this of us. Development should be about others, not ourselves; we can participate, where appropriate, in influencing their lives and giving advice when we are invited, but even caution is needed in giving advice, because advice can easily turn to compulsion and manipulation. We must be aware of our impositions, meaning how our cultural values may differ from others we try to help, and how forceful we are, or can be, in influencing their ideas and actions and ultimately their lives.

We should question our methods and our assumptions, including any change orthodoxies that have not been humbly and thoughtfully challenged. As outsiders, we are influential and often are automatically given a status that we do not deserve. It is wise for us to move slowly and carefully. Even we as well-intentioned idealists, wanting only good outcomes, can diminish or even rob another's agency, thus claiming the glory for ourselves. From the very beginning, we have known that this approach is not in keeping with what is good, right, and just. Let us utilize this gospel principle in informing our development theory.

I end this chapter by stating that I do not claim any special insight or understanding into these important topics. I am intrigued and challenged with the questions and issues surrounding the ethics of change and at the same time convinced that more careful discussions are needed by those of us involved in international development and especially by those of us who consider ourselves idealists.

David A. Shuler is the International Field Studies program coordinator at Brigham Young University. This essay was presented at "The Gospel, Professional Ethics, and Cross-Cultural Experience," the International Society's fourteenth annual conference, August 2003, Brigham Young University, Provo, Utah.

Chapter 19

The Paradox of Religious Pluralism and Religious Uniqueness

Elder Charles Didier

I would like to thank the International Society for the invitation to address this distinguished audience. I use the word *distinguished* on purpose as it means literally "to separate by pricking." Your mark of distinction, of excellence, is your testimony of the divinity of Christ and His restored Church on the earth today. Using this mark in your professional field is making a difference in the way The Church of Jesus Christ of Latter-day Saints is being known, recognized, and established in the nations of the world.

As for myself, my field is as general as it can be as a General Authority, and my only distinction is to prick the hearts of people with the word of God, as mentioned in Jarom 1:11–12:

> Wherefore, the prophets, and the priests, and the teachers, did labor diligently, exhorting with all long-suffering the people to diligence; teaching the law of Moses, and the intent for which it was given; persuading them to look forward unto the Messiah, and believe in him to come as though he already was. And after this manner did they teach them.
>
> And it came to pass that by so doing they kept them from being destroyed upon the face of the land; for they did prick

their hearts with the word, continually stirring them up unto repentance.

This proselyting message will never change; it is eternal in our mortal perspective. It is, of course, associated with the verb *to prick*, which also means to affect with anguish, grief or remorse, or repentance. Where did it start?

Physical and Spiritual Needs

From the very beginning of the history of mankind, man has been characterized by physical and spiritual needs, as we may refer to the so-called primitive man of Africa, Australia, and Neanderthal or to our biblical religious ancestors Adam and Eve. Their physical needs were their first priority in order to survive, and the earth became their first resource. Three essential questions were asked on a daily basis.

The man: "What are we going to eat tonight?"

The woman: "What am I going to wear tomorrow?"

Both of them: "Where are we going to find shelter and protection from the elements around us?"

But after being satisfied with an answer to their physical needs, namely, from the earth, there came the quest for knowledge about themselves, their existence, their hopes and pains, their future. How to face the challenges of life and especially death? Spiritual or philosophical needs emerged rapidly and were answered by revelation from God or by worshipping manmade idols. It seems that there was always an inborn need for worship or religion. It is the Greek historian Plutarch who wrote, "In history I have found cities without ports, cities without palaces, cities without schools, but never have I found cities without places of worship."

Religious Pluralism

Religious—as well as social, economical, or political—pluralism developed from the beginning in one form or another. The one religious form, the original, came by direct revelation from God giving knowledge of who to worship and how to worship and giving mankind a plan of happiness, also called the plan of redemption. Another religious form was a deviation from divine revelation that could be defined as human divination leading to a worship of manmade idols or man-created gods. This deviation, by the name of apostasy, would take place by defection from true knowledge or renunciation of true faith. It is interesting to note that despite eras of apostasy, they were always followed by a restoration of the true nature of God and His plan of redemption for His children. Such a period of establishing or restoring true religion was called a "dispensation"—God literally dispensing divine knowledge for the benefit of His children. Thus, in this religious pluralism, people had to deal with a fact called divine revelation and not only the uniqueness of it but also that this divine revelation had been witnessed by men called prophets, whose testimonies were recorded in sacred books.

Atheists, pagans, and idolaters did not have such written or revealed evidence except their own. In the Book of Mormon, Alma the prophet, confronting Korihor, the anti-Christ, asks him, "And now what evidence have ye that there is no God, or that Christ cometh not?" The answer is plain and direct, "I say unto you that ye have none, save it be your word only" (Alma 30:40). Evidence throughout the centuries testifies of the existence of God—even though some may choose to deny this existence.

For example, returning to our beginnings, we read of what happened to our religious ancestors, Adam and Eve, as they were pondering and praying about their spiritual needs. From the book of Moses in the Pearl of Great Price, we read: "And Adam and Eve, his wife, called upon the name of the Lord, and they heard the voice of the Lord from the way toward the Garden of Eden, speaking unto them, and they saw him not; for they were shut out from his presence. And he gave unto them commandments, that they should worship the Lord their God, and should offer the firstlings of their flocks, for an offering unto the Lord. And Adam was obedient unto the commandments of the Lord" (Moses 5:4–5).

Unique Role of Christ's Church

Religious uniqueness has always been declared by revelation from God, by angels—his messengers—or other means, and through prophets called by Him. Religion, a revealed system of beliefs, ordinances, rites, and a way of life, was to become an integral part of life to save man from his mortal and imperfect condition. A Savior and Redeemer was announced to bring to pass the immortality and eternal life of man through the Atonement. His name would be Jesus Christ, the Messiah, the Son of God.

Jumping over the centuries, we find the same reality today. The recent dedication of the Nauvoo Illinois Temple, a house of worship, is a vivid and modern example of what happened yesterday with Adam and Eve and what has continued in all the various dispensations of the gospel. May I first refer to the words uttered by the prophet of the Restoration, Joseph Smith, in his dedicatory prayer of the first temple in this modern dispensation of the fulness of the gospel, the Kirtland Temple:

> Remember all thy church, O Lord, with all their families, and all their immediate connections, with all their sick and afflicted ones, with all the poor and meek of the earth; that the kingdom, which thou hast set up without hands, may become a great mountain and fill the whole earth;
>
> That thy church may come forth out of the wilderness of darkness, and shine forth fair as the moon, clear as the sun, and terrible as an army with banners;
>
> And be adorned as a bride for that day when thou shalt unveil the heavens, and cause the mountains to flow down at thy presence, and the valleys to be exalted, the rough places made smooth; that thy glory may fill the earth. (D&C 109:72–74)

Is that prayer different from the dedicatory words of President Gordon B. Hinckley, our present prophet, for the Nauvoo Illinois Temple? Let us review a short excerpt:

Now, Beloved Father, this is Thy house, the gift of Thy thankful Saints. We pray that Thou wilt visit it. Hallow it with Thy presence and that of Thy Beloved Son. Let Thy Holy Spirit dwell here at all times. May Thy work be accomplished here, and Thine eternal purposes brought to pass in behalf of Thy children, both the living and the dead. May our hearts reach to Thee as we serve within these walls. May all who are baptized in behalf of those beyond the veil of death know that they are doing something necessary under Thine eternal plan. May those who are here endowed understand and realize the magnitude of the blessings that come of this sacred ordinance. Seal upon them the covenants which they make with Thee. Open their eyes to a clear perception of Thy divine purposes. As they move into the beautiful celestial room, may their minds be brought to an understanding of Thy glorious plan for the salvation and exaltation of Thy children.

May those who gather at the altars in the sealing rooms, whether in their own behalf or in behalf of their forebears, comprehend by the power of the Spirit Thy divine will concerning the eternity of the family—fathers, mothers, and children, joined together in an everlasting union. May they receive a vision of Thine infinite 'plan of happiness' which Thou hast designed for Thy faithful sons and daughters.

Again, from the beginning until now, all that has been done to exercise the true worship of a living God and His Son Jesus Christ has been accomplished through the establishment of the Church of Christ upon the earth. Modern revelation confirms it over and over, as I quote from the Doctrine and Covenants: "And also those to whom these commandments were given, might have power to lay the foundation of this church, and to bring it forth out of obscurity and out of darkness, the only true and living church upon the face of the whole earth, with which I, the Lord, am well pleased, speaking unto the church collectively and not individually" (1:30).

One God, one Savior, one plan of salvation, one church, one priesthood, one set of ordinances of salvation. That uniqueness has always been the subject not only of questioning this assertion but especially of criticism leading even to persecution. Elder Dallin H. Oaks once said, "Anyone who preaches unity risks misunderstanding." We may add that we are not only risking misunderstanding but also risking life—as we have witnessed in the cases of Joseph Smith the Prophet and even Jesus Christ, the Son of God.

How do we deal with that paradox of uniqueness declared by God and pluralism advertised by the world as being politically correct? Is it religiously correct to condemn and silence or persecute nonbelievers or members of other faiths?

One of the early Apostles, Paul, said, "For I am not ashamed of the gospel of Christ: for it is the power of God unto salvation to every one that believeth; to the Jew first, and also to the Greek" (Romans 1:16). Another Apostle, James, asked the following question, "Know ye not that the friendship of the world is enmity with God? whosoever therefore will be a friend of the world is the enemy of God" (James 4:4). Lehi warned his son Jacob, "For it must needs be, that there is an opposition in all things" (2 Nephi 2:11).

Opposition and Persecution

As simple and innocuous as it may seem, establishing the Church of Christ among religious pluralism has not only been met by skepticism but also by opposition, persecution, destruction, and violence by believers and nonbelievers. Religion or church are too often associated with chauvinism and exclusion. Being recently in Palmyra and Kirtland, I rediscovered the reality of the persecution endured by the early Saints trying to establish the restored Church of Jesus Christ.

Has the situation changed in the beginning of this twenty-first century? Are new religious movements or the restored Church exempt from religious or state persecution? Apparently not, as it is quite evident in view of the destruction of sacred sites, sacred lives, and sacred values all around the world in our days. The devastating human effects of religious wars, that we thought belonged to the dark ages of civilization, are alive and doing well in the Middle East, Nigeria, Kashmir, Sri Lanka, India, Indonesia, and Bosnia-Herzegovina, to mention only a few. The more insidious of these wars are also being fought in the Western nations dealing with religious freedom and human rights versus the amazing explosion of religious plurality among the traditional religions. Paradoxically, this awakening of various new religious movements has been accompanied by a growing extension of the exercise of religious freedom and rights and also with increased restrictions to limit that new freedom to worship how, where, or what we may. Religious exclusiveness related to nationalism, patriotism, or favoritism is not new and will continue, as we saw in a 2000 incident in Russia between the Orthodox and the Catholic churches. Tolerance does not seem to belong to the religious vocabulary!

The major monolithic religions—Judaism, Islam, and Christianity—also seem to build more than ever before the physical and spiritual walls of intolerance, hate, and distrust among them. All three are major revealed religions based on words of prophets recorded in their sacred records: the Torah, the Qur'an, and the Bible. In essence, all have the same source and foundation!

How can ordinary people who are members of these religions deal with constant references to war? The most challenging temptation of this twenty-first century will be to turn to oneself and to use reason to deal with religion or to simply negate the role of religion, churches, and priesthood. The recent scandals affecting priesthood leaders and church shepherds in the Catholic Church will neither help the growing desertion of their faithful nor prevent growing distrust for church leaders of other confessions.

The dogma of the existence of God is a message of love to help us be transformed to become like Him. A dogma is a promise; it is hope that will change life by faith. It is up to the individual to accept it or to tear it down. Logical reasoning, relativism, and the modern propensity to discard judgments to be politically correct are the temptations to change the divine nature of God into a natural god, the divine instrument of love and salvation into a worldly instrument of friendship and unconditional salvation, and the divine righteousness into hedonism. That is much easier to believe when there is almost nothing left to believe in.

The Lord has warned us about this calamity in very clear terms: "They seek not the Lord to establish his righteousness, but every man walketh in his own way, and after the image of his own god, whose image is in the likeness of the world, and whose substance is that of an idol, which waxeth old and shall perish in Babylon, even Babylon the great, which shall fall" (D&C 1:16).

What is the Lord's solution? He called a prophet, Joseph Smith. He gave him commandments. He told this prophet and his followers to proclaim the restored truths unto the world that the fulness of His gospel might be proclaimed by the weak and the simple unto the ends of the world, and before kings and rulers. Then, in His preface to the doctrines, covenants, and commandments given in this dispensation, the Lord said: "For verily the voice of the Lord is unto all men, and there is none to escape; . . . and the voice of warning shall be unto all people, by the mouths of my disciples, whom I have chosen in these last days. . . . Wherefore the voice of the Lord is unto the ends of the earth, that all that will hear may hear" (D&C 1:2, 4, 11).

Religious pluralism and religious uniqueness, despite being a major cause for contention and wars, can coexist—even if at first glance it seems unsolvable as a paradox. The one and only truth can exist without excluding or condemning the unbelievers and others. Religious freedom has a double edge but addresses both sides of the table and should assure communication, friendship, and peace despite the differences.

So are there any doubts about the uniqueness, the reality, or the necessity to share and expose the gospel of salvation to mankind? The Lord has spoken in our day. His Church will continue to be established in all the nations of the earth, missionaries will continue to share their testimonies, there will continue to be persecution, but we have a spiritual duty and a spiritual assignment to declare the message of the Restoration—that Jesus is the Christ, that Joseph Smith was the prophet of the Restoration, and that The Church of Jesus Christ of Latter-day Saints is the church led by Jesus Christ. It is our motivation to do so without imposing our message or restraining the agency of others.

Religious Freedoms Today

The eleventh article of faith is a declaration of love and respect as "we claim the privilege of worshiping Almighty God according to the dictates of our own conscience, and allow all men the same privilege, let them worship how, where, or what they may" (Articles of Faith 1:11). It is not different from the various international declarations trying to cope with the mortal challenge for an individual to decide for himself or herself, without the intervention of the state, a church, or a court, to join, belong, or leave a religion or a church. The Universal Declaration of 1948 states, "Everyone has the right to freedom of thought, conscience and religion; this right includes freedom to change his religion or belief." It has been repeated in every possible assembly of government and church leaders, as it was recently in Rome in the International Symposium on Human Rights in Islam. In his message to the symposium, Kofi Annan, Secretary General of the United Nations, stated, "Human rights are the expression of those traditions of tolerance in all cultures that are the basis of peace and progress. Human rights, properly understood and justly interpreted, are foreign to no culture and native to all nations." He then went on to refer to Imam Ali, the fourth khalifa after Prophet Muhammed, who "instructed the governor of Egypt to rule with mercy and tolerance towards all his subjects . . . 'for they are of two kinds: either they are your brothers in religion or your equals in creation.'"

Apparently everyone agrees today, too often in words only, that religious freedom and the exercise of human rights can or should be applied equally to all political regimes, cultures, nations, and particularly religions. The Vienna Declaration and Programme of

Action of 1993 states: "All human rights are universal, indivisible, interdependent and interrelated. The international community must treat human rights globally in a fair and equal manner, on the same footing, and with the same emphasis. While the significance of national and regional peculiarities and various historical, cultural and religious backgrounds must be borne in mind, it is the duty of States, regardless of their political, economic and cultural systems, to promote and protect all human rights."

There is still a major difference between the word of the law and its intentions and the reality of the world and its traditions. We can help by building bridges of communication, friendship, and peace instead of elevating walls of incomprehension, hate, and war. It is not only our duty but also our responsibility to claim our religious uniqueness.

Conclusion

What is the conclusion of this very short examination of religious plurality and religious uniqueness, that unique paradox? We must look and listen as Joseph Smith did when he prayed to know which of all the sects was right, that he might know which to join. The vision was of the Father and the Son, the message was the greatest ever given again to mankind: "This is My Beloved Son. Hear Him!" (Joseph Smith—History 1:17). It was the message of love: "For God so loved the world, that he gave his only begotten Son, that whosoever believeth in him should not perish, but have everlasting life" (John 3:16).

Jesus Christ is the Son of God sent to bring to pass the immortality and eternal life of man. He is the central part of the plan of salvation, and the ordinances of salvation are found in His church, The Church of Jesus Christ of Latter-day Saints. This message is unique and is an invitation for the honest and sincere to find out for himself or herself as Moroni the prophet concluded his exhortation:

> Remember how merciful the Lord hath been unto the children
> of men, from the creation of Adam even down until the time
> that ye shall receive these things, and ponder it in your hearts.
>
> And when ye shall receive these things, I would exhort
> you that ye would ask God, the Eternal Father, in the name of
> Christ, if these things are not true; and if ye shall ask with a
> sincere heart, with real intent, having faith in Christ, he will
> manifest the truth of it unto you, by the power of the Holy
> Ghost.
>
> And by the power of the Holy Ghost ye may know the
> truth of all things. (Moroni 10: 3–5)

The invitation is not coercive. It is given with respect for others' beliefs; it is given in the spirit of love and recognition that we
may be different in our religious thoughts but we are essentially the
same—all are spirit children of our Heavenly Father. Our quest for
happiness and peace is also the same, and eternal life is a result of
agency and choice.

May the Lord help us to remember our religious uniqueness
among the religious pluralism of our days, but may we also do it the
Lord's way and not the world's way, as He commanded us to love our
neighbor as ourselves.

© by Intellectual Reserve, Inc.

*Elder Charles Didier is a member of the First Quorum of the Seventy.
This essay was presented at "Muslims and Latter-day Saints: Build-
ing Bridges," the International Society's thirteenth annual conference,
August 2002, Brigham Young University, Provo, Utah.*

Chapter 20

The Church in a
Cross-Cultural World

President Dieter F. Uchtdorf

THE THEME OF this year's conference, "The Gospel, Professional
Ethics, and Cross-Cultural Experience," is certainly an area of special concern for The Church of Jesus Christ of Latter-day Saints and
its worldwide membership. It has special significance for Latter-day
Saint professionals who are more and more involved in international
affairs due to the ongoing process of globalization and the integration
of markets, transportation, and communication systems as we have
never witnessed before. In a way, this development enables countries,
corporations, institutions, and individuals to reach around the world
faster, farther, and deeper than ever before.

Many of us are crossing these borders of different cultures frequently. Elder Neal A. Maxwell would suggest that Latter-day Saint
international professionals should have their citizenship first in the
kingdom of God, but then carry their passport with all its consequences into the professional world and not the other way around.
This also reminds me of a comment made by Elder Dallin H. Oaks
after his call to the Quorum of the Twelve Apostles that he wanted to
be remembered as an Apostle who formerly was a judge and not as a
judge serving as an Apostle.

The dictionary defines *culture* as the sum of ways of living, built
up by a group of human beings and transmitted from generation to

generation. *Cross-cultural* is defined as pertaining to or contrasting two or more such cultures, and the dictionary suggests that *ethics* is the body of moral principles or values held by or governing a culture, group, or individual.

I commend all of you who are participating in the International Society. I have read several of your newsletters, published presentations, and papers from prior conferences. In my thinking, you are not only building links and bridges between nations and countries but also between cultures and traditions and, most important, between revealed truths and the world of your professional lives.

Division versus Integration

As I grew up in Europe following the Second World War, the political system then was symbolized by a single word—*division*—and by a name and a location—*the Berlin Wall.* It was the Cold War system. The globalization we are experiencing now is a different system. The world has become an increasingly interwoven place. Today, whether you are a country, institution, or a company, your opportunities come increasingly from who you are connected to and how you are connected. This system of globalization is also impressively characterized by a single word—*integration*—and by a name and a location—*www,* or the *World Wide Web.*

So in a broad sense, we have come from a world of division and walls to a system built increasingly around integration. This type of globalization is bringing the world closer together. Borders are coming down, and the rewards will be measured in better standards of living, less poverty around the world, more respect and deference for diversity of culture, and peace for all mankind. I believe we all agree that we still have a long way to go.

Globalization is facilitated by openness and trust. Yet openness is today considered as much a liability as a virtue. The tragic and traumatic impact of 9/11 and the Iraq War have brought increased focus on insecurity and uncertainty, which translates into extreme caution for anyone considering travel and investments. The emphasis is not so much on opportunities but on avoiding risks of any kind. We have also discovered in the past that some of the links and connections that made globalization work so effectively across cultures can also transmit a crisis. The Asian currency crisis of the late 1990s was transmitted through a worldwide financial system that had become much more integrated than almost anyone understood. That made it possible for the crisis to spread quickly through Asia, triggering a huge economic collapse in Russia and coming close to bringing Wall Street to its knees.

In the recent past, a similar impact coming from Asia, this time not just financial, had huge worldwide ramifications for all walks of life. The SARS virus is easily transmitted through our open global travel network. The SARS virus can hitch an airplane ride and get anywhere in twenty-four hours.

We are also living in a cynical time. Trust in public institutions, corporations, and organized religion is declining. We read daily newspaper accounts and hear media reports that describe the decline of moral decency and the erosion of basic ethical conduct. They detail the corrupting influence of dishonesty, from small-time childish stealing or cheating to major embezzlement and fraud, child or spouse abuse, and misappropriation of money or goods.

A Time of Great Opportunities

In this time of uncertainty, mistrust, fear, rumors of war, and political road rage, is there still hope for integration and openness across different cultures? Is there still room for virtues and divine principles?

Yes, there is, but we must understand that the axiomatic and eternal principle of agency demands that there be "an opposition in all things" (2 Nephi 2:11) to ensure that meaningful choices can be made, not only between good and evil but also from among an array of righteous alternatives.

Moral agency refers not only to the capacity "to act for [ourselves]" (2 Nephi 2:26) but also to the accountability for those actions. Exercising agency is a spiritual matter (see D&C 29:35); it consists of either receiving the enlightenment and commandments that come from God or resisting and rejecting them by yielding to the devil's temptations (see D&C 93:31). Without awareness of alternatives, an individual could not choose, and that is why being tempted by evil is as essential to agency as being enticed by the Spirit of God (see D&C 29:39).

We believe that every man and woman, irrespective of race, culture, nationality, or political or economic circumstance, has the power to determine what is right and what is wrong. In the Book of Mormon we read, "For behold, the Spirit of Christ is given to every man, that he may know good from evil; wherefore, I show unto you the way to judge; for every thing which inviteth to do good, and to persuade to believe in Christ, is sent forth by the power and gift of Christ; wherefore ye may know with a perfect knowledge it is of God" (Moroni 7:16).

Church leaders have counseled wisely about how to handle temporal matters to produce rich spiritual revenue. President N. Eldon Tanner taught, "Material blessings are a part of the gospel if they are achieved in the proper way and for the right purpose."[1] And President Spencer W. Kimball said that money is "compensation received for a full day's honest work. It is . . . reasonable pay for faithful service. It is . . . fair profit from the sale of goods, commodities, or service. It is . . . income received from transactions where all parties profit."[2]

One reason for today's decline in moral values is that the world has invented a new, constantly changing, undependable standard of moral conduct, often referred to as "situational ethics." Now individuals consider good and evil adjustable according to each situation. Some wrongly believe that there is no divine law, so there is no sin

---

1.   N. Eldon Tanner, in Conference Report, October 1979, 117–18.
2.   Spencer W. Kimball, in Conference Report, October 1953, 52.

(see 2 Nephi 2:13). This is in direct contrast to the proclaimed, God-given, absolute standards which we find in the Ten Commandments and in other revealed sources that represent the commandments of God.

For Latter-day Saints, obedience to divine imperatives and the pursuit of ultimate happiness are correlated elements in the maturing of human beings. We believe that this ethical maturity derives from experience, including religious experience; from rational and practical deliberation; from the mandates, both general and specific, that recur in scriptures; and from the counsel given by living prophets.

Divine laws are instituted by God to govern His creations and kingdoms and to prescribe behavior for His offspring. The extent of the divine laws that He reveals to mankind may vary from dispensation to dispensation, according to the needs and conditions of mankind, as God decrees, and as they are given through and interpreted by His prophets. These laws are important to the individual and for the social aspects of the human family eternally. The scriptures teach, "That same sociality which exists among us here will exist among us there [in the eternal worlds], only it will be coupled with eternal glory, which glory we do not now enjoy" (D&C 130:2).

Modern revelation brings the human existence to a clear, divine, and eternal perspective. Latter-day Saints believe in an ethic of divine approbation; to discern the will of God and receive assurance that one is acting under God's approval are the ultimate quest of discipleship. This may be called Spirit-guided morality.

Children of a Loving Heavenly Father

Latter-day Saints believe that all human beings are God's children and that He loves all of us. He has inspired not only people of the Bible and the Book of Mormon but other people as well to carry out His purposes through all cultures and parts of the world. God inspires not only Latter-day Saints but also founders, teachers, philosophers, and reformers of other Christian and non-Christian religions. The restored gospel holds a positive relationship with other religions. Intolerance is always a sign of weakness. The Latter-day Saint perspective is that of the eleventh article of faith: "We claim the privilege of worshiping Almighty God according to the dictates of our own conscience, and allow all men the same privilege, let them worship how, where, or what they may" (Articles of Faith 1:11).

The Church teaches that members must not only be kind and loving toward others but also respect their right to believe and worship as they choose. George Albert Smith, the eighth President of the Church, publicly advocated the official Church policy of friendship and tolerance: "We have come not to take away from you the truth and virtue you possess. We have come not to find fault with you nor to criticize you. . . . We have come here as your brethren . . . to say to you: 'Keep all the good that you have, and let us bring to you more good, in order that you may be happier and in order that you may be prepared to enter into the presence of our Heavenly Father.'"[3]

On February 15, 1978, the First Presidency of the Church issued the following declaration: "The great religious leaders of the world such as Mohammed, Confucius, and the Reformers, as well as philosophers including Socrates, Plato, and others, received a portion of God's light. Moral truths were given to them by God to enlighten whole nations and to bring a higher level of understanding to individuals. . . . Our message therefore is one of special love and concern for the eternal welfare of all men and women, regardless of religious belief, race, or nationality, knowing that we are truly brothers and sisters because we are the sons and daughters of the same Eternal Father."[4] In the words of Orson F. Whitney, an Apostle, the gospel "embraces all truth, whether known or unknown. It incorporates all

---

3. George Albert Smith, *Sharing the Gospel with Others*, comp. Preston Nibley (Salt Lake City: Deseret Book, 1948), 12–13.
4. Spencer J. Palmer, *The Expanding Church* (Salt Lake City: Deseret Book, 1978), frontispiece.

intelligence, both past and prospective. No righteous principle will ever be revealed, no truth can possibly be discovered, either in time or in eternity, that does not in some manner, directly or indirectly, pertain to the Gospel of Jesus Christ."[5]

President Spencer W. Kimball set the tone in relationships with other religions and cultures. In a major address to Church leaders, he said, "The Church has not been to demand rights but to merit them, not to clamor for friendship and goodwill but to manifest them to give energy and time beyond rhetoric." Citing a statement by the First Presidency, President Kimball also said: "With our wide ranging mission, so far as mankind is concerned, Church members cannot ignore the many practical problems that require solutions. ... Where solutions to these practical problems require cooperative action with those not of our faith, members should not be reticent in doing their part in joining and leading in those efforts where they can make an individual contribution to those causes which are consistent with the standards of the Church."[6]

"Go Ye Therefore, and Teach All Nations"

The Church has a history of reaching out to other nations and cultures beginning immediately after the Church was organized again in April 1830. Early missionaries fearlessly taught the gospel in Native American lands before the Church was fully organized. As early as 1837, the Twelve Apostles were in England; in 1844 they were in the Pacific Islands; by 1850 they had been to France, Germany, Italy, Switzerland, and the Middle East. This was during a time when the Church was facing severe persecution and extreme financial difficulties.

---

5. As quoted in Daniel H. Ludlow, ed., *Encyclopedia of Mormonism* (New York: Macmillan, 1992), s.v. "World Religions (Non-Christian) and Mormonism."
6. Spencer W. Kimball, "Living the Gospel in the Home," *Ensign*, May 1978, 100.

The Church has become a great cosmopolitan church. It rejoices in the tremendous growth of the work across the world. We are thankful for the deep faith and faithfulness of members of the Church. We all look upon one another as brothers and sisters, regardless of the land we call home. We belong to what may be regarded as the greatest community of friends on the face of the earth.

Church members now live in nearly every country of the world. Church congregations around the world will increasingly reflect the diversity of the nations in which they are located. There are members in at least 150 of the 230 countries of the world. Church members speak approximately 170 different languages as their first language. Therefore, the Church as a whole, worldwide, is becoming more diverse in terms of national, racial, cultural, and linguistic characteristics of its members.

Across all the different nations, we are guided and united by the ethical principles of the thirteenth article of faith: "We believe in being honest, true, chaste, benevolent, virtuous, and in doing good to all men; indeed, we may say that we follow the admonition of Paul—We believe all things, we hope all things, we have endured many things, and hope to be able to endure all things. If there is anything virtuous, lovely, or of good report or praiseworthy, we seek after these things" (Articles of Faith 1:13).

This article of our faith is one of the basic declarations of our theology. It is an all-encompassing statement of the ethics of our behavior. There would be less rationalizing over some elements of our personal conduct which we try to justify with one excuse or another if we would closely follow this declaration. The restored gospel offers the more excellent way; it suggests we seek answers to life's crucial questions from God, who is the source of all true wisdom. "Fear not to do good. . . . Look unto me in every thought" (D&C 6:33, 36).

Diversity by its very nature implies differences. Not all differences are of equal value; some differences can be very positive, and some can be destructive. For example, Latter-day Saints, though we are "required to forgive all men" (D&C 64:10), cannot accept and tolerate the gross evils that are so prevalent in societies today. We hear often of the need for people to be tolerant of differences they observe in others. We agree insofar as tolerance implies genuine respect for another, but we disagree if tolerance means acceptance of sin, which God Himself rejects. "For I the Lord cannot look upon sin with the least degree of allowance" (D&C 1:31).

Ethical decline is accelerated when individuals and eventually societies become indifferent to divine values once widely shared. Now is the time to stand up and be counted and not to step aside or duck. We actually have an obligation to lift people out of endangering routine and help them face the challenges of the future. Leaders and followers are both accountable to Him who gave us life. In a democratic society much is required of leaders and followers, and individual character matters so much in both.

The ultimate, key source for Christian behavioral ethics, and therefore for Latter-day Saints, is found in Jesus Christ's Sermon on the Mount, which sacred message He reemphasizes by providing us with a second witness in the Book of Mormon. Based on those principles, a world community could be established where we are "of one heart and one mind, and [dwell] in righteousness" (Moses 7:18).

There is no question about it; we cannot separate ourselves from others. Our common interests are too great. The English poet John Donne said, "No man is an Island, entire of itself; every man is a piece of the Continent, a part of the main."[7]

By crossing boundaries, continents, and countries, we are establishing contact with different cultures, religions, and traditions. Naturally some challenges arise. In many countries, The Church of Jesus Christ of Latter-day Saints is viewed as an American church. Church leaders strongly emphasize that it is a universal church for all people everywhere, with a responsibility to share the gospel with all of God's children. There is an increased awareness of cultural differences as well as a willingness to work within those differences. The

---

7.   Angela Partington, ed. *The Oxford Dictionary of Quotations*, 4th ed. rev. (Oxford: Oxford University Press, 1996), 253.

Apostle Paul pronounced that all men and women are God's beloved children. To the Athenians, Paul said, God "hath made of one blood all nations of men for to dwell on all the face of the earth" (Acts 17:26).

Nephi expressed the same vision: "[Christ] inviteth them all to come unto him and partake of his goodness; and he denieth none that come unto him, black and white, bond and free, male and female; . . . and all are alike unto God" (2 Nephi 26:33).

Sadly, however, deep divisions of race, ethnicity, politics, economic status, and cultures still separate people throughout the world. These divisions corrode, corrupt, and destroy relationships between neighbors and prevent the establishment of societies where there is "no contention in the land, because of the love of God which did dwell in the hearts of the people" (4 Nephi 1:15).

We can be a positive influence as we meet the people of the world. Often people of other cultures look up to us, and it is important that we are not looking down on them.

It takes great courage to put away old hatred, divisions, and tribal traditions that constrict and confine people into a blind succession of destructive behavior toward others. Jesus, who knew perfectly the corrosive effects of such behavior, gave us a higher law when He said: "Ye have heard that it hath been said, Thou shalt love thy neighbour, and hate thine enemy. But I say unto you, Love your enemies, bless them that curse you, do good to them that hate you, and pray for them which despitefully use you, and persecute you; that ye may be the children of your Father which is in heaven: for he maketh his sun to rise on the evil and on the good, and sendeth rain on the just and on the unjust" (Matthew 5:43–45).

Today the power of the restored gospel brings to pass the kind of miracle Paul described to the Saints at Ephesus: "Without Christ, [we are] aliens, . . . having no hope. . . . [But] through [Christ] we both have access by one Spirit unto the Father. Now therefore ye are no more strangers and foreigners, but fellow citizens with the saints, and of the household of God" (Ephesians 2:12, 18–19).

The World a Global Village

The world is becoming, to some degree, a global village with a diverse population. Even in the United States it is expected that by the year 2050 the so-called racial minorities will have taken over and will surpass in numbers the Anglo majority. The children and grandchildren of today's Americans will live in a society where everyone is a member of a minority group. Therefore, we must look beyond superficial stereotyping, which influences too much of our thinking about the worth of those who seem on the surface to be different than we are and sometimes leads us to judge them prematurely. We must learn to look at others through the eyes of love, not as strangers and foreigners but as individuals, fellow children of God, of one blood with us. The Apostle Paul taught, "By love serve one another" (Galatians 5:13).

Becoming a worldwide religion in spirit as well as in organizational matters is much more than building chapels and translating documents. As we embark to experience the universal brotherhood we seek, all of us must be prepared to make some alterations in our views of one another. We will need to increase our empathy and cross-cultural sensitivity and progressively discard prejudices incompatible with brotherhood. The different cultural and ethnical backgrounds bring challenges into members' lives.

We also need to make a clear distinction between our cultural and other preferences and the gospel of Jesus Christ. The gospel has flourished and has been blessed and sanctioned by God under numerous kinds of governments and economic and cultural systems. There must be some accountability, of course, between these preferences and systems and the gospel. In political terms, one key is freedom: freedom unfettered by practices that limit the exercise of religious conscience or that relegate classes of citizens to servitude, bondage, oppression, or exploitation—freedom that is compatible with the gospel. Governments that actively foster freedom of conscience and opportunity and protect it for all of its citizens are our implicit friends. This is true whether they happen to agree with the political policy of the United States or not. This is not an American church. The Church is beyond the nation-state because no state is an official representative of God. So why is it to our advantage to make a distinction between the gospel we possess and our own political, economic, and cultural preferences?

A Global Church of Jesus Christ

To become a worldwide Church in various cultures and nations, the doctrinal truths of the restored gospel will be the guiding star, not our political background, not even some of the present Church programs. It is the Spirit that counts.

A diverse Latter-day Saint people cannot have brotherhood if one of its segments insists on being always right, all the time, on everything. The gospel is transcendent truth—man-made political and social institutions are not. In social, cultural, and political areas, we cannot expect that widely divergent people should adhere to the same specific perspectives. It is certain that some aspects of culture, ideology, and political practices are more compatible with gospel principles than others, and from that point they are temporally preferable, but only the principles of the restored gospel of Jesus Christ constitute eternal truth.

Jesus Christ is the central figure in the doctrine of The Church of Jesus Christ of Latter-day Saints. Complete salvation is possible only through the life, death, Resurrection, doctrines, and ordinances of Jesus Christ, and in no other way. "We talk of Christ, we rejoice in Christ, we preach of Christ, we prophesy of Christ, ... that our children may know to what source they may look for a remission of their sins" (2 Nephi 25:26). Jesus is the model and exemplar of all who seek to acquire the divine nature. Thus, the Messiah's mission to "preach good tidings unto the meek," to "bind up the brokenhearted, to proclaim liberty to the captives, and the opening of the prison to them that are bound" (Isaiah 61:1; see also Luke 4:18–19) extends into our days and into the life beyond.[8]

---

8. See Topical Guide, "Salvation for the Dead" and "Spirits in Prison."

Jesus Christ is the God of the whole earth and invites all nations and people to come unto Him. To worship Christ, the Son of God, and to acknowledge Him as the source of truth and redemption, as the light and life of the world, is the only way and the answer to all the challenges of our time (see John 14:6; 2 Nephi 25:29; 3 Nephi 11:11).

The charge and commandment given by the Savior Himself to His Apostles in the meridian of time applies equally to us today: "Go ye therefore, and teach *all nations*, baptizing them in the name of the Father, and of the Son, and of the Holy Ghost: . . . I am with you alway, even unto the end of the world" (Matthew 28:19–20; emphasis added).

Did the early Apostles, then, live up to this charge? Their real test came when God answered the prayers of a Roman centurion from Caesarea called Cornelius, a just man who feared God and was of good report, and instructed him to send for Peter to teach and to baptize him. After initial doubt and resistance, followed by fervent prayer and willingness to embrace divine revelation, "then Peter opened his mouth, and said, Of a truth I perceive that God is no respecter of persons: but in every nation he that feareth him, and worketh righteousness, is accepted with him" (Acts 10:34–35).

The people of the earth are all our Father's children. They are of great diversity and many varied religious persuasions. They are our brothers and sisters. May we cultivate tolerance, respect, and love for one another and stand up for the truth with sweet boldness to magnify the charge given to us by the Lord today is my humble prayer.

© by Intellectual Reserve, Inc.

President Dieter F. Uchtdorf is Second Counselor in the First Presidency. This essay was presented at "The Gospel, Professional Ethics, and Cross-Cultural Experience," the International Society's fourteenth annual conference, August 2003, Brigham Young University, Provo, Utah.

Scripture Index

Index

Christianity, 82, 136
African, 104
afterlife beliefs in, 10–11
community of, 16, 74, 90, 137–38
culture of, 71, 75
European, 45, 74
worldwide, 4, 74, 92
Christians, 92, 299
Christiansen, James, 191
Chul, Seo Hee, 193
Church Board of Education, 189, 192,
208, 215–16, 219, 231
Church Educational System (CES),
189–91, 197, 214–15, 219, 230–
31, 234
Church Humanitarian Services, 153,
157, 176
Church of Jesus Christ of Latter-
day Saints, The. *See also* Church
Educational System (CES);
gospel, restored; Latter-day Saints;
Restoration
administration of, 19, 25, 77–82,
196, 201
as a world religion, 4, 143–44, 185,
304–6
auxiliaries of, 20, 73, 76, 79–81, 89,
111, 162, 200
culture of, 72, 74–75
employment and, 164–69
globalization of, 197, 201, 205, 238,
257, 290, 301
growth of, 4–5, 11, 20–21, 27–28,
65–67, 78–80, 83, 102, 183–84,
250, 254
in relation to national
governments, 54–55, 88–90, 93–
103, 107, 134
in the developing world, 71–72, 77,
105, 109
mission of, 29, 65, 72–73, 219, 300
misunderstandings of, 105–6, 109–
10, 118–19, 257–58, 302, 305
organization of, 26, 52, 82
programs of, 73, 76, 90, 111, 152,
161, 199

Public Affairs Department of,
109, 111
revelation and, 11–12
role of, 67, 76, 150
schools of, 42–43, 186–87, 197,
199, 222–28
scriptural canon of, 11–12, 72
welfare and, 153, 162, 164, 169–
74, 234
Church of the Holy Sepulchre, 137
Church Welfare Services, 153, 162,
169, 176
Civil War (U.S.), 60
Clark, J. Reuben, Jr., 170
Clarke, J. Richard, 107
coercion, 128–29, 293
Cold War, 68, 126, 242, 250, 295
Collier, James Lincoln, 262–63
colonialism, 32, 68, 108, 120, 136,
269, 273
communism, 61–64, 116, 119–21,
250–51. *See also* Soviet Bloc; Soviet
Union
Confucius, 299
conversion, 17, 93, 117, 127, 129, 132
Council of Europe, 118, 120
Cowdery, Oliver, 34, 184, 223–24
Crosby, Caroline, 42
Cuba, 256
cults, 117–19
cultures
definition of, 269–70, 272–73,
294–95
imposition on, 273–77
safeguards against imposition on,
277–78
values of, 270–73, 281
Czechoslovakia, 48, 194

D

Darwin, Charles, 114
Day, Frank D., 190, 192
democracy, 69, 71, 91, 135, 280
Democratic Republic of Congo, 172
Denmark, 49, 59
Deseret, 210

KV-515-298

Mountain Disaster

Mountain climbing is an exciting and rewarding activity, but it can be dangerous. If a thick mist suddenly covers the mountain, it's very easy to lose your way …

Rob saw Alex fall from the ledge. He hit his head as he fell.

"Alex!" cried Jenny.

For a terrible moment, Rob thought Jenny was going to fall too. Then she began to climb down towards the still figure lying on the rocks below. Rob followed, hardly able to believe what had happened.

Rob, Alex and Jenny were seventeen and very experienced climbers. They had been walking along a ledge and because it was wide, they had not needed to rope themselves together. So how could Alex have slipped off, just like that?

SURVIVAL!

Written by Anthony Masters
Illustrated by Tim Clarey, Tim Gaudion
and Colin Sullivan

Contents

Alex lay on the ground, his face a deathly white, blood pouring from a deep cut on his forehead. Jenny pulled the first-aid kit out of her rucksack.

"Hurry up!" snapped Rob. "He's losing a lot of blood."

Jenny began to wipe the cut on Alex's head with cotton wool.

"It's a very deep cut," said Rob. "We must try to stop the bleeding."

"I'll pull the cut together with some strips of tape," said Jenny. "Then I'll bind it all up tightly. Alex really needs stitches."

"We need to call for help," said Rob. "Where's the mobile?"

"Alex had it," replied Jenny.

She searched Alex's coat pockets and found the phone. Rob and Jenny stared at it. "It must have broken when he fell," said Jenny quietly.

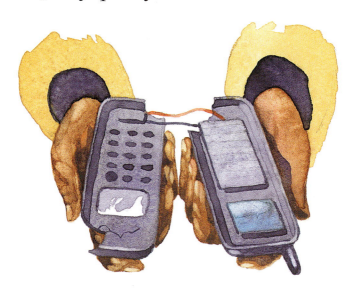

Rob and Jenny had not seen any other climbers on the mountain that afternoon – there was no one to call to for help.

They looked at each other. Then they looked down at Alex. He was very pale. Then his eyes began to close.

"He could have concussion," said Jenny.

Or worse, thought Rob.

"We told the Rangers what time we were starting off – and what time we planned to be back." Rob tried to be calm and reassuring. "But we've got a few hours before they'll start looking for us."

"We need help faster than that," said Jenny, still trying to close the cut with the strips of tape.

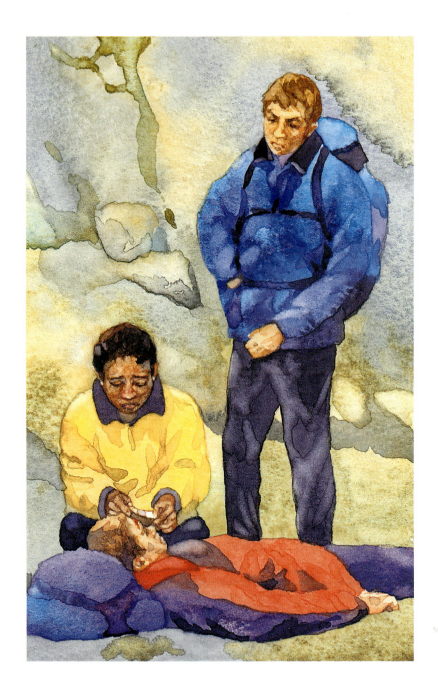

9

Alex groaned but didn't open his eyes. Then he started to snore.

"That's not a good sign, is it?" said Rob.

Jenny shook her head. "We ought to wrap him up. I've got another coat in my rucksack."

"One of us should go for help," said Rob. "I'll go. You stay here and try to stop that bleeding. I'll be as quick as I can."

Rob looked down at Alex. Alex's breathing seemed uneven now, and the snoring sound was worse.

"You'd better get moving," said Jenny. "Be careful," she added.

"I'll be fine," Rob replied.

Rob began to hurry down the steep
mountain path. He made good progress
at first. But the weather was closing in
and misty rain was beginning to blot out
the landscape.

After a while, the path narrowed and
Rob found himself on top of a ridge. The
mist was thicker and the rain heavier ...

This is weird, thought Rob. He didn't
remember this ridge on the way up.
Could he have missed a turning? The
mist made it impossible to see clearly.
Sometimes he could see a few metres
ahead, but at other times he could
hardly see at all.

Rob didn't know what to do. Should
he retrace his steps, or carry on along
the ridge?

Rob decided to go on along the ridge.
Maybe he hadn't noticed it as they'd
climbed up the mountain.

After walking on for another few
minutes, the mist suddenly shifted. Rob
stumbled and came to a sudden stop.
He was standing over a sheer drop.

Panic swept over him and he turned back the way he had come. He hoped he could find his way back to the path. Rob felt in his pocket for his compass. He hadn't thought he would need a compass. The way down the mountain had seemed so obvious.

As he searched his pockets, Rob realised that he had made a very foolish mistake. He had left the compass in his rucksack with Jenny. No experienced mountain climber would have done that. Mist could always close in – and it had!

Rob could have kicked himself for being so stupid. Alex and Jenny were depending on him and he had let them down.

Suddenly, the mist shifted again. To his relief, Rob saw a large rock that looked like a giant hand. He remembered it from when they had climbed up earlier. He saw a path near the rock leading down the mountainside. He was sure that this was the path they had climbed up only a few hours before.

Rob hurried down, almost jogging, looking at his watch, trying to make up for lost time. Then he came to yet another stop. The path had become wider and seemed to be going up the mountain, not down. He'd got it wrong again!

"Alex?" whispered Jenny.

His breathing definitely seemed to have become more shallow.

"Alex?"

Jenny knew she had to try to get him to talk, but his eyes were still closed and his face was very pale.

"Alex?" Jenny whispered again. "Speak to me. You've got to speak to me. Please, Alex."

If only he'd talk there'd be a chance. But now he seemed deeply unconscious.

Once again, Rob turned back, trying to keep calm, searching for the hand-shaped rock. He was now certain the right path lay further over to the left. Stabs of fear hit him, making him stumble and scatter loose stones. He had to find the right path. He had to get help – quickly!

Then Rob saw shadows in the mist, coming down the mountain. He thought for a wonderful moment that Alex had made an amazing recovery. Here he was, walking down towards Rob, with Jenny just behind.

Instead, two strangers came into view. Quickly, Rob began to explain.

"It's OK," said one of the climbers. "We've got a mobile. We'll call for help. Then we'll get back up the mountain and see what we can do. By the way, my name is John and this is Alan."

"I feel so stupid not bringing my compass," explained Rob.

"Don't worry about it," said Alan. "This bad weather just blew up. If there was no mist you wouldn't need a compass."

Half an hour later, Rob, John and Alan were back at the spot where Alex had fallen. The rainy mist was lifting a little.

"I'm so pleased to see you," said Jenny. "Alex is in a bad way."

"We've contacted the emergency services," said Alan. "Help will be on its way soon."

Rob knelt down beside Alex. He was sure that Alex was going to die.

An hour passed before a helicopter managed to land. A paramedic leapt out to examine Alex. "We'll get him to hospital right away," he said. "But I'm afraid we can only take one of you with him."

"You go, Jenny," said Rob. "You've been looking after him."

23

As he walked down the mountain with Alan and John, Rob still felt bad. "I should have had my compass with me and we should have had more than one mobile phone," he said. "If you two hadn't turned up, I'd still be wandering about."

"Don't blame yourself," said Alan. "It's easy to make mistakes when you're stressed."

"You won't make the same mistake again," said John.

"Too right I won't," said Rob.

Dive into Danger

Potholers know that exploring caves can be a risky sport. An underground cave that may seem perfectly safe can suddenly become a death trap.

Adam's powerful torch beam swept
the underground cave. "Isn't it
beautiful?" he whispered.

The cave was more than beautiful,
thought Jack. It was amazing. He
had never seen anything like this
before in his life. The ceiling must
have been over forty metres high and
the cave's dark lake looked peaceful
and still.

On the far side, Adam's torch beam picked out a dark shore. The whole place was like a huge church and Jack almost expected to hear the singing of a choir at any moment.

"I bet not many people have seen this," said Jack.

"Only potholers," replied Adam.

Adam and Jack were keen on potholing. They loved exploring these strange, magical places deep underground. Adam had explored this cave a few months ago with some other potholers and an instructor.

"Looks like we've got the place to ourselves today," he said.

There had been a lot of rain that week, but it had cleared up and the day on the surface was bright and sunny.

Both Adam and Jack were wearing waterproof clothing, helmets with lamps, and coils of rope. The scramble down into the cave had been fairly easy and they both felt exited.

"I've never seen anything like this," said Jack, as they continued to look around the cave.

"Think of all those people walking across the moors who don't realise what's below them," said Adam.

There was a steady drip of water running down the cave walls. Underneath a nearby ledge, Jack could see strange shapes moving that made his heart thump. "What are they?" he gasped.

"Bats," laughed Adam.

Suddenly, they both heard a deep
rumbling sound followed by silence.
Then came the roaring of water.

Adam's torch swept the lake as they
listened to the terrifying noise, confused
about where it was coming from. Then
the torch lit the mouth of the tunnel
where they had come in. To their horror,
water was crashing through it into
the cave.

"That's our way back to the surface!" shouted Jack.

The water seemed to be getting fiercer by the minute. They would never be able to struggle against it.

As they gazed around, what a few moments before had been a beautiful underground cave, now seemed like a death trap. We could drown here, thought Jack.

"Look at the bats," shouted Adam. They had risen in a fluttering cloud, flying to the roof of the cave.

If only we could fly, thought Jack.

"That rumble must have been a rock fall. This water must be flooding down from another underground lake higher up," said Adam. Again he shone his torch. "Look at that!"

The water now filled the whole mouth of the tunnel, carrying with it mud and chunks of rock.

Then came another, louder rumble and a grinding crash.

"That's another fall," said Adam, his voice shaking.

"Isn't there any other way out?" gasped Jack. "I thought you knew this cave."

"There's a chance," Adam replied, "I just hope we can make it in time."

"What are you on about?" yelled Jack, watching the water flooding into the lake. He could see the level was rising fast.

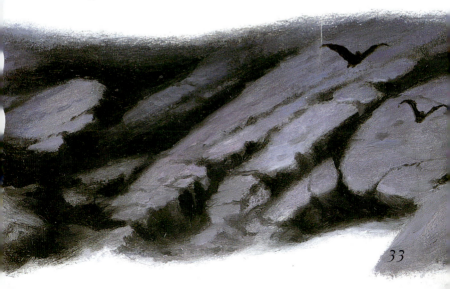

Adam looked around the walls of the cave yet again.

"What do you mean 'a chance'?" repeated Jack, imagining them both drowning as the water completely filled the cave.

Adam was still silent.

"Aren't you –" began Jack.

"Shut up! I'm trying to find the way out," snapped Adam.

Jack tried to get a grip on himself, but it was difficult. He could hear more rumbling in the distance, and the noise of rushing water seemed to fill his head.

"We're trapped!" he shouted, gazing at Adam in despair.

"No, we're not," said Adam quietly. He was pointing the torch beam at another ledge on the opposite side of the lake.

"I've been looking for that ledge.
That's the way out the instructor
showed us. I'm sure it is." Then he said
shakily, "We're going to have to take
a dive."

"You mean dive into that dark
swirling water?" asked Jack.

"It's OK," said Adam. "We made the dive when we came here with the instructor. He showed us how to do it. Don't you remember me telling you?"

"You said you swam down an underground stream. But you didn't mention any diving," said Jack.

"There's nothing to it." Adam said, trying to sound sure of himself.

"No?" said Jack uncertainly.

Adam's powerful torch once again swept the rapidly flooding underground cave. "See that ledge over there?" he said. "Beneath it there's an entrance to another cave."

"Won't that be flooded?" asked Jack.

"I don't know," replied Adam. "But in that cave there's a tunnel that leads to the surface. If we can get through to that tunnel, we'll be OK."

"How long will we be under the water?" asked Jack.

"About a minute," said Adam. "Come on, it will be fine. We did the dive with the instructor."

Jack didn't say anything.

"Come on," shouted Adam urgently. "It's our only chance."

"OK," said Jack. "Let's do it."

Adam began to swim towards the ledge at the other side of the lake. Jack followed him nervously.

When Jack arrived on the ledge,
Adam was already pulling off his helmet,
headlamp and waterproof suit. Trembling,
Jack did the same.

"Don't think about it," Adam yelled
above the noise of the water. "Just go
for it."

They paused, shivering, looking down at the icy water, trying to see the entrance to the other cave.

"Down there?" asked Jack anxiously.

"Yes, down there," said Adam. Then he crouched down and launched himself into the water. He kicked out his legs behind him and suddenly disappeared from sight.

Jack looked down, a cold, sick feeling spreading inside him. For a moment he couldn't move. Then he held his breath and dived, kicking his legs just as Adam had done.

Almost immediately, Jack found an underwater gap in the rock, but when he tried to push himself through, he felt the rocky sides grip him. Was he going to get stuck? Panicking, he kicked and struggled but the rock held him fast.

Jack knew he mustn't open his mouth. He had to hold his breath. He thrashed about, the sharp rocks scratching and cutting his skin.

He kicked out hard again and suddenly found himself wriggling through the narrow passage, his lungs feeling as if they were going to burst at any minute.

43

Jack couldn't hold his breath a second longer. He kicked hard and then found his head was above the water. He could breathe again.

Jack saw that he was in a low-roofed cave with a tunnel above him. The tunnel sloped sharply upwards. This was the way out.

When Jack reached the surface, Adam was sitting on a rock, waiting for him.

"What took you so long, Jack?" he said with an annoying grin.

"It was just a bit of a tight fit," said Jack, as he staggered up into the sunlight he had thought he would never see again.

Buried Alive!

The desert is one of the cruellest places on earth. It is blazing hot in the day and deadly cold at night, and you never know when a violent wind might create a sandstorm ...

The jeep's engine spluttered to a stop. The three people in the jeep looked at each other. Outside, the sand dunes stretched far into the distance.

Jane Mason got out of the jeep into the burning African heat and opened the bonnet. She called out to Ben and Chris, "The head gasket's gone – again!"

"But we've only just replaced it," said Ben.

"Maybe the spare was faulty," said Chris.

Sweat poured down their worried faces. How long could they survive in this heat?

Jane Mason was a writer. She was making a trip to explore the remains of an ancient desert village. She planned to write about it for a magazine. With her were Chris Scott and Ben Dexter. They were students studying geography. They had asked Jane if they could travel with her into the desert.

They had left the road earlier that morning and were making their way across the sand. All three of them knew that, in the desert, any problems with the jeep could be a disaster. They had taken plenty of spare parts with them. For two head gaskets to go was sheer bad luck.

"Can't we push the jeep back to the road?" asked Ben.

"It's much too far," replied Jane

"And the sand is too deep," said Chris.

"I'm going to light some flares," said Jane.

"But who's going to see them?" asked Chris.

"Somebody will," said Jane.

"But we didn't pass anybody this morning," said Ben.

Jane didn't answer. She had to try something.

The flares zoomed up into the cloudless sky. Surely someone would see them, she thought.

"How much water have we got left?" asked Chris.

"Four gallon bottles. But we have to be careful," replied Jane. "We don't know when we'll be rescued. We could be here some time."

They fired off a few more flares and waited. But no one came.

After a while, Ben said, "This isn't
working. No one's going to see our flares
because there's no one out here. I'm
going to walk to the road. I'll see if I
can spot any trucks."

"It's far too risky," said Jane.

"And you'll never make it in this heat," said Chris.

"Have you got any better ideas?" asked Ben. "We could be out here for days. I've got to give it a try. I'll take some water and something to eat in my rucksack."

"We should really stay together," said Jane.

"And die together?" snapped Ben.

Jane shrugged her shoulders and Ben started to pack his rucksack.

Ben looked at his watch. It was
midday. It would be dark by six o'clock.
The road could only be a few miles
away. For a moment, he paused. He
knew he couldn't make much progress in
this heat. He would have to pace himself
very carefully but anything was better
than just sitting around.

"Follow our tracks," said Jane. "Then you'll reach the marker posts by the roadside."

"In other words I can't miss it," grinned Ben.

"In other words you must be careful," Jane insisted.

"I'll be back," said Ben confidently, "and I'll bring back a truck or two. Just think, we could be in a hotel tonight, having a shower and a huge dinner."

Ben set off towards the road. The desert seemed to swallow him up immediately. He looked at the tracks. It should be easy to follow them back to the road, he thought.

Ben trudged on, his rucksack getting heavier with every step. It was much more difficult than he had thought. The heat was intense, and he needed to stop and have a drink of water every few minutes.

When he had been walking for about half an hour, Ben felt a breeze blowing on his face. He looked up and saw that the sky was going dark.

The sand began to swirl around Ben's ankles in the stiffening breeze. Ben had never been in a sandstorm before. He gazed around him. He would never make it back to the others. He had to find shelter. If he didn't, he could be buried alive.

Ben broke into a stumbling run. The wind was stronger now and the sand was making a strange moaning sound. Painful pellets of sand flew up into his face.

He tried to run faster, but his feet sank into the soft, shifting sand and he fell. He got to his feet and noticed his water bottle lying in the sand. To his horror, he saw water pouring out if it. Ben realised he must have forgotten to tighten the lid. When he fell the lid had come off. Ben snatched the bottle up and saved the last few drops.

Suddenly he remembered a wrecked truck that they had passed, some time after the jeep had left the main road. How far away was it? Could he get to the truck before the sand buried it?

Ben hurried on, but the tracks had disappeared and he couldn't see where he was going. Then, in the distance, he saw the truck. Head down, eyes stinging, sand in his mouth, he staggered on.

The truck was lying on its side with one back door open. Already it was half full of sand, but the rocks behind it were keeping off the worst of the storm. Ben knew that if he could get inside the truck, he would have shelter. He pushed some of the sand aside and got in.

Ben curled up, clutching his knees. He was shaking with fear. He pulled off his rucksack. He desperately needed a drink. He took one gulp and then shook the bottle. There was nothing left. What if the storm lasted for days?

Hours later, the sandstorm seemed to ease off slightly. Finally, there was silence and Ben struggled to his feet. By now there was a huge pile of sand blocking the doorway of the truck. Ben managed to dig most of it away with a large spanner he had found on the floor. Shoving the spanner into his rucksack, he set off to find Jane and Chris.

Outside, the landscape seemed different. The sand was even deeper and the dunes had changed shape. Ben was desperately worried about the others. Their jeep could be buried in the sand.

After a long walk, Ben stood staring
at his compass. Surely this was where
the jeep should be, but there was no sign
of it. Slowly, Ben realised that the mound
behind him must be the buried jeep. Jane
and Chris had been buried alive!

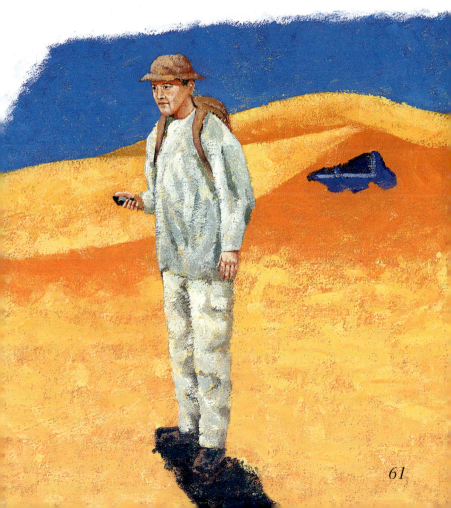

Ben began to tear at the sand with
his bare hands, his heart hammering.
He had to find out if Jane and Chris
were still alive.

He was almost collapsing with
exhaustion when suddenly he saw a
terrified face behind the windscreen.

Ben couldn't get the doors open.
The sand was far too deep. Then he
remembered the spanner. He waved it
at Jane to show her what he was going
to do.

Ben attacked the windscreen with all the energy he had left. The glass finally shattered.

"Thank goodness you're alive!" he gasped.

"We didn't think we were going to make it," said Jane.

"Neither did I," replied Ben.

Then they heard the powerful roar of an engine. A jeep was coming over the sand towards them, its headlights flashing.

"We saw your flares," the driver shouted. "But the sandstorm slowed us up."

"I'm so glad you found us," said Jane. "We thought we were going to die out here."

"How come you weren't inside the jeep?" the driver asked Ben.

Ben, Chris and Jane looked at each other. "It's a long story," said Ben.